BRITAIN, FASCISM AND

BRITAIN, FASCISM AND THE POPULAR FRONT

Edited by

Jim Fyrth

LAWRENCE AND WISHART
LONDON

Lawrence and Wishart Limited
39 Museum Street
London WC1A 1LQ

First published 1985

© Lawrence and Wishart, 1985

Each essay © the author

Photoset in North Wales by
Derek Doyle & Associates, Mold, Clwyd
Printed in Great Britain by
Oxford University Press

All round the barren hills of Aragon
Announce our testing has begun.
Here what the Seventh Congress said,
If true, if false, is live or dead,
Speaks in the Oviedo mauser's tone.

Three years ago Dimitrov fought alone
And we stood taller when he won.
But now the Leipzig dragon's teeth
Sprout strong and handsome against death
And here an army fights where there was one.

We studied well how to begin this fight,
Our Maurice Thorez held the light.
But now by Monte Aragon
We plunge into the dark alone,
Earth's newest planet wheeling through the night.

(From *Full Moon at Tierz: Before the Storming of Huesca*,
written by John Cornford, Aragon Front, Spain, 1936.)

'Popular Front' – 'People's Front': A Note

In the summer of 1934 the French Communist Party signed an agreement with the other left parties to form 'le Front Populaire'. In Spain the same style 'Frente Popular' was used. These are most adequately rendered into English as 'people's front', since 'popular' has another, more usual, meaning of 'liked by the people' (OED). Unfortunately the people's front was not sufficiently 'popular' in this sense. In the 1930s, therefore, 'people's front' was more generally used in Britain. But since the war 'popular front' has come into vogue. We have, therefore, used 'Popular Front' in the title of these essays and when referring to France or Spain. Elsewhere we have generally restored 'people's front'.

CONTENTS

Introduction: In The Thirties

JIM FYRTH

The years between 1928 and 1933 were bad, not only because of unemployment and hunger, but because the organisations which working people had built over the previous century failed them. In Britain, trade union membership declined, leaders were cautious, many members preferred work under bad conditions to no work at all. The Labour Government, elected in 1929, had, in common with European social-democratic parties, no policy to deal with the depression. In 1931 it split and fell, some of its best known leaders joining with the Conservatives and some Liberals to form a 'National Government' which turned out to be the harshest administration for a century.

The Narrow View
Communist parties were in thrall to a strategy, adopted at the Sixth Congress of the Communist International (Comintern) in 1928, which reduced Marxism to a narrow form of 'class politics'. In developed capitalist countries, it was held, a large working class faced a small, ruling, capitalist class, with their political interests divided along economic lines – 'class against class'. The world crisis would lead to a sharper class struggle and so to a new wave of working class revolutions. The social democrats, who had helped to restore capitalism in the 1920s, would try to divert the workers from revolution and so were the worst of the 'class enemies', except for the left-wing socialists (and the left-wing nationalists in the colonies) who were even worse because they hid their reformism in revolutionary phrases. In the revolutionary crisis the 'middle strata' (peasants, intellectuals, shop-keepers and others) would vacillate, joining whichever side seemed strongest, no special approach was necessary to win them as allies. In Britain, where there was no 'peasant problem', some of the 'middle strata' would be forced into the working class by the

9

economic crisis, most would join the capitalists. Some individual intellectuals, professionals, even aristocrats would, as the *Communist Manifesto* had predicted, throw in their lot with the workers. They would be expected to cross the barriers of class to join the workers in their struggle. They had no special role in, for example, their own intellectual fields, or in winning the majority of their own social groups to the socialist cause.

But the revolutionary revival did not come. Instead political reaction advanced and by 1932 half of Europe had authoritarian right-wing governments. In 1933 came the worst blow. Hitler became Chancellor of Germany and the strongest working class movement in Europe was destroyed. In 1934 Dolfuss's Austrian fascists crushed the Viennese workers, in France the fascist leagues tried to seize power and in Spain an extreme right-wing government suppressed the miners' uprising in Asturias. Each of these defeats was greeted by Communists as another sign that the revolution was maturing.[1]

The Communist Party of Great Britain (CPGB or CP) had some successes during this period, notably in leading the unemployed, through the National Unemployed Workers' Movement (NUWM) which organised the great Hunger Marches and demonstrations against the Means Test. Communists played a leading role in the Lancashire cotton strike of 1932. The Busman's Rank and File Movement, formed in 1932, and the Railway Vigilance Committees owed much to the party's initiative and help. The foundation of the *Daily Worker* and its survival against all odds was a considerable achievement, but membership fell from 10,730 in October 1926, to 2,555 in November 1930, and then rose again with the beginning of less sectarian policies.

On straightforward 'class issues' the dedication of Communists could work wonders. But the growing dangers of fascism and war demanded more. No Marxist would doubt that fascism was a product of capitalism and its class relationships. But Jewish shopkeepers whose windows were broken by working class toughs in black or brown shirts, intellectuals who saw their books burned by an uneducated mob, Christians persecuted for refusing to recognise that the state was above conscience, did not see it like this. Quite the contrary; fascism posed as a form of socialism and its anti-capitalist rhetoric was directed at the working class and lower-middle class. The drive to war was fuelled by the demands of imperialist have-nots (Germany, Italy and Japan) against imperialist haves (England and France), and by a desire to wipe out the Soviet Union. But there were a multitude who did not see it that way yet who, remembering the horrors of 1914-18, were worried by the resurgence of militarism. Even more directly economic questions such as unemployment and malnutrition appeared to a growing body of people, who were far from being socialists, as morally and humanely objectionable features of society, about which something must be done.

If war and fascism were to be prevented and if poverty and unemployment were to be attacked, all these different groups of people and the organisations to which they belonged had to be brought together to make a combined stand, whatever their long-term wishes for the future might be. And the danger was so great that they could be brought together – but not if the Comintern's 'class against class' policy was persisted with.

Towards Unity

Fortunately and wisely, as these essays show, the left in Britain, as on the Continent, in Ireland and India, began – hesitatingly and with many contradictions – to change its practice and, between 1932 and 1934, took the first tentative steps towards unity against the common enemy. For Communist parties the decisive turning point was the Seventh World Congress of the Comintern in 1935 which adopted the strategy of the united front of working class parties and the popular front of these parties with all who would combine against fascism and war. But, as the contributors to this book show, the Congress itself was the result of discussions and changes in practice during the preceding years.

When Hitler came to power the Independent Labour Party (ILP), which had disaffiliated from the Labour Party in 1932, appealed to all working class bodies for a united front against fascism. The Communist Party did likewise, in response to the Comintern decision that Communist parties should approach social-democratic parties. The ILP and CPGB did work together, albeit somewhat uneasily, but the Labour Party and TUC refused. The Labour Party replied with two pamphlets, *Democracy v. Dictatorship*, which argued that there was nothing to choose between communism and fascism and *The Communist Solar System*, which listed and forbade Labour Party members to join all those organisations which it said were 'Communist fronts'. When, at the 1934 Labour Party Conference, a delegate asked why Labour Party members could share platforms with Conservatives and

Liberals but not with Communists, Herbert Morrison replied, 'It [the CP] is the only political party that sets out to make difficulties for the Labour Party, the trade unions and the Co-operative Movement'.[2]

In spite of official Labour strictures, a united peace movement of Communists, socialists, pacifists and supporters of the League of Nations was slowly built up through the National Congress Against War in March 1933, the Peace Ballot of 1934, the campaign against the private manufacture and export of arms in 1934-35 and the demand for League of Nations sanctions to prevent the Italian invasion of Abyssinia in 1935. However, unity did not come smoothly. Communist support for the 1933 Congress Against War led the Balham Group, the first British Trotskyist sect, to accuse the CP of 'entrusting the leadership of the anti-war movement to petit-bourgeois pacifists'.[3] Although the CP took part in the National Peace Congress which followed the Peace Ballot the party had advised socialists to write on the ballot forms (which asked for views on collective security) 'the only complete safeguard is the abolition of capitalist society'.[4] And when the Communist Party did support League of Nations sanctions against Italy and called for the Suez Canal to be closed to Italian ships, the Labour left did not follow suit, Aneurin Bevan declaring, 'If I am going to ask workers to shed their blood, it will not be for medieval Abyssinia or fascist Italy, but for making a better social system.'[5] It took Franco's rebellion in Spain in 1936 to bring the Labour left to support collective security.

Left-wing unity against fascism at home was easier to achieve, although the leaders of the labour movement tended to close their eyes in the hope that it would go away. Nevertheless, the ILP, CP and Labour left joined in huge demonstrations against Mosley. After his meeting at Olympia in June, 1934, the CP invited well-known Labour people to join a 'Co-ordinating Committee for Anti-fascist Activities'. John Strachey became secretary and Lord Marley (a Labour peer), Leah Manning (NUT President), Ellen Wilkinson MP and Harry Adams (builders' leader) were among members. They issued a successful call to 'drown Mosley in a sea of working-class activity' when his blackshirts rallied to Hyde Park in September.

In 1933 an international inquiry into the Reichstag fire (which Hitler had blamed on the Communists and used as an excuse for suppressing opposition), was held in London, chaired by the left Labour MP D.N. Pritt, organised by the Communist Isabel

Brown and involved distinguished judges. The inquiry exposed
the guilt of the Nazis and helped secure the release of George
Dimitrov and other accused Communists. The Women's
Congress Against Fascism and War led to the formation of a
broadly-based Women's Committee Against Fascism and War in
Britain. The 1934 Hunger March was the occasion of a big and
widely-supported Congress of Action Against Hunger, Fascism
and War in Bermondsey town hall and led also to the formation
of the National Council of Civil Liberties, with Labour and
Liberal support, to monitor the conduct of the police and oppose
all measures tending towards fascism. These campaigns and
others of a like kind laid the foundations of what was to become
the people's front movement in Britain.

But Sectarianism Lives On

Communist thinking moved rather more slowly towards unity
than practice did. At that time Raji Palme Dutt was responsible
for many of the CP's policy statements, although he was not so
highly regarded after 1932 when he had declared that the trade
unions were organs of the ruling class. The Dutt Papers in the
British Library, as well as the 'Notes of the Month' in his journal,
Labour Monthly, show the developments and contradictions in one
line of ideas, which had considerable influence among
Communists. When, in March 1933, the Comintern recommended member parties to approach social-democratic parties
with a view to unity against fascism – a break with the 1928 policy
– Dutt wrote to Pollitt that the statement was 'a damned good
thing and urgently due ... the only pity is we could not have
reached it sooner', but added, 'we want to be ready to meet the
reformist leaders because we want to win the workers behind
them ... But we are perfectly aware of the reformist leaders the
whole time as the enemies of the workers.'[6]

In October 1933, he wrote to Pollitt that the old Communist
arguments condemning bourgeois democracy as a sham were
'out of date' because, in the face of fascism, the workers
naturally thought democratic rights important.[7] In the same year,
when another Hunger March was mooted Dutt warned Pollitt
that to make it a really united march, 'a genuinely broad
committee is needed',[8] and Pollitt brought together nineteen
leading labour movement figures to sponsor the march.[9] But
when the Bermondsey Congress met in support of the march –
and it was a genuinely representative gathering – Dutt wanted it

to 'raise the question of Soviet Power ... we need (he wrote) a strong INSURRECTIONARY tone to the manifesto'. A CP resolution attacking the Labour Party and TUC as saboteurs of the march was withdrawn only under ILP pressure.

Dutt's draft of the May Day Manifesto called stridently for the overthrow of capitalism and the establishment of Soviet power.[10] Yet, that summer, under the influence of events in Austria and France, he wrote that the urgent need in Britain was an 'Anti-Fascist Front', which should include 'all unorganised workers and all elements of the petit-bourgeoisie, employers, small traders, technicians, professionals, intellectuals and even bourgeois liberal elements who are prepared to enter into the common fight against fascism under the hegemony of the working class', and wrote to the Comintern expressing this view.[11] The anti-fascist potential of classes other than the workers was being recognised at last – but only if they put themselves under working-class leadership. Nor did this stop Dutt from criticising other leading Communists who objected to calling Labour leaders' 'social-fascists', nor from characterising Roosevelt's New Deal as fascist (a view shared at that time by some left Labour people and by some American liberals).[12]

Sectarian thinking in 1934-35 was demonstrated in attacks on the Socialist League. This had been formed in 1932 by ILP members who wanted to stay in the Labour Party when the ILP disaffiliated and was a centre of Labour left thinking for the next five years. In 1933 it published its programme *Forward to Socialism*, a coherent socialist strategy which aroused great hostility from the right and which Dutt saw as a right-wing conspiracy, using the Labour left to divert the workers from moving further left.[13]

The Turning Point

It was well that, as these essays show, leading Communists in Britain and elsewhere were thinking more realistically, with the result that the French Popular Front was formed in 1934 and the policy of seeking united fronts of socialist and working class organisations, leading to people's fronts of all anti-fascists became the policy of the Comintern at its Seventh Congress in August 1935. The Congress decisions led to an entirely new approach to social democrats and to the 'middle strata', peasants, intellectuals and the 'middle classes', and to questions of democracy, nationalism, patriotism and history.

All this was welcomed with a sigh of relief by most members of the CPGB. But there was no public recognition that the previous policy had been disastrously wrong. The situation, it was argued, had changed so the policy had changed,[14] an attitude not calculated to win the confidence of potential allies. Nevertheless, from this time in Britain the Labour left, many liberals and others besides the Communists more and more thought and acted in terms of people's front politics. In various developing forms the idea of unity in opposition to fascism and for progressive social policies guided the left for the next decade, except for the twenty months from October 1939, when the Communist Party returned to a more sectarian policy. Even then, however there were strands of left unity and the People's Convention movement of 1940-41, in which the CP was involved, had or aimed to have some characteristics of people's front politics.

This was the most fruitful period in the history of the British left and of the Communist Party in particular. In the four years with which these essays are mainly concerned there was a renaissance of the left wherever the policy was applied; in the women's movement against fascism and war and in campaigns on housing, birth control and abortion, as well as in traditional forms of class struggle in mining, engineering, passenger transport and among council tenants. New forms of anti-imperialist organisation were developed in the India League, the China Campaign Committee, and others.[15] There were new groupings of intellectuals and a 'people's front' culture in many fields as intellectuals took part in Spanish Aid and other campaigns.

The people's front movement was strong among students. In January 1936, Labour and Communist student groups united in the University Labour Federation. In a year it grew from 16 branches with 1,500 members to 28 branches with 3,017 members (there were far fewer students than now). The ULF was very active in anti-fascist and peace movements, with the unemployed and in industrial conflicts. But university Liberals and Conservatives, Christians and League of Nations supporters often joined in. Edward Heath, for instance, led a Conservative student delegation to Spain in support of the Republic. Many young intellectuals joined the left and, contrary to myth, only a minority changed course after 1939. David Widgery in *The Left in Britain* (mainly about the new ultra-left) asserts that there was no left-wing student movement in the 1930s. All students were busy trying to ape Oxbridge traditions, and joining the CP was merely another student lark.[16] Like much of the ultra-left 'history' of this period, Widgery's account touches truth at no single point.

Much of the ultra-left criticism of 'popular-frontism' is based on such myth-making. Trotsky then believed, as his followers have continued to believe, that the working class was eager to respond to revolutionary calls but was misled by Communists and social democrats. The facts that, in Britain, no group of workers listened to the calls of the ultra-left and that the ILP, which followed the revolutionary line, shrunk in numbers and influence, while the various Trotskyist sects grew in numbers as they split and declined in membership, seem not to weigh with today's inheritors of Trotsky's mantle.[17] In contrast, support grew steadily for those following the people's front policy. From 1935-39 Communist Party membership grew from 7,700 to 17,756; *Daily Worker* circulation rose from 30,000 to 80,000 with 100,000 copies sold at weekends; the Left Book Club, founded in 1936, had 57,000 members in April 1939; *Tribune*, founded in 1936, had a circulation of 30,000 at the outbreak of war. The people's front idea was also supported by the *New Statesman* and the *News Chronicle* and by the Co-operative Sunday *Reynolds News*, with the *Manchester Guardian* and others showing interest.

From United Front to People's Front

What did the term people's front mean in Britain? From 1935 it was widely used by Liberals and some Conservatives as well as by Labour people to mean a parliamentary alliance against the National Government and a number of attempts were made at Westminster to form such a grouping.[18] This view was rejected by the Labour left, one of whose best known publicists, G.D.H. Cole, wrote 'electoral pacts are consequences, not causes of real movements among people ... A People's Front is a state of mind, a political attitude, and not a piece of electoral machinery.'[19]

The Communist Party went further. From 1935-38 a formal people's front of all anti-fascists was not its first objective. Such unity, it argued, must be based on three conditions:

> first a united front of working class parties and organisations must be formed to give correct direction to a wider alliance;
> such a wider alliance would be real only if it was the result of broadly based mass movements against fascism and war and for social change;
> any alliance must leave the Communist Party, like others in the alliance, free to conduct its own independent campaigns for its

full political programme, while adhering strictly to the terms of the alliance.

Without these conditions a people's front could create the illusion of anti-fascist unity while being, in reality, under the control of the political centre and so could possibly be turned in opposition to the militant working class movement. But the way to a people's front could be paved by propaganda and by co-operation in particular campaigns with all who were against fascism, war and the policies of the National Government.[20]

Two attempts were made, between 1935 and 1937, to achieve a united front of labour movement organisations. Both, after raising initial hopes, failed. The first followed immediately after the Seventh World Congress. The Communist Party withdrew all its candidates chosen for the November 1935 general election except for Willie Gallacher in West Fife and Harry Pollitt in Rhondda East. In seventy constituencies unofficial united front agreements were made with local Labour Parties. Gallacher was elected and played a notable part at Westminster for the next fifteen years. Pollitt had a large vote and many Welsh Communists thought that Arthur Horner, leader of the Welsh miners, could have won the seat had he been the Communist candidate.

A few days after the election, the Central Committee of the CP applied for affiliation to the Labour Party. The Labour Party replied that it saw no reason why anything had changed since 1922 when its Conference had rejected affiliation by fifteen to one. But the application roused enormous interest both within and without the labour movement and for the next three years there was no Labour or trade union organisation where the question of united front and people's front was not hotly argued. The matter was widely discussed in the press, and in the run-up to the 1936 Labour Party Conference the miners', train drivers', engineers', clerks' and furnishing workers' unions, as well as the Socialist League, Fabian Society, Scottish Socialist Party and sixty divisional (constituency) parties all declared their support for Communist affiliation. It looked as though nearly half the votes would be cast in favour and Herbert Morrison warned the PLP that affiliation might have to be conceded.[21] However, the major figures in party and unions, Dalton, Citrine and Bevin, were adamant. At the conference every kind of manipulation of votes was used and only five speeches on the subject were allowed. Affiliation was rejected by 1,728,000 votes to 592,000.

The 1936 Labour Party Conference in Edinburgh was a disaster for progressive causes and a triumph for the right-wing. It supported the policy of non-intervention in the Spanish war, so voting to withold arms for the Republic, in spite of the pleas of Spanish Socialist Party delegates and clear evidence of Italian and German support for Franco. It put curbs on the Labour League of Youth and also qualified Labour opposition to re-armament, so letting go of the main lever for changing the government's foreign policy.

To provide a new focus for the left, Cripps, Bevan, Laski, George Strauss and William Mellor founded *Tribune*; shortly afterwards Mellor, the editor, met Pollitt to discuss a new path to unity. Cripps chaired talks between the Socialist League, ILP and CP, which launched the Unity Campaign of 1937. This got off to a tremendous start with Cripps, Pollitt, Maxton, Brockway, Bevan, Gallacher and others touring the country speaking to crowded meetings. Cripps later said, 'It did really seem in the first electric weeks that the miracle could be worked, that the Labour Party could be taken by storm'.[22] It could not! The Labour Party executive at once disaffiliated the Socialist League and made membership incompatible with Labour Party membership. The Labour League of Youth, the University Labour Federation and several divisional parties were threatened with disaffiliation and an attempt was made to expel Cripps. At the same time the ILP and CP divided over the uprising in Barcelona, in May 1937, of the ultra-left POUM and some anarchist groups against the Spanish Popular Front government. The ILP supported the POUM and the CP supported the Spanish government's suppression of the uprising.

Yet in spite of these set-backs people's front type movements were growing rapidly 'from below'. In the spring and summer of 1936 there was a new wave of the peace movement, with Peace Councils formed in many parts of the country. In June a National Peace Conference at Leeds heard speakers from all parties and peace organisations as well as messages of support from Anthony Eden and the Archbishop of Canterbury. In September a British delegation to a Brussel's Peace Conference, supported by the Communist Party, included seven mayors, three lord provosts, representatives of 64 peace councils and 60 League of Nations Union branches with several national trade unions and trades councils.

In May 1936, the publisher Victor Gollancz formed the Left Book Club. By the end of 1937 some 50,000 people were buying a monthly left-wing book and receiving the Club's journal. These were being discussed in 750 groups, many of them in working class districts; there were special groups of cyclists, actors, architects, scientists and others. These groups campaigned for a people's front and took part in all the movements for aid to Spain and China, solidarity with the Czechs, opposition to Mosley and campaigns against poverty and unemployment. They often formed Labour Party branches where none existed and moved them to the left where they did exist. They became the focus for the spread of new ideas in the left. John Strachey's *Theory and Practice of Socialism*, one of the Club's major choices, and his pamphlet *Why You Should be a Socialist*, sold a quarter of a million copies each.

Mass Movement

From 1936-38 Britain experienced the most widespread mass movements since the mid-nineteenth century days of Chartism and the Anti-Corn Law Leagues, though they have been written out of the record by orthodox historians. These movements included, among others, the demonstrations against Mosley, the support for the 1936 Hunger March – the first to be recognised by the Labour leadership – the Jarrow march of the same year and the campaign in support of Czechoslovakia. But the most widespread and representative was the Aid Spain campaign, the biggest movement of international solidarity in British history. There were more than a thousand local committees uniting people of all views. Tens of thousands of people organised meetings, collected food and money, sent medical aid, received Basque children and denounced non-intervention. Altogether millions of people contributed food and money. Working class organisations, shop stewards and trade union branches took weekly collections. Almost every Labour Party branch, Women's Section and Co-op Guild acted in some way, often together with Communists, Liberals and religious people. Women played a specially important part in the movement. Medical teams went to Spain. More than two thousand Britons joined the International Brigades.

In all this the Communist Party played a crucial, and in some spheres a leading, part, but acted in unity with people of all parties and beliefs, and of none. The party did not attempt to push relief organisations further than they were prepared to go, or beyond the purpose for which they were formed. Nor did it, as does today's ultra-left, carry slogans for one campaign while participating in another. It conducted its own independent Spain campaign while joining in the united actions, and so won increasing support and membership.

By 1938 it was clear that the Labour leadership would go to any lengths to prevent either a united front or a people's front. One of its arguments was that the Communist policy had not really changed, it was all a sham to seduce Labour voters from the Labour Party, an idea that flew in the face of all that was happening at the time, and the opposite accusation from that of the ultra-left. Attlee, who did take part in united campaigns, argued rather differently, in *The Labour Party in Perspective* (1937), that the Popular Front governments in France and Spain aimed merely at reforms within the capitalist system, whereas the Labour Party 'cannot hope to make a success of administering the capitalist system, because it does not believe in it' (!), but that he would not rule out a people's front 'as an impossibility, in the imminence of a world crisis' – which apparently there was not![23]

On the other hand, the political climate of 1938 was very different from that of 1935. There were widespread mass movements and, while there was still strong support amongst the establishment for the fascist dictators, one of the first opinion polls (1938) showed that only 7 per cent of the public supported Franco against 57 per cent supporting the Republic. A growing group of Conservatives was against the government. Fascist aggression was clearly seen in Spain; Japan had invaded China; Hitler was preparing to invade Austria and threatening Czechoslovakia.

It was in these circumstances that in January 1938 at a Left Book Club rally, Pollitt called for a people's front 'of all peace and progressive forces with no prior condition'. This, he explained at a London District conference in June, must be a mass movement for a government of a new kind. It was not a retreat from socialism but a Leninist policy of 'seeking allies to carry forward the struggle as a whole', with independent socialist propaganda carried on at the same time. Even in a revolutionary situation a people's front would be appropriate.[24]

In February the party coined the slogan 'Chamberlain Must Go', which quickly became the call throughout the left.[25] On 27 March Sydney Elliott, editor of *Reynolds News*, proposed a 'United Peace Alliance' of all anti-fascists, on foreign policy only at first, and for an alliance at the next general election. This was welcomed by the Communist Party and most Liberals and supported by the *News Chronicle*, the *Yorkshire Post* (owned by the family of Anthony Eden's wife), *New Statesman*, *Tribune*, and by sixty divisional Labour Parties in the Home Counties alone. Some hundred local People's Front Committees were formed, embracing people of all left and centre parties. Even the Labour Party National Executive said it might accept the idea if enough Tory MPs revolted against Chamberlain and Morrison recommended that the PLP reconsider its attitude to the CP. Cripps and Bevan, supported by two hundred smaller unions, called for an emergency Labour Party Conference (there was no conference in the crisis year of 1938). When the infamy of the Munich Agreement was appreciated the tide for a people's front flowed more strongly. Even Churchill put out feelers to the left and the CP accepted the idea of Churchillite allies.[26] In the autumn Vernon Bartlett won the Bridgewater by-election as an Independent Progressive on a people's front programme, with the support of the local Labour Party acting against headquarters instructions. A.D. Lindsay, Master of Balliol, standing as Popular Front candidate against Quentin Hogg in the Oxford by-election halved the Tory majority. A public opinion poll early in 1939 showed that 72 per cent of those asked now supported the Spanish Republic.

By the end of the year some sort of unity against Chamberlain's policies seemed within reach. Then in January 1939, Cripps published a Memorandum calling for a front of Labour, Liberal, Communist and Independent Labour Parties, with a special appeal to youth. Rejected by the Labour Party NEC, he sent it to all Labour MPs, candidates, parties and affiliates. The leaders of the Liberal, Co-operative and Communist Parties and many intellectuals, including Keynes, supported him, as did a huge Youth Pilgrimage to London, uniting Labour, Liberal, Communist and University labour youth organisations.

The NEC moved with speed unprecedented in the decade. Cripps, Bevan, Strauss, Trevelyan and others were expelled and all Labour members and organisations given seven days to withdraw from the people's front campaign or be expelled.[27]

A few weeks later Hitler invaded Czechoslovakia and soon afterwards the fascists finally defeated the Spanish Republic. Throughout the summer the Communist Party and those on the left who were not too demoralised tried to rally opinion for an Anglo-French-Soviet alliance, and public opinion was strong enough to push Chamberlain to make some gestures, though patently insincere ones, in that direction. In August, the Soviet Union, faced with the failure of its collective security policy of the previous five years, signed a Non-Aggression Treaty with Germany. The people's front campaign, it seemed, had failed. War followed in September.

Failure and Success

Why did it not succeed? It is tempting to put the main blame on the determination of the Chamberlain government to persist in 'appeasement' of the dictators even beyond the point where it had self-evidently failed: tempting also to point to the obduracy of a Labour leadership of which Nye Bevan said 'it is too respectable and statesmanlike, too frightened of offending the middle class', which G.D.H. Cole accused of 'constantly disowning its own protagonists for the crime of courage'[28] and which did all it could to discourage any kind of direct action. Bevin, Citrine and other right-wing trade union leaders dominated conferences with the block-votes of the large unions. The Labour left, although influential in the constituencies, was unable to move this leadership. When there was any possibility of its doing so it was stamped on. It was itself weakened by pacifist tendencies and relied too much on volatile individuals such as Cripps, Gollancz and Strachey. But the reasons went deeper.

In March 1939, D.L. Manuilsky, chief Soviet delegate to the Comintern, said that,

> despite these successes [Spain campaign etc, J.F.], the CPGB ... has not succeeded in breaking through to the main sections of the British working class, which bear tremendous responsibility for the fact that the policy of British reaction on the blockade of the Spanish Republic was not thwarted in good time by action on their part.[29]

How much influence did calls for a united front and a people's front have? Orwell and others have alleged that the Communist policy of unity against fascism and war won no serious support from Labour Party people or from the working class.[30] Anyone who took part in the Aid Spain campaign or who, like this writer, has looked at the documents of the campaign and interviewed its activists, knows that this is false. What is true is that, while very large numbers of Labour people took part in individual campaigns together with Communists and others, by no means all of these were won completely for the people's front strategy. Many Labour and trade union stalwarts who supported the working class united front thought the people's front meant dropping socialist aims and were too suspicious of liberals, let alone dissident Conservatives and Churchill's followers, to go the whole way to an alliance of all anti-fascists.[31] Exact reckoning is not possible, but there were perhaps half a million political and trade union activists, most of whom were involved in one or another of the anti-fascist and working class campaigns and very many of whom supported some form of unity against fascism and against the Chamberlain government.[32] There were some two million readers of newspapers and journals which supported the people's front strategy – though, of course, figures overlap.

But beyond all these there were four million trade union members and twelve to fifteen million unorganised blue and white collar workers and, of course, the rest of the population. Many contributed to Spanish Aid, supported individual campaigns and were anti-fascist in outlook. But the CP and the left generally failed to find either the organisation or the language which would reach those millions, many of whom were insular, imperialistic and deferential in their attitudes (royal occasions were immensely popular).

Though it grew rapidly, the Communist Party remained small and so did its industrial base even though there were active party groups in mining, engineering, aircraft, printing, shipbuilding, the docks and transport. Most industrial workers never came into contact with Communists. The Labour Party was the party of the trade unions and Communists were excluded from it. When they stood their own candidates they were accused of splitting the vote. But there were weaknesses apart from size. Communists were often dogmatic and talked as if all workers were political, over-simplified issues and held stereotyped views of people. The party's refusal to admit past mistakes was immature and so was its attitude of Communist infallibility and its apparent belief that almost all injustice and wickedness was the product of class society and would fade away under socialism.

Admiration for Soviet survival and achievements was carried to uncritical lengths. Of course, the price of anti-Sovietism in the 1930s was terribly high, at a time when the hope of averting war lay in Anglo-Soviet alliance. And it was necessary to defend the only socialist state and the only country helping Republican Spain. Nor is there any evidence that British Communists knew the extent of Stalin's decimation of Soviet Communists and intellectuals. Belief that the Moscow trials of the time were fair and the charges genuine went far beyond the Communist Party,[33] though the trials raised doubts among many people's front allies.[34] More seriously, admiration for the October Revolution delayed an understanding that the people's front could become a long-term strategy for achieving socialism and was not a temporary device after which there would be a return to the classic revolutionary path.[35]

Yet the weaknesses and the failure to achieve immediate goals, should not mask the achievements of the Communist Party and its people's front allies from 1935-39. Their political record is better than that of any other group during those critical years. Many individual campaigns were successful and, whether successful or not, they awakened thousands to the dangers and injustices of the time. They led to a renewal of the labour and radical movements which has been long-lasting,[36] and Marxism became an essential part of British political thought.

The events of the 1940s proved that the strategy of unity was correct and necessary for the defeat of fascism. And it was the men and women of the 1930s campaigns who, in the forces and factories, reached out to the millions and so did most to break down the dominance of conservative views and to generate a new radical climate. It was this which made 1945 and the post-war advances possible. And if the promise of the post-war years turned out to be greater than their performance, some of the reasons for that, too, lie in the pre-war years.

Then and Now

It is as dangerous to believe that history repeats itself as it is to learn nothing from history. The 1980s are not the 1930s. But if the dangers are different they are at least as great and if the possibilities are different they are even greater. There is immense danger of war – terminal war – and the foreign policy of the British government, founded largely on the same anti-Soviet stance as in the 1930s (though without the same world influence), is not one that lessens the danger.

The Thatcher government is neither fascist nor proto-fascist, although it is more reactionary than the Chamberlain government, against which the people's front movement in Britain was directed. It is dismantling as many as it can of the social gains made during and since the war, including those made by women since the 1960s. It is attacking and shackling the trade unions and the labour movement more radically and speedily than any British administration since the Whig governments of the 1830s. It is eroding democratic rights, pulling down democratic institutions and strengthening the coercive powers of the state to a greater extent than any government since the aftermath of Waterloo. It is trying to create a low-wage economy, destroying productive industry and elevating market forces – under the control of finance capital and the multinationals. And it is trying, with some success, to construct a society in which self-seeking individualism replaces working-class solidarity and a system of social support for all in need.

The Thatcherites can do these things because the labour movement, the political left and all democrats are tragically divided, not only into rival parties but within each party, and because, aided by servile media, it has been able to shift public opinion to the right with populist demagogy. This frightens the less political with bogeymen, from pickets to muggers and even bishops and dons when appropriate. It plays on racial prejudice. It prates about democracy and individual rights as an excuse for weakening trade unions and sending the police against strikers. It demands law and order (for the working class) while unemployment and broken communities create the conditions for crime, and talks about the caring family, as an excuse for closing hospitals and old people's homes. Behind the rhetoric lies a right-wing ideology very different from traditional Conservative philosophy. To construct a social basis for such an outlook the government seeks to build up the class of small property owners (council house buyers, small businessmen, British Telecom shareholders etc), a strategy followed by reactionary governments from Napoleon to Tsar Nicholas II.

As in the 1930s, the labour movement has been unable to stem this tide. As then, it has lost members and been swamped electorally, though it has not been so utterly defeated as then and is stronger, healthier and further to the left – even though it has failed to organise the unemployed.

In all these features there are parallels with the 1930s, but there are important differences. There are now several socialist states and most former colonies are now independent even if still economically exploited. In Britain there are influential new political forces – the peace, women's, black, ecological, nationalist and other movements. There are new trends in the churches and among professional workers and intellectuals. These all oppose Thatcherite policies in some way, but they are independent of the labour movement and even suspicious that it recognises them only if they are useful to it.

How is Thatcherism to be understood and rolled back? Some on the left see it as a qualitatively new stage of capitalist rule in Britain – produced by the world economic and political crisis and the changes in British society. Others see it only as the policy of a harsher Tory government, unable to make concessions because of the crisis, and so intensifying policies of class confrontation begun by Labour and Tory governments since the late 1960s. Those who see it as a new and more dangerous phase tend to call for a 'broad democratic alliance', a modern form of the people's front, to defeat Thatcherism. Those who disagree tend to see the answer in more vigorous 'class politics'.

For those on the far, far left this is not a problem since they see a revolutionary wind rising with major social conflicts such as the miners' brave and splendid struggle of 1984-85. And when the revolution does not arrive the treachery of Labour leaders and Communists can be blamed.

All these ideas do echo the arguments of the 1930s. But what do terms like 'broad democratic alliance' and 'class politics' mean today? The crux of the matter is the relationship of the labour movement and the traditional left to the new political movements and to other parties and groups opposed to Thatcherism and war.

Many Labour people think that the voters will become disillusioned with Thatcher and that then the Labour Party can on its own and, as it were, 'in one mighty bound', rout both the Tories and the Alliance parties, win back the majority of the working class and recapture enough seats in the southern half of the country to become the government. They tend, therefore, to see the role of the new movements as being to canvass for Labour votes and trust the next Labour government to take care of their interests.[37] The Labour Party had similar views in the 1930s. But do, for instance, CND and the women's movement have any cause to trust a Labour government? The new movements do not see their role in traditional political terms and still less in class terms. In spite of this some on the left do see them in that way and argue that, for instance, working class women and blacks have more in common with working class men and working-class whites, in all their main concerns, than with women or blacks of other classes. They should, therefore, fall in behind the labour movement.[38] Their concern for autonomy is seen as 'divisive' and 'petit-bourgeois'.

But many others think that alliances, wider even than those of the 1930s, are needed. The labour movement should recognise the others as autonomous, should join with them in campaigns of mutual interest as equals and should learn from other movements. At the same time the left should continue its own work for a socialist Britain, exploring and explaining what that means and fighting on class issues in such a way as to draw in wider support from diverse social groups. They argue that the labour movement cannot demand political leadership but must win it by convincing those outside the labour movement of its rightness, sincerity and dedication in fighting against every sort of injustice and oppression.

Would allying with groups outside the labour movement on these terms mean, as it did in the 1930s, working for a programme of democratic advance and radical reforms that were not necessarily socialist, and even being prepared for electoral agreements with non-socialists? Neither the French or Spanish Popular Fronts won their elections on programmes of socialism, and the CPGB's policy for a people's front was not one for socialism. Millions of people around the world were attracted to socialism and tens of thousands joined Communist parties because their experiences in anti-fascist and anti-war campaigns convinced them that the political explanations and the hopes for the future of socialists and communists were right. Those who stand for intensified 'class politics' today tend to argue that any such talk of radical and democratic but not fully socialist programmes, let alone suggestions of electoral agreements, is a 'revisionist' retreat. The world is further along the road to socialism now and a definitely socialist programme can win majority support if enthusiastically enough propagated alongside vigorous class politics.[39] Is this so? Or is it a recipe for isolation and defeat and so for a generation of Thatcherism or worse?

However these questions are answered, all democrats, all socialists, all on the left, have to ask themselves why in Britain, after more than three hundred years of radical and democratic movements, after two hundred years of trade unionism, after a hundred and fifty years of working class political organisation and century of marxist parties we have the present situation?

Those who have contributed to this book are not necessarily

agreed on how to solve these problems or the way ahead for the left. But the essays are published, on the fiftieth anniversary of the Congress which was the turning point towards a people's front strategy, in the belief that it is useful to study the experience of the people's front and the failures and successes of that strategy if the left is to find its way forward today.

NOTES

1. 13th Plenum of Comintern EC, report by O. Kuusinen, *Inprecorr*, 30 January 1934; also Dutt Papers, British Library (CUP) K4 (hereafter 'Dutt') 7 March 1933; also R.P. Dutt, 'Notes of the Month', *Labour Montly* (hereafter 'LM Notes'), November 1933, attack on Leonard Woolf for suggesting that the breakdown of capitalism was leading to fascism and not to proletarian dictatorship.
2. Dutt, 15 October 1934, article to *Communist International*: also *Inprecorr*, 24 November 1934.
3. Reg Groves, *The Balham Group: How British Trotskyism Began*, London, 1974, pp. 82-3. The Balham Group had been expelled from the CPGB in 1932.
4. *Daily Worker*, 14 November 1934 (hereinafter 'DW').
5. Michael Foot, *Aneurin Bevan, Vol 1*, London 1962, pp. 210ff.
6. Dutt, 13 March 1933. For Dutt's differences with Pollitt and Gallacher on trade unions, see A.L. Morton, 'The 1930s', *Marx Memorial Library Bulletin*, No. 106, Spring 1985.
7. Dutt, 2 October 1933.
8. Dutt, 2 August 1933.
9. J. Mahon, *Harry Pollitt*, London 1976, pp. 183-4.
10. Dutt, 14 February 1934, letter to Pollitt on Bermondsey; May Day Manifesto, Dutt, 17 April 1934.
11. LM Notes, July 1934; also Dutt to Pollitt 13 June 1934 and 20 July 1934; see also James Jupp; *The Radical Left in Britain, 1931-41*, London 1982; p. 73; also Pollitt in *Communist International*, 20 March 1935, calling for a new approach to the middle classes.
12. Dutt, 20 July 1934 and 2 November 1934: also R.P. Dutt, *Fascism and Social Revolution*, London 1934, Chap. VIII and pp. 247-51.
13. Dutt, 16 May 1934, letter to Varga: LM Notes, June 1934; also LM Notes, February 1935 for a more moderate view of left-Labour 'parliamentary illusions'.
14. See, for example LM Notes, October 1935.
15. See, for example, J.M. Kenyatta, *Hands off Abyssinia*, LM September 1935. Kenyatta was Secretary of African Friends of Abyssinia; also CC Report on 14th Congress CPGB.
16 David Widgery, *The Left in Britain*, Harmondsworth 1976, pp. 305-6.
17. Jupp, op. cit., pp. 101-2. Also Warwick University Modern Records Centre; Tarbuck Papers MS 75, Maitland-Sara Collection MS 15 and D.D. Harber MS 151, also catalogue notes on these.
18. See Ben Pimlott, *Labour and the Left in the 1930s*, Cambridge 1977, pp. 3-4.

19. G.D.H. Cole, *The People's Front*, London, 1937, p. 334.

20. Dutt, Statement for 14th Congress discussion, 26 June 1936 and 5 June 1936, article in *Advance*. Also LM Notes, January 1936; Pollitt, *Inprecorr*, 30 May 1936; Jupp, op.cit., p. 79.

21. *Inprecorr*, 25 August 1936; Pimlott, op.cit., pp. 87ff.; Bevan, *Daily Herald*, 5 August 1936: for Morrison, D.N. Pritt, *From Right to Left*, London 1965, p. 100: but see below note 27, did Pritt confuse this with the 1938 Statement?

22. Foot, op.cit., p. 246-7.

23. C.R. Attlee, *Labour Party in Perspective*, London, 1937, pp. 121ff.

24. DW 17 January 1938; Pollitt, LM, July 1938; CP Letter to Labour Party Affiliates, 9 June 1938.

25. DW, 22 February 1938; and CPGB statement, 23 February 1938.

26. G. Carritt, 1984, interview with the author on the work of British Youth Peace Assembly in 1930s.

27. Pimlott, op.cit. chap. 18; Foot, op.cit. pp. 288-91. For Morrison's statement on the CP, see Neil Maclean M.P., reports to Scottish Socialist Party Conference, *Forward*, 26 March 1938.

28. Cole, op.cit., p. 80.

29. Report to 1939 Congress of CPSU(B), in DW, 17 March 1939.

30. G. Orwell, *Road To Wigan Pier*, chapters 10-12, especially chapter 11. J. Coombes, 'British Intellectuals and the Popular Front' in F.W. Gloversmith (ed.), *Class Culture and Social Class*, Hassocks, 1980; see also A.J.P. Taylor, *English History, 1914-45*, Oxford 1965, p. 398, 'Yet it [the Spanish Civil War] remained very much a question for the few, an episode in intellectual history ... Most English people displayed little concern.' The statement is wholly false.

31. See, for example, National Union of Foundry Workers; *Journals* 1936-39; this right-of-centre union supported the united front but opposed the people's front: also Dutt, 15 April 1938 and 26 January 1939, answering claims that the peace front meant 'dropping socialism'.

32. For quantative estimates of left groupings see Jack Cohen, *Inprecorr*, 19 September 1936 and Jupp; op.cit., pp. 171-7.

33. See, for example, Wickham Steed in *Spectator*, 16 July 1937: F. Elwyn Jones, *The Battle for Peace*, London 1938: Joseph E. Davies (US Ambassador to Moscow), *Mission to Moscow*, London 1942, among others.

34. For example, Dutt, 26 October 1937, letter to Harold Laski shows the latter contemplating withdrawing support from the USSR.

35. Draft Programme for the 16th Congress, published 29 August 1939; see also Pollitt interviewed in *Picture Post*, 2 August 1939. The Spanish civil war suggested that armed conflict was inevitable on the path to socialism, see for example, LM Notes October 1936.

36. Pimlott, op.cit., p. 5; Jupp, op.cit., p. vii; Will Paynter, *My Generation*, London 1972, p. 107.

37. For example, Frank Allaun on the role of CND, *Guardian* letters, 28 January 1985.

38. See the interview with Eric Heffer, *Morning Star*, 13 February 1985.

39. See, for example, statement by Tony Benn after 1983 general election that, while Labour lost the election, its votes had been for a full socialist programme, *Guardian*, 20 June 1983. He argued that this meant the regeneration of the Labour Party.

1935 – The Turning Point

MARTIN MYANT

The Seventh World Congress of the Communist International opened on 25 July 1935 and lasted almost a month. It ranks as one of the most important events in the history of the Communist movement. The great bulk of the 510 delegates in attendance felt uplifted to be part of a great international gathering and were left with a feeling that the Comintern was abandoning old errors and developing a new, more realistic approach that could lead the way out of its political isolation. The central figure in this was the Bulgarian Dimitrov whose speeches were met with prolonged and adulatory ovations the like of which had never been seen before in a Comintern congress. The real point, however, was that the experiences of so many Communist parties pointed in the same direction.

This is missed by those historians who have tried to reduce the whole change to a shift in Soviet foreign policy. The threat to the Soviet Union from Nazi Germany undoubtedly was the main factor persuading Stalin of the need for a shift in Comintern policy, but the detailed form of that policy emerged from the practical struggles of individual Communist parties. In fact, a more serious criticism of the Seventh Congress is that it was too cautious and did not mark a final break with the dogmatic and sectarian policies of the preceding years. In many respects the new line emerged out of a compromise between 'old' and 'new' ideas. Great care was taken not to be too explicit in condemning past policies and ideas which were the responsibility of Comintern – and Soviet –leaders.

Class against Class
Nevertheless, the dramatic changes in the capitalist world during the seven years since the Sixth Congress in 1928 were a powerful

stimulus to rethinking. Starting with the Wall Street crash of October 1929, the world economy had plunged into its deepest ever depression, with unemployment rising to record levels of 16 million in the USA, 5½ million in Germany and 3 million in Great Britain. Linked with this industrial crisis was a catastrophic drop in agricultural prices ruining farmers and farm workers. Colonial and dependent countries, tied to the export of raw materials, were hit particularly hard. This economic and social catastrophe, on top of the disruption and disillusion left by the war, created the basis not for the anticipated socialist revolution, but for the Nazi triumph in Germany. There seemed a real possibility that fascists would come to power in France and other countries too.

In most advanced capitalist countries the majority of the working class supported social democratic parties which, in a number of cases, had held government posts and in some had formed governments. In so far as they had a theoretical foundation to their policies it typically revolved around the notion that capitalism had entered a new, crisis-free, 'organised' phase. Socialism was still said to be the ultimate aim, but in practice it was never an immediate issue. Talk of revolution was positively shunned, not least in Germany where Social Democrats had used some of the most reactionary elements of the Kaiser's army to suppress the post-war revolutionary upsurge. In the depths of depression the Labour and Socialist International's Fourth Congress, held in Vienna in 1931, signally failed to find a radical policy. Instead, it was principally concerned with protecting Germany and Austria from collapse by appealing to the Western powers to overcome the financial crisis with 'an immediate and generous international action to save the economy, democracy and peace'. The alternative was said to be 'catastrophe and civil war'.[1]

The anti-Communism of the powerful reformist parties was mirrored at that time in the crude sectarianism of the Comintern. Since its foundation in 1919 it had been dogged by bitter internal disputes. The positions changed over the years but, at the risk of some over-simplification, there was a 'left', condemned by Lenin at the Third Congress in 1921, advocating at that time the 'theory of the offensive'. It believed that activity by a minority could galvanise the majority of the working class into action. The position was based on a false and idealised belief that revolution was imminent and whenever it gained dominance it inevitably led the Communist movement into sectarian isolation.

On the other side stood those who saw the need to find more subtle ways to win mass support. That meant taking a more realistic view of the objective conditions, and they developed ideas of a united front to defend the people's immediate interests and then of a 'worker-peasant' government that could be one stage towards working class power. The accusation against the 'right' was that it advocated an opportunist policy which blurred the distinctiveness of the Communist movement and left vague the ultimate aim. Although supported by Lenin, the 'right' did suffer from the obvious disadvantage that they were seeking unity with social democrats who were held responsible for the failure and suppression of the post-war revolutionary upsurge.

After Lenin's death the Comintern, still unable to lead a world revolution, became increasingly embroiled in the battles and mutual denunciations within the Bolshevik leadership. The clear triumph for the left-sectarian position in the Comintern coincided with Stalin's battle against the 'right opposition' in the Soviet Union and was codified in the resolutions of the Sixth World Congress held in 1928 and in the slogan 'class against class'.

Communists had, of course, always maintained that their policies were based on the principles of class struggle. Now, however, they were insisting that only they – with their aim of revolution, involving armed conflict and leading to the 'dictatorship of the proletariat' – could represent the working class. This was reflected in the blanket condemnations of social democracy, the left wing of which was characterised as 'the most dangerous fraction' because it was 'used to execute particularly subtle manoeuvres for deceiving the working class'.[2] Under such circumstances unity with other social forces or political movements was a practical impossibility. In fact, it was usually insisted that a united front could only be created 'from below', in opposition to the leadership of other parties. This gave the position a certain psychological appeal as it amounted to the clearest possible proclamation of the distinctiveness of the Communist movement. It was, however, never based on an objective analysis of the world situation. The subsequent claim to have foreseen capitalism's deepest ever economic crisis is incorrect: the Comintern merely predicted, in very general terms, that the 'contradictions in the capitalist countries (would) become more acute', leading to war between imperialist states and against the Soviet Union.[3]

The general unreality of its policies crucially weakened the Comintern's ability to lead a successful fight against fascism. In fact, the Comintern increasingly lost sight of the distinctiveness of fascism. It began to revive Stalin's view, expressed in September 1924, that social democracy was 'objectively the moderate wing of fascism' and his insistence that the 'main blow' should be directed against 'compromising parties'.[4] This culminated in the acceptance of the term 'social-fascism' by the Tenth Plenum of the Comintern's Executive in July 1929. The term itself had been used often enough before in the Communist movement, but only as a glib insult. It was still not accepted as an analytical category at the Sixth Congress. Its elevation followed the killing of 32 participants in a Communist demonstration in Berlin after Prussia's Social Democrat chief of police, Zorgiebel, had ordered his men to fire. The Communist reaction was one of understandable fury, but it also indicated a complete failure to conduct a sober analysis of either fascism or social democracy. It opened the way for the full revival of Stalin's erroneous views from 1924.

Despite this triumph for sectarianism, there were continual tensions within the Communist movement. The Comintern's constitution gave it the power to impose its decisions on member parties and this was often necessary to ensure acceptance of the class against class line. Thus, for example, the Comintern Executive supported the minority at the Fifth Congress of the Polish party in September, 1930, insisting that 'the fight with social-fascism' was the principal arena of struggle. Two years later the Comintern was again involved in condemning the leading Polish Communist, Kostrzewa, for allegedly helping 'opportunists and Trotskyists' after she had suggested that the Polish Socialist Party did have some interest in fighting the Nazis. Like others who questioned Comintern policy, she was effectively excluded from any position and right to express her views within the party. Those, such as Isaac Deutscher, who actually associated themselves with Trotsky's criticisms of the line on 'social-fascists' were expelled.[5]

There was, however, an almost universal reluctance to stick rigidly to the logic of the Comintern's line. Even in Germany, despite all the talk of left-wing social democracy being the main enemy, Communists were actually engaged in street fights with Nazis. At one time Nazi deputies even came to blows with the Communist group in the Prussian parliament. The German

Communist Party (KPD) was criticised from the Comintern and the KPD leadership itself criticised regional organisations for not really accepting the notion of 'the fascisation of social democracy'.[6]

In spite of the sectarian line, there were some important successes. As the depression bit into people's living standards, Communists often appeared as the only force actively fighting to defend them against the consequences of economic crisis. Throughout the advanced capitalist countries of Europe Communists were prominent in organising mass movements of the unemployed. They isolated themselves from much of the population by trying to link every movement to the aim of proletarian revolution, but that did not matter too much when other political movements were shunning the unemployed completely. However, once Communists succeeded in mobilising workers who were still in employment, they inevitably encountered other parties and trade unions. Such was the case in a miners' strike in Czechoslovakia in 1932, after which Gottwald, the Communist Party's general secretary, hinted at the need to seek unity with socialist leaders and tried unsuccessfully to persuade the rest of the Comintern leadership that talk of 'social-fascists' hampered the whole working class and anti-fascist struggle by making grass-roots unity more difficult.[7]

The New Line Emerges

The real momentum for change could only come when Communists, and the Soviet leadership, looked with horror at the seemingly irresistible rise of fascism. The KPD was taken completely by surprise by Hitler's rapid consolidation of power. Its immediate response was to place the blame on the broad shoulders of the German Social Democratic Party (SPD). There was considerable justification for this. The Social Democrats were the biggest workers' party and they had consistently underestimated the Nazi threat. The Berlin police chief, Grzezinski, actually claimed in November 1930 that 'there is no Nazi danger, there is only a Communist danger'.[8] SPD Executive member W. Schiff subsequently characterised communism as worse than fascism and maintained that the German people did not rise against Hitler because they feared 'Communist slavery'.[9]

As Hitler was coming to power the Social Democrats shunned extra-parliamentary action and shrank away from using their military-style defence units which were apparently 400,000 strong.[10] They feared defeat, but also victory which could have culminated in revolution. They ended up subserviently acknowledging Hitler's government, hoping to be 'allowed' a legal existence, while still pouring scorn on the KPD. Meanwhile, the KPD Central Committee in May 1933 was still characterising social democracy as the 'chief social prop of the dictatorship of capital',[11] while the Comintern Executive in April claimed that

> the organisation of an open fascist dictatorship, which is destroying all democratic illusions among the masses and so liberating them from the influence of social democracy, is accelerating Germany's development towards proletarian revolution.[12]

These condemnations of social democracy were shielding the KPD and the Comintern from criticism of their own mistakes and therefore a major barrier to the mounting pressures for a change in Comintern policy. So when the Labour and Socialist International (LSI) offered better relations after Hitler's assumption of power, the Comintern Executive published on 5 March 1933 a hesitant statement recommending to individual parties that they should approach social democrat leaders in their own countries with proposals for joint action against fascism and the capitalist offensive.[13] This was welcomed by, among others, the Communist Party of Great Britain (CPGB) which approached the Labour Party, TUC, Co-operative movement and the ILP for united front action. Only the last named responded and the two parties began working together, although the relationship was tense, particularly when the Comintern leadership tried, unsuccessfully, to push the ILP into rejecting completely the LSI and affiliating to the Communist International, ideally by means of a merger with the CPGB.

The change at this time was more limited in some of the larger sections of the Comintern. Thus the French Party was reprimanded for toning down its criticisms of the socialist leaders and the Czech party was sharply criticised when it approached Social Democratic leaders and also for suggesting that the KPD might mend its ways.[14] Meeting in November 1933, the Comintern Executive reiterated old ideas and played down or ignored attempts that had been made to create a genuine united front.

A clear example of new moves in the direction of genuine unity had begun as early as 1932 with the Communist-inspired peace movement, which included massive congresses in 1932 in Amsterdam and in June 1933, in the Pleyel Hall in Paris, attended by 2,000 and 3,000 delegates respectively. A British Congress was held in Battersea Town Hall also in June 1933. This 'Amsterdam-Pleyel Movement' was later to be seen as one of the germs for the subsequent idea of the people's front, being sponsored by liberals such as Bertrand Russell and Albert Einstein, as well as by Communists, and attended by socialists, liberals and non-party people.

Although pressures for a change in Comintern policy had been mounting for some time, the decisive break was possible only when the Soviet leadership realised the extent of the danger posed by Nazi Germany. The Soviet government had hoped that the good relationship between the two countries, built up in the early 1920s, might continue and even that Hitler's anti-Bolshevik rhetoric was mere window-dressing, while his real hostility was directed towards the Western powers which had humiliated Germany with the Treaty of Versailles at the end of the First World War.[15] Germany had had a special place in Soviet thinking, not only as a likely arena for revolution, but more immediately as a possible ally. However, it was the parties of the German 'right' which seemed most interested in the Soviet connection and had developed relationships based on the Treaty of Rapallo, signed between Germany and Soviet Russia in 1922. German Social Democrats had increasingly looked to the west and the Comintern's Sixth Congress had warned that Germany might be moving into a counter-revolutionary imperialist bloc for war against the Soviet Union.[16] There was, therefore, a link between the 'class against class' condemnation of social democrats and Soviet diplomacy.

By the beginning of 1934, however, Stalin was clearly suggesting that Nazi Germany posed a major threat to the Soviet Union[17] and he became far more responsive to the need for a broad, world-wide anti-fascist movement. The feasibility of this was clearly demonstrated by the response to Dimitrov's courageous and famous performance in the Leipzig trial of December 1933. Irrespective of the mutual slanging and apparent ineffectiveness of the mass workers' parties, ordinary people around the world were prepared to show their united support for a man who could stand up to the Nazis. He arrived triumphantly in Moscow on 27 February 1934 with a standing such as no other foreign Communist ever achieved inside the USSR. He pressed at once for broad working class unity against fascism and is reported to have overcome initial hostility from Stalin who quickly helped him on his way to the top of the Comintern, ignoring personal jealousies and political opponents.[18] Although Stalin was apparently still suspicious of Dimitrov's views, he could hardly have picked a better man to reorientate the Comintern towards an active fight against fascism, which now seemed essential if the Soviet Union was not to suffer another invasion.

Dimitrov's ideas had already been given forceful backing by events themselves when French fascists made a bid for power. Unlike the German Nazis they lacked a united organisational structure, but there were about half a million members of the various 'leagues'. On 6 February 1934, élite units from all over the country assembled in a demonstration 20,000 strong which culminated in an attempt to storm the Bourbon Palace where parliament was meeting. The aim was the establishment of a 'provisional government'. Instead the attack was repulsed and 17 were killed in shooting with the police, but it was followed by a serious shift to the right in the French government.

Speaking that day in parliament the French Communist Party (PCF) general secretary Maurice Thorez called 'on all proletarians and on our brothers, the socialist workers, to come out into the streets to repel the fascist gangs'.[19] The government banned a Communist demonstration called for 9 February, but thousands of Socialists took part alongside the Communists and joint demonstrations were held in many other parts of the country. As L'Humanité reported the next day, 'the united working class showed how energetically it could fight so as to smash fascism'.

On the 12 February the Socialist leadership of the trade union federation, the CGT, called for a general strike which, after much heart-searching, the PCF agreed to join. The organisers claimed $4\frac{1}{2}$ million participants. This mighty demonstration of popular feeling was a major blow against French fascism. It also marked a somewhat hesitant new beginning for the Communist movement. Thorez, who had shortly beforehand risen within the PCF with the help of the Comintern, was at first cautious. His party had previously been criticised for establishing contacts with Socialist leaders. He did not condemn the 'class against class' approach, and even continued to use the term 'social-fascist' until the end of April. There was, however, a very strong grass-roots desire for unity and particularly the left-wing Socialists were keen to develop it. The split in the workers' movement was nothing like as deep as in Germany and there were good relations in many localities.

With the help of a little prodding from Dimitrov,[20] Thorez became more imaginative and dropping the insistence that a united front could only be created from below, he signed a pact on 27 July committing the PCF and the Socialist Party to unity of action in the fight against fascism and in defence of democratic liberties. Shortly afterwards Thorez went against the advice of the Comintern leadership, conveyed to him by Togliatti, the experienced Italian leader, who advocated a little more caution,[21] and set about creating still broader anti-fascist unity to include the large Radical Party. It was in this context that the term *Front Populaire* or Popular Front first appeared in *L'Humanité* of 24 October 1934 in an article by the long-standing Communist leader Marcel Cachin. The alliance was formally born on 14 July 1935 when 10,000 delegates swore to remain united to defend democracy, to disarm and dissolve the fascist leagues, to give the working people bread and the youth work and to ensure peace in the world. The mass demonstration that followed was half a million strong: it far outnumbered a fascist demonstration held elsewhere in Paris on the same day.

These developments in France strongly influenced preparations for the long overdue Seventh Congress. Dimitrov had Stalin's blessing and the backing of the Ukrainian Manuilsky who, as the highest-ranking Soviet representative in the Comintern, never deviated from Stalin's line. With valuable support from Togliatti, Dimitrov gave encouragement to Thorez and, by July 1934, was privately suggesting the need to 'revise' the tactics of 'class against class'.[22] He faced a fierce rearguard action from within the Comintern leadership and from a number of Communist parties. The majority of the KPD leadership, based at the time in Paris, continued until the end of 1934 to direct its main attacks against left-wing Social Democrats. The most sectarian were the Hungarians, led by Bela Kun, who right to the end could accept a united front 'only with advocates of the dictatorship of the proletariat'.[23]

Fascism and Democracy

As the Seventh Congress assembled there was a lot of confusion at all levels in the Communist movement. On the one hand there was talk of a change of 'tactics', but at the same time even its leading advocates were suggesting that the Comintern's previous policies were still correct and valid. To develop the ideas of the people's front further and to ensure the political defeat of advocates of 'old' ideas, it was essential to state clearly how far the movement was adopting a new orientation.

In this context the opening report on the work of the Comintern Executive since the Sixth Congress was disappointing. Delivered by Pieck, one of the first KPD leaders to accept Dimitrov's approach, it claimed that the 'class against class' tactics had been correct but that 'a number of sectarian mistakes' had been committed by individual parties. He thereby evaded any direct criticism of the role of the Comintern leadership. There followed six days of discussion during which criticisms of the Comintern were consistently veiled as self-criticisms from individual parties. The only exception in the published records was the British delegate, J.R. Campbell, who responded to criticisms of 'clumsy and sectarian tactics' in trade unions by calling on the Executive to 'examine its own work in those seven years in the same objective spirit as it examines the work of the various parties'. He claimed that incorrect policies had 'been imposed on us in Britain as being fundamentally correct'.[24] Pieck did not accept these points, but the final resolution approved the Executive's proposals after March 1933 while tactfully omitting to mention the previous five years.

The next, and most important part, of the congress business was Dimitrov's report entitled *The fascist offensive and the tasks of the Communist International in the struggle of the working class against fascism*: it was followed by eight days of discussion with 60 participants. His analysis of fascism, of the need to defend democracy and of the means to create a united or people's front were themselves powerful enough. Dimitrov gave it all much greater force by combining analysis with anecdote and by implying an irreversible break from the dull and obscure language that had characterised much of the Comintern's propaganda. He managed, without saying anything too explicit, to make it quite clear that he was not just announcing a tactical shift. He was not suggesting just that the new situation required a new line. He was looking for a completely different approach that would have been just as valid even without the fascist threat.

The aim was for Communist parties 'to come out and act as *real political parties of the working class*, to become in actual fact a *political factor* in the life of their countries.[25] They had to 'overcome *the isolation of the revolutionary vanguard* from the masses of the proletariat and all other working people'. To achieve that it was essential to take the masses 'as they are, and not as we should like to have them'. People had to be approached in a way they could understand around issues they cared about.

The greatest obstacle to this in the Communist movement was dogmatism which created 'cut-and-dried schemes' and 'lifeless formulas'. Dimitrov clearly linked this to 'self-satisfied sectarianism ... satisfied with its doctrinaire narrowness, its divorce from the real life of the masses; sectarianism which professes to know all and considers it superfluous to learn from the masses'. Such sectarianism, he claimed, *'will not and cannot* understand that the leadership of the working class by the Communist Party does not come of itself'. Instead, Communists must *'earn and win the confidence of the working masses* by everyday mass work and a correct policy'.

Dimitrov made it clear that sectarianism was still alive, especially in continuing nervousness over the united front, and it must have been quite obvious that he was attacking the ideas of the 'class against class' period. It was no longer just the 'infantile disorder' about which Lenin had harangued the Comintern's Second Congress. It had become a 'deeply rooted vice'. Although he showed the close links between dogmatism and sectarianism, Dimitrov understandably shied away from suggesting how ultra-leftism had grown into this 'mature' disorder rather than disappearing as the movement grew up. That would have required a critical reassessment of Comintern history which was not his purpose at that time.

If these points constitute Dimitrov's lasting message, then his immediate concern was with the fascist danger. That surprised a few delegates who may have expected a continuation of past practice with optimistic trumpetings about imminent revolution. Indeed speaking in 1935, before the world had even heard of the gas chambers, it might have seemed that Dimitrov was exaggerating the danger. He therefore listed the grisly details of fascist horrors up to that time.

His definition of fascism as 'the open terroristic dictatorship of the most reactionary, most chauvinistic and most imperialist elements of finance capital' was first used by the Comintern in December 1933 and is said to have been devised by Stalin. It was criticised in the course of discussion and Dimitrov himself emphasised that no general characterisation of fascism could excuse the need for a concrete analysis of each specific case. Togliatti had previously pointed out that Spanish fascism was based on the large landowners while the Spanish delegates at the congress claimed that it was based on the military and Catholic hierarchies. Thorez and Cachin indicated that French fascism also had a military form, relying as it did on senior army officers.

The great benefit of Dimitrov's definition was that it enabled him to distinguish clearly and dramatically between fascist and democratic methods of rule. It is not 'an ordinary succession of one bourgeois government by another', he insisted, directly contradicting Comintern statements of a few years previously, 'but a substitution of one state form of class domination of the bourgeoisie – bourgeois democracy – by another form – open terrorist dictatorship'.

To achieve this, fascism made demagogic appeals to the people's most urgent needs and feelings. These were adapted to the specific circumstances of each country and frequently gave fascism a progressive appearance. Dimitrov showed a very clear awareness of fascism's mass appeal, but he saw its real essence in deep hostility to the workers' movement and to all forms of democracy. Subsequent events were to support this view when many fascists quickly forgot their chauvinism and became the most enthusiastic collaborators with foreign occupation. Although he did point to the internal contradictions of fascism, he was implicitly rejecting the view that had gained dominance in the Comintern in the mid-1920s which had emphasised fascism's 'petty bourgeois' base and revolutionary rhetoric, a view leading to unrealistic hopes that its internal conflicts would quickly cause it to collapse, thereby hastening the revolutionary process.

Dimitrov himself had, in fact, emphasised in 1923 that fascism 'is the complete negation of democracy and of all political rights and freedoms for the masses ... far from being only *anti-Communist*, it is at the same time *anti-popular* in essence'.[26] Such thoughts remained undeveloped and were soon almost forgotten, but Dimitrov could resurrect them with a stirring appeal to defend bourgeois democracy.

> How great were the sacrifices of the British working class before it secured the right to strike, a legal status for its trade unions, the right of assembly and freedom of the press, extension of the franchise and other rights ... The proletariat of all countries has shed much of its blood to win bourgeois-democratic liberties, and will naturally fight with all its strength to retain them.

There was strong support for example from Gottwald who was 'naturally for the defence of those democratic rights attacked by fascism'.[27] There were, however, doubts expressed, for example by Bela Kun who went no further than a grudging acknowledgement that 'bourgeois democracy represents only a different mixture of deceit and violence than fascism'.[28]

The point was that, although Dimitrov's views seem entirely sensible, he was breaking from firmly established Comintern positions. As he acknowledged, the opponents of the Russian Bolsheviks had relied heavily on the slogan of the defence of democracy. The reaction against that was reflected in the resolution of the Comintern's First Congress in 1919 which dismissed such issues as freedom of assembly and freedom of the press: until the exploiters were expropriated and the state machine smashed they were apparently of little value. Parliamentary forms were equated with 'the dictatorship of the bourgeoisie' and were to be swept away and replaced by soviets'.[29] The specific experience of the Russian revolution was thus generalised for the whole Communist movement. At the Sixth Congress democratic demands were treated as if they were irrelevant to the working class in the advanced countries because it was on the verge of 'a direct transition to the dictatorship of the proletariat'.[30]

The People's Front

There were still fears that the fight for democracy might somehow degenerate into an opportunist policy losing sight of the ultimate aim. That, however, did not show itself in opposition to Dimitrov's strategy for the defeat of fascism. The precise details were to vary from one country to another, but the central message was that where fascism had triumphed it had done so primarily because the working class was split and also because it was isolated from its natural allies such as the peasantry. As fascism was 'the most vicious enemy' of 90 per cent of the people, it should be perfectly possible to unite the overwhelming majority against it. This obviously could not be done on the basis of a Communist programme for immediate socialist revolution. Instead, the key was to create the widest possible unity around issues of immediate concern and that could hardly be achieved without unity with the leaders of other political parties.

The most obvious allies were among the social democrats. Dimitrov saw two principal camps emerging among these, one

favouring continued class collaboration while the other favoured
unity with Communists. This reversed the policy of greatest
hostility to the left wing of social democracy, but also made it
absolutely clear that there was no hope of unity with social
democracy as a whole. For some speakers this showed the
continuing relevance of 'class against class', although the slogan
was being given a substantially different meaning. It was not used
at all by Dimitrov, but his insistence on a selective approach
towards other parties would seem to have conflicted with the
broadest possible *anti-fascist*, rather than anti-capitalist unity, and
was not reflected in French experience.

There was anyway continuing distrust amongst social
democrats of the Communists' motives. It was always an open
question whether offers of unity were not just, as the Comintern's
first President, Zinoviev, once described them, a tactical
manoeuvre to expose the social democratic leaders. In fact, as
Pieck admitted at the Seventh Congress, such proposals
frequently had been linked with conditions known to be
unacceptable to social democrats. It is therefore not surprising
that, when the Comintern approached the Labour and Socialist
International in October 1934 with an offer of common action to
help the fight in Spain, where the coal miners of Asturias were
being ruthlessly suppressed, the immediate response was
suspicious, questioning as to whether this was not yet another
manoeuvre. Thorez, representing the Comintern, replied rather
ambiguously 'that this is neither a new line nor a manoeuvre on a
grand scale on Moscow's part. There has not been and will not be
any change in the policy of the Communist International.'[31] Fully
a month later, and despite Communist protestations that unity
against fascism should have absolute priority, the offer was
rejected with the comment that the Spanish workers' movement
had by then been defeated. In fact, although socialists from
France, Austria, Italy and Spain were in favour of unity, there was
firm opposition from others, especially the British Labour Party.
The right had preferred inaction while brushing aside offers of
unity on the grounds of programmatic differences or with general
proposals for a full merger of parties, which Dimitrov insisted
was not possible at that time, so that such discussions would only
make unity on immediate issues more difficult.

Despite this concern with organised social democracy,
Dimitrov stated that the aim was certainly not just a coalition of
political parties. The key objective was 'the militant activity of the

working class itself'. This could involve many organisational
forms including 'elected non-party class bodies of the united
front, at the factories, among the unemployed, in the working
class districts, among small towns-folk and in the villages'. This, it
was hoped, would bring in vast masses of unorganised working
people. Perhaps because it reminded him of the soviets in the
Russian revolution, this was the only element of Dimitrov's
proposals that Trotsky liked. It was also one that proved
impossible to put into practice.

The Congress also called for trade union unity and, where
possible, the merging of rival unions – aims more easily
realisable. In fact, the previous practice of insisting on
independent 'Red' trade unions was probably criticised more
strongly than any other aspect of Communist activity. At the Sixth
Congress the 'reformist' unions had been denounced as 'organs
of the bourgeois state'. Shortly afterwards Stalin justified creating
separate Communist unions on the grounds that the decisive
revolutionary struggle was imminent.[32] In practice, however, the
effect was simply to isolate the most militant workers from the
mass of their colleagues. Despite propaganda about the crisis of
the Amsterdam trade union international, the early 1930s saw a
growth in membership of the reformist unions in many countries
as workers sought protection against lower wages and
unemployment. The new line, modelled on the most recent
French experience, was therefore for full trade union unity on
terms that included democracy, freedom of opinion and no
victimisation for membership of a particular political party. The
united unions were to be independent from parties, but that did
not mean political neutralism. They were to fight for the workers
against capital, but it was now implicitly accepted that
Communists were not the only ones capable of doing this.

Alongside this working class unity Dimitrov saw the possibility
of, and the need for, much broader anti-fascist unity. In fact, in
those countries where the working class was only a small minority
this was clearly absolutely essential. It meant abandoning the
mistaken view, deeply rooted in the Hungarian, Romanian,
Greek, Bulgarian and Yugoslav parties, that the peasants and the
urban petty bourgeoisie were somehow a reserve for fascism. To
some extent this had become a self-fulfilling prophecy as peasants
had suffered disastrously from the world depression and many
did turn to fascism.

The Bulgarian Kolarov explained in a major speech on work in the villages, that Communists should drop talk of proletarian revolution, soviet power and the collectivisation of agriculture. Instead, they had to accept the peasants' own judgement of what their immediate demands should be. He condemned those who refused to support actual peasant struggles and who dismissed their 'limited' demands as representing a narrow, reformist approach. Instead, Communists should be fully involved in issues like the deferment of taxes and duties, the lowering of rent and the availability of cheap loans. Such was to be the basis for a really broad 'people's front' extending beyond the working class to involve anyone, even capitalists, who could be won as allies against fascism. An additional novelty in the congress's resolution, already reflected in French experience but clearly going beyond earlier notions of a united front, was that unity could involve alliances with *parties* representing the peasants and petty bourgeoisie. This obviously sat uneasily alongside the alleged continuation of the 'class against class' approach.

The idea of the people's front had significance way beyond the anti-fascist struggle. Although the congress was preoccupied with Europe as the centre of the threat to peace and to the USSR, there was some attempt to apply its principles to colonial and dependent countries. The Chinese representative, Wang Ming, scathingly attacked the failure of all but the Japanese and American parties to give help to the Chinese revolution. His and other reports contained a lot of criticism of the former assumption that the national liberation struggle would quickly merge into a soviet revolution and also of the view, at one time propagated by Stalin, that the left wing of the national bourgeoisie was actually the most dangerous enemy.[33] It had been only a short step from that to condemn many leaders of the liberation movement, such as Gandhi in India, as agents of imperialism.[34]

The alternative in its most complete form was presented by the Brazilian representative who outlined his party's experience in creating a 'National Liberation Alliance'. Its manifesto, published before the World Congress on 5 July 1935, called for an anti-imperialist government that would nationalise foreign enterprises, divide up large land-holdings, implement social reforms such as the eight-hour day and extend democratic rights. This anti-imperialist and anti-feudal perspective was frequently referred to as a model for Communist parties throughout Latin America.

Revolution?

Many delegates went out of their way to insist that the anti-fascist struggle was not a purely *defensive* fight. On the contrary it was seen as the means to create the conditions for great advances in the future. There was, however, a clear implication that the aim – as repeated by Dimitrov – of 'the revolutionary overthrow of the rule of the bourgeoisie and the establishment of a soviet government' was not on the immediate agenda. Some speakers, most notably Pieck, still talked of a rising revolutionary tide, but the Soviet delegation tried to minimise such 'unrealistic' suggestions; thus, for example, the title of the first section of the main resolution was changed from 'Fascism and the Growth of Revolutionary Forces' to 'Fascism and the Working Class'.[35] The fear, presumably, was that such thoughts could divert attention away from the immediate issue of the fascist threat into romantic notions of an armed uprising which if attempted, for example in France, could have had catastrophic consequences.

Instead, the immediate hope was that unity around anti-fascist demands could culminate in the formation of governments that Communists could support. Their exact programmes were left vague, obviously differing for each country, but would include economic measures beneficial to the workers, a purge of fascists from the state machine and the disarming of fascist organisations. The most complete programme, not surprisingly, was being developed in France, where the central social demand was for heavier taxes on the rich to pay for improved services such as free milk for the children of the unemployed: this was already being distributed in Communist municipalities. The target became the '200 families' who were said to dominate French industry and politics. The campaign fitted well with Thorez's insistence on the need to concentrate on the immediate demands of the working people and it also looked like very good anti-capitalist propaganda, but it was not directly linked to the transition to socialism.

Dimitrov's attempt to find such links provided the least satisfactory part of his presentation. The fundamental problem was that he was still tied by the unwritten understanding that there should be no direct criticism of the Comintern's earlier line and that seemingly included its long-standing condemnation of 'worker-peasant governments', actually coalitions of Communists and left-wing Social Democrats, that had emerged in the German states of Saxony and Thuringia in 1923. The KPD, egged on from Moscow, had used them as the basis for an unsuccessful attempt at armed insurrection throughout Germany and had later been condemned by the Comintern for entering governments which lacked a programme of immediate revolution. The paradox was that, while proposing a united front with a still broader class base and more diverse tasks, Dimitrov was obliged to repeat Zinoviev's criticisms of 'right opportunism' and insisted that the 'government of the anti-fascist Popular Front could only be formed in the midst of a political crisis with the state apparatus already disorganised and paralysed'. He placed it 'on the eve of the victory of the Soviet revolution' and was adamant that it could not be formed under 'normal' conditions. The logic of his criticism of events in Saxony and Thuringia was that such a government's primary task should be arming the workers. That was simply not the central issue in France at the time, and it was highly unlikely that enough allies could be won for such a programme. It led to the bizarre paradox that grave doubts were expressed about whether Communists could participate in the government that they more than anyone else were working for.

Dimitrov expressed the vague hope that the government of the united front could become one of the most important transitional forms leading to the proletarian revolution. But the united front government itself was not to implement fully socialist measures although genuine socialists in social democratic parties would have found such measures very difficult to oppose. The French Socialists actually called for the socialisation of the banks and big industry, but Thorez had replied:

We are for expropriation pure and simple of the capitalist expropriators, but we consider that one condition must be fulfilled in order to socialise, just one little condition: the possession of power, the seizure of power.[36]

His reluctance could have had a very reasonable justification as, again in the face of Socialist scepticism and despite his continuing use of the 'class against class' slogan, he wanted to create a broader front incorporating non-socialists. He was, however, relying on a theoretical justification that reflected the superficially radical dogma, established over the years within the Comintern, that socialist measures were possible only under a dictatorship of the proletariat led exclusively by a Communist Party. That itself must have made firm and lasting unity with other political parties much more difficult.

War

The other main reports were delivered by Manuilsky, on the construction of socialism in the USSR, and by Togliatti on the preparations for a new imperialist world war. Manuilsky's speech aroused no controversy. His account of economic and social advance, contrasted with the stagnation of capitalism, struck a chord with delegates who had already been deeply impressed by visits to factories newly built in the Soviet Union's great industrialisation drive. Togliatti had to cover more difficult ground.

Although he claimed to be building on previous Comintern policy, his call to fight for the *prevention* of war amounted to a major change. Communists had campaigned persistently against war, but they had previously regarded it as an inevitable consequence of capitalism. Togliatti repeated that theory, but added an analysis of the world situation which pointed to Nazi Germany in alliance with Italy and Japan as the main threats to world peace. Japan had invaded Manchuria in September 1931 and Germany was secretly rearming. Both of these moves could be interpreted as a threat to the USSR and Togliatti made the general comment that the coming war, however it might start, 'will inevitably become a war against the Soviet Union'. With revolution nowhere on the horizon, nobody doubted that the defence of the USSR was a prime duty of the Comintern.

Neither did anybody challenge Togliatti's suggestion that transforming 'imperialist war into civil war' by 'revolutionary mass actions', as the Sixth Congress had proposed, would be made much easier by 'conducting a struggle for the defence of peace prior to the outbreak of war'. He could thereby claim that 'We defend peace, not because we are flabby Tolstoyans, but because we are striving to ensure the conditions for the victory of the revolution.' There were however, only thirty participants in the discussion and Togliatti complained that it had remained largely at the level of generalisations. Very little was said on what actually could be done about Japanese aggression in China or about arms supplies to the Italian fascists then preparing their attack on Ethiopia.

During the discussion itself one of the major issues was the Franco-Soviet pact signed on 2 May 1935, after which Stalin had expressed 'complete understanding and approval of the national defence policy pursued by France with the object of maintaining its armed forces at a level consistent with its security requirements'. This seemed to conflict with the PCF's long anti-militarist record: the party apparently 'had certain misgivings' and its opponents tried to cause as much embarrassment as possible. Togliatti helpfully quoted Lenin on the possibility of reaching a military agreement with one imperialist bloc against another, but the real issue was that Stalin's comments could be read as implying that the PCF should break from its long-standing practice of voting against any military budget.

Again, Togliatti rejected this, arguing that Communist parties could take differing tactical positions on specific questions. The French Communist, André Marty asked:

> What guarantees have we that this army will not be thrown against the workers and peasants in battle tomorrow? What guarantees have we that the army will cease oppressing and harassing the enslaved peoples of the colonies?

The pact, it was concluded, did not indicate that the French army had changed sides. There was even a strong fascist influence within it. Military budgets could therefore only be supported alongside the democratisation of the army which was to be one of the major tasks of a Popular Front government.

In general, however, Togliatti insisted on the 'complete identity of aim between the peace policy of the Soviet Union and the policy of the working class and the Communist parties of the capitalist countries'. This meant not only defending the Soviet Union in general but also 'its whole policy and each of its acts'. He thereby implicitly justified Soviet domination over the Comintern as the Comintern itself certainly had no practical means of questioning Soviet foreign policy. He could be said to have justified in advance the change of line in 1939 when the needs of Soviet diplomacy were allowed to dictate a sudden reversal of Comintern policy away from the fight against fascism.

The more immediate problem with Togliatti's position, and indeed with the whole line of the Seventh Congress, remained the tactics in those countries threatened by external aggression. They clearly were to be defended. As Dimitrov insisted, Communists should never allow their internationalism to appear as support for 'national nihilism', but ultimately a choice had to be made between defending an existing state machine, albeit improved by further democratic reforms, and working for its dissolution and the establishment of 'soviet' power. Thus in Czechoslovakia, shortly after the Seventh Congress, the Communist Party took the very sensible step of supporting an anti-fascist candidate for President, although he had no interest in unity with Communists, and of voting in parliament for strengthening the armed forces. The party was soon condemned for right opportunism and so made more foreceful criticisms of social democracy and of the 'left wing' of the bourgeoisie, and linked calls for a people's front with the unrealistic notion of 'Jacobin' defence, to be based on the dissolution of the existing army. By the time of the Nazi threat of 1938 the Czech Communists had reverted to calls for the broadest possible anti-fascist unity and for stronger armed forces, as the Czech people turned to the regular army as the only body capable of defending their country.

After the Congress

The Comintern's Seventh Congress ended with a clear and enthusiastic acceptance of Dimitrov's line. Resolutions were passed unanimously and on the face of it the movement had never been so united. The next few months saw a major campaign by legal parties to popularise its decisions. It soon became clear, however, that the achievement of the people's front in practice was far from easy.

There was a very positive response from some left-wing social democrats, but the Labour and Socialist International did not shift. Adler, its secretary, sent a letter to all its members urging them not to believe the resolutions of the Seventh Congress because 'there has been no change in the opinions of the Communist International': it was just adopting 'more flexible tactics'. In Britain the *Daily Herald* had already warned against the 'Trojan horse' of the united front while Kautsky called again for 'a united front for the defence and renewal of democracy' which was to be directed primarily against the Soviet Union. Generally speaking right-wing social democrats could not understand the Seventh Congress; they saw either a capitulation by the Comintern from revolution or a cunning trick that represented only a superficial change. They had some justification as the Comintern itself referred only to the 'tactic' of the united and people's front. Nevertheless, despite ambiguities and hesitations, the speeches by Dimitrov and others represented the start of a fundamentally different strategic approach to revolutionary politics in a non-revolutionary period.

The hostility and criticisms from social democrats made it easier for sectarian Communists to ignore the Comintern's new line. Thus the Central Committee of the Hungarian party argued that in their conditions it was not possible to speak of a fight for democracy and a people's front: the conclusion was that their policies had been correct before and required no changes. More generally, there was a strong tendency to proceed as if nothing had changed once the first formal approaches to other parties had been rebuffed. Kuusinen, a Finn who had been in the Comintern leadership since its foundation, warned at a meeting of the Presidium on 20 November 1935 against the tendency to take 'the road of least resistance' just producing generalised propaganda for a people's front. The need was to find the means to generate the necessary mass action. 'Self-satisfied sectarianism' should not make way simply for 'self-satisfied passivity'.[37]

There was, however, a still deeper problem as the Comintern leadership itself began to play down the significance of the Seventh Congress. This was at one time attributed by the Soviet historians Leibzon and Shirinya to the power and personality cult of J.V. Stalin, and there is strong, but largely circumstantial, evidence for this. He had been involved in developing the new line and Thorez later claimed that he had encouraged the PCF in its 'courageous policy of unity'.[38] Nevertheless, he never publicly approved of the congress's decisions and remained silent throughout its proceedings, although every mention of his name was met with 'tumultuous applause'.[39] He did not even mention the congress at the Eighteenth Congress of the CPSU in 1939 where it was referred to mainly in the context of alleged dangers of 'right opportunism'.

Stalin, it is frequently claimed, had over the years very little interest in the Comintern, but he must have seen its value in the mid-1930s. That did not mean devaluing its role into a mere appendage of Soviet diplomacy, as Stalin seems to have been convinced that a political struggle was required to halt the spread of fascism. It would, however, be no surprise if Stalin had warned against strengthening the critique of policies he had previously advocated. That could explain why Manuilsky, when speaking at meetings of Moscow and Leningrad party activists immediately after the congress, referred to the continuing relevance of Stalin's thesis that fascism and social democracy are not antipodes but twins.[40] This, along with a claim that Comintern policy had been fully correct even before the congress, contrasted strikingly with Manuilsky's statements at the congress itself.

The impact of the 'cult of the personality' is also very clear in the limitations on democracy inside the Comintern. On the face of it, with a new Executive firmly committed to the people's front, there was an ideal basis for further development of the new line. In fact there never was another congress, although the statutes specified one every two years. There was not even a major policy discussion within the Executive. Probably the clearest violations of democracy affected the Polish Party, where the 'right', although its positions had been vindicated at the congress, was never allowed back into the leadership. The Comintern conducted no political fight against the sectarians it had previously helped to power. Instead, the whole party was dissolved in June 1938 by the Comintern and its leaders perished in Stalin's purges alongside other leading figures in the Comintern, such as Kun, who were always uneasy about the people's front. Manuilsky claimed that 'agents of Polish fascism managed to get positions of leadership',[41] but it was accepted in 1956 that the charge had been false.

All this, however, cannot detract from the enormous advance that was being made. The essential message of the Seventh Congress was very simple and clear. Communist parties were to become an active – possibly even a leading – force in their national political lives by creating unity around the anti-fascist struggle. This was the basis for an enormous advance by the Communist movement and by the left generally in the latter part of the 1930s. Despite its ultimate defeat, the Popular Front government in Spain showed a degree of anti-fascist unity which led to a democratic republic distinct from the usual form of bourgeois democracy, but also quite different from the Communists' conception of the dictatorship of the proletariat. Thus, alongside its powerful condemnations of sectarianism and dogmatism, the Seventh Congress must be seen as a vital starting point for new ideas on the transition to socialism that could be built on, especially after the Comintern's dissolution in 1943.

I would like to acknowledge the helpful criticisms of an earlier draft of this chapter from Jim Fyrth, Monty Johnstone and Noreen Branson. I also benefited from the memories of Finlay

Hart and Idris Cox who were both at the Seventh World Congress.

NOTES

1. J. Braunthal, *History of the International*, London 1967, Vol. II, pp. 360-4.
2. J. Degras (ed.), *The Communist International 1919-1943 Documents*, 3 vols, London 1956-65, Vol. II, p. 483.
3. Ibid., p. 456.
4. J.V. Stalin, *Works*, 13 vols, Moscow, 1952-55, Vol. VI, p. 294 and pp. 402-3.
5. M.K. Dziewanowski, *The Communist Party of Poland*, Cambridge Mass 1959, pp. 136-7 and J. Kowalski, *Trudne lata*, Warsaw 1966, p. 105.
6. Quoted in M. Hájek, *Jednotná fronta*, Prague 1969, p. 183.
7. Hájek, op.cit., p. 186 and Z. Hradilák, 'On the process of the constitution of the 'definitive' form of the Communist Party of Czechoslovakia (1929-1936)', *History of Socialism Yearbook 1968*, Prague 1969, pp. 50-3.
8. Quoted in Hájek, op.cit., p. 197.
9. Quoted in B.M. Leibzon and K.K. Shirinya, *Povorot v politike Kominterna* Moscow 1975, p. 215.
10. Braunthal, op.cit., p. 373.
11. Quoted in E.H. Carr, *The Twilight of Comintern 1930-1935*, London 1982, p. 91.
12. Degras, op.cit., Vol. III, p. 262.
13. Ibid, p. 253.
14. Hradilák, op.cit.
15. Carr, op.cit., p. 52.
16. Degras, op.cit., Vol II, p. 458.
17. Stalin, op.cit., Vol. XIII, p. 309.
18. Leibzon and Shirinya, op.cit., p. 93.
19. M. Thorez, *Oeuvres*, Book II, Vol. VI, Paris 1951, p. 48.
20. Leibzon and Shirinya, op.cit., pp. 93-4 and A.P. Dimitriev and K.K. Shirinya, 'Vopreky istoricheskoy pravde', *Voprosy istorii KPSS*, 1972, No 1, p. 128. These two sources also provide general accounts of the development of the new line.
21. For a discussion of this event see Carr, op.cit., p. 199.
22. From notes of 1 July 1934, reproduced in *Marxism Today*, July 1972.
23. Quoted in Leibzon and Shirinya, op.cit., p. 116.
24. Degras, op.cit., Vol. III, pp. 351-2 and *Inprecorr*, 28 August 1935.
25. Quotes from the congress, unless otherwise stated, are from *Seventh Congress of the Communist International abridged stenographic report*, Moscow 1939. This version omitted parts from some of the most important speeches and Campbell's contribution was absent altogether.
26. G. Dimitrov, *For a United and Popular Front*, Sofia nd, p. 12.
27. K. Gottwald, *Spisy*, 15 vols, Prague 1951-60, Vol. VI, p. 180.
28. Leibzon and Shirinya, op.cit., p. 211.
29. Degras, op.cit., Vol. I, pp. 7-16.
30. Degras, op.cit., Vol. II, p. 505.

31. M. Thorez, *Oeuvres*, Book II, Vol. VII, Paris 1952, p. 39.
32. Stalin, op.cit., Vol. XI, pp. 311-4.
33. Stalin, op.cit., Vol. VII, pp. 146-51.
34. Leibzon and Shirinya, op.cit., p. 257.
35. K.K. Shirinya, *Strategiya i taktika Kominterna v borbe protiv fashisma i voyni*, Moscow 1979, pp. 65 and 73.
36. *Seventh Congress of the Communist International*, p. 223.
37. Leibzon and Shirinya, op.cit., p. 365.
38. M. Thorez, *Fils du peuple*, Paris 1960, p. 102.
39. R.P. Dutt, in a letter to *The Times Literary Supplement*, 5 May 1966, claimed that the British delegation publicly protested against the 'excessive adulation' and the 'assumption of infallibility' surrounding Stalin's name. Idris Cox has confirmed that the British delegation generally frowned on the cult of Stalin's personality.
40. *Inprecorr*, 17 December 1935.
41. *The Land of Socialism Today and Tomorrow*, Moscow 1939, p. 89.

What the Papers Said

TONY ATIENZA

It was a lovely summer; a scorching August. Every paper had 'Heatwave' headlines and pictures of crowded beaches. If you accosted the *News Chronicle*'s Lobby Lud on the promenade you could win yourself £10. In Drury Lane Ivor Novello dreamed on through 'Glamorous Nights'; you could swoon to young Clarke Gable at the London Pavillion. After five hard years of depression this could at last be recovery: look how splendid the Jubilee had been in May, real royal razzmatazz! Twelve thousand guests graced the royal garden party in July, where the *Daily Herald*'s Hannan Swaffer saw 'the Russian Ambassador and Madame Maisky presented ... So ... did the Soviet and the British monarchy exchange greetings.' That would set the ultra-left a-flutter.

It was too good to last: on 31 July at Old Trafford the Test versus South Africa ended in a draw; by the end of August came news of storms and flooded roads. On 27 July the *Daily Herald*'s main front page news was the death 'on his wedding anniversary, among his guests' of Lieutenant-Colonel Sir Dennis Boles of Bishop's Lydeard, Master of the West Somerset Fox Hounds. There were still two million unemployed and last January they counted 1,472,891 on poor relief.

There was, indeed, plenty of worrying news, whatever paper you read from *The Times*, under the firm control of Geoffrey Dawson, at one political pole, to the little *Daily Worker* at the other. Since Geoffrey Dawson once, unexpectedly, described *The Times* as 'something of an organ of the Left', one should recall the existence of the *Daily Mail* on the extreme right.

During this summer the serious national dailies were increasingly anxious about Mussolini's threats towards Abyssinia; they were anxious, too, at the spread of fascist ideas and influence throughout Europe. The crucial debates on these two linked problems revolved around the role of the League of Nations on the one hand and the possibility of a united front on the other. In this latter case the attitude of the press to the Seventh World Congress is enlightening.

Already on 17 July the *Manchester Guardian* carried the following report under the headline 'THE COMMUNIST INTERNATIONAL – AN EARLY MEETING?'

> The Soviet Press today lifted a corner of the blanket of silence which covers the intentions concerning the oft-postponed seventh congress of the Communist International by indicating that it is still planned for the near future. ... the chief aim of the Comintern ... is to push forcefully and persistently 'united front' tactics.[1]

The Times covered Russian news through its correspondent in Riga, capital of semi-fascist Latvia, five hundred miles from Moscow, a feat once described as 'reporting a boxing match in the Albert Hall from the steps of the Albert Memorial'. His report ran:

> RED INTERNATIONAL'S CHANGED TONE –
> EFFECT OF M. STALIN'S FOREIGN POLICY.
> The Executive Committee of the Communist International has issued a new manifesto in connexion with the impending world congress of the International, the date of which has been postponed more than once. The manifesto is the weakest and vaguest which the Communist International has issued and is significant as reflecting the crisis in the organisation's policy which first became noticeable a year ago. The Soviet entry into the League of Nations and the collaboration with the French and other Governments have created difficulties for the Communist International in carrying on open activities against these Governments.[2]

On Friday of the following week the *News Chronicle* was quoting *Pravda*, 'on the eve of the opening in Moscow of the Seventh World Congress ... '

> *Pravda* asserts that ... 'The workers now understand that to succeed in the struggle against Fascism it was essential to present a united front, based on a revolutionary policy.
> 'Communists' it is emphasised, 'must fight whole-heartedly to save the remnants of bourgeois democracy from the advance of Fascism.'
> It is presumed that the change in policy is the result of the success of Fascism in Germany.[3]

A discerning enough comment!

On 27 July *The Times* reported the opening of the Congress

COMINTERN IN CONGRESS – MODIFIED TACTICS –
CO-OPERATION WITH SOCIALISTS.

The long-delayed seventh world congress of the Comintern (the first since 1928) opened in Moscow yesterday in the presence of M. Stalin ... The congress is on a smaller scale than was intended. The original programme provided for the arrival of over 1,000 white and coloured delegates, but only about half that number are now assembled.

The Congress opened with a speech by the German Communist, Herr Pieck ... The tone of the new programme differs markedly from the notorious militant programme of 1928, and Herr Pieck's speech was decidedly 'diplomatic'.[4]

Thus by the first weekend of the Congress, readers were aware of the tenor of the early discussions. Naturally their particular interest lay in the attitude of the British Communist Party: the *Manchester Guardian* on Monday 29 July said that on the Sunday J.R. Campbell,

admitted that the party had made serious mistakes in tactics in its approach to the trade unions, but claimed that the hunger march which it organised had succeeded in drawing hundreds of local unions into the sphere of Communist influence.[5]

Predictably *The Times* Riga correspondent did not have his copy ready for another two days and he seems a little confused; on 31 July the headline was 'WORLD COMMUNISTS AND WAR'. The report ran:

The chief delegates ... in Moscow are reiterating the Communist shibboleth used at the Sixth Congress seven years ago: 'Prevent imperialist war by class war.'

The British delegate, Mr. Campbell, urged the necessity of an energetic campaign against nationalism and the Hitler Government as the chief organizer of war. The British Labour Party, he said, had lost caste by collaborating with a bourgeois Government in condoning German and Japanese military plans. The British Communist Party had successfully used unemployment and the industrial depression to organize strikes and hunger marches, and its membership had increased by 33% in the last six months.

The German delegates, describing the determined anti-Fascist struggle by the persecuted and illegal Communist Party, and the methods employed to secure its existence, averred that they had discovered common ground with the Social Democrats. Enumerating imminent war dangers, the Czechoslovak delegate struck an anomalous note, contending that Soviet Russia was the protector of the national independence of small states against Fascism, while delegates of other countries classed nationalism with the chief foe, Fascism.[6]

The same day the *Manchester Guardian* leader writer took a broader but firmly critical approach.

> What Karl Marx said of the Democrats in his day is true of the Communists in our own day – that they emerge from the most shameful defeat with looks of triumph on their faces.

After listing recent ineffective – indeed disastrous – Communist policies, mainly in Germany, he continues scolding:

> One might have thought that [the Congress] would have taken stock of the ruin it has brought about, but not at all; the congress explains amid much cheering that despite minor errors ... the Communists were always fundamentally right and everybody else fundamentally wrong. Perhaps the future of Europe will be some form of Communism, but that it will never be with the Communism of the Third International is made much more certain by the International itself and its congresses in Moscow than it could ever be made either by Hitler or Mussolini.[7]

The next news of importance in Britain came a week later with Harry Pollitt's speech to the Congress. On 8 August the *Manchester Guardian* reported:

> ### THE UNITED FRONT –
> ### BRITISH COMMUNISTS PLEDGE SUPPORT.
> A pledge that the British Communist party will faithfully carry out 'United Front' decisions that are in the interests of the working class and participate in elaborating decisions if the Labour Party consents to admit revolutionary organisations was made in a speech by Mr. Harry Pollitt ...
> Mr. Pollitt declared that the greatest task of the British Communist party was to engage youth in active support of the United Front.
> Dimitroff ... said: The struggle against Fascism in England is a struggle against the National Government, which is lowering the standards of living of the masses.
> The Communists are ready to discuss with the Labour Party a programme aiming at establishing a Labour Government.[8]

The next day the *News Chronicle* was also reporting that

> Mr. Harry Pollitt, leader of the British Communists, is henceforth to teach his followers love of their country. ... he disclaimed that Communists are friends of all countries but their own.
>
> 'We love our country', he declared, 'and are prepared to offer our lives in an effort to eliminate poverty and unemployment.
>
> 'Henceforth it will be the policy of the British Communist Party to popularize among British youth England's great traditions and the personalities connected with the struggle for progress and democratic rights.'[9]

The *Manchester Guardian* headline that day, 'MR. POLLITT ON THE NEW COMMUNISM – LOVE OF COUNTRY', was followed by an agency report:

> An appeal to the Labour party to open its ranks and admit British Communists in order that there might be a joint fight against Fascism was made by Mr. Harry Pollitt ...[10]

The only big daily that purported working class sympathies, the *Daily Herald*, carried no news of the Congress until it was over; even the Co-operative *Reynolds News*, a Sunday paper which often carried items of interest to the left, simply stated on 11 August,

> Mr. Harry Pollitt ... says that another approach is to be made by the Communist Party of Great Britain for common political action.[11]

Towards the end of the Congress the promotion of Dimitrov to the general secretaryship of the International was reported in the *News Chronicle*;

> DIMITROFF HAILED – NOW A WORLD LEADER OF COMMUNISTS.
> When the Congress of the Communist International closed last night, after sitting for 27 days, the delegates of 65 nations raised a storm of cheers for Dimitroff, the Bulgarian who was acquitted in the Reichstag fire trial.
>
> Dimitroff ... called on the world's Communists ... to prepare 'for a victorious world proletarian revolution' ... [He] has emerged from the Congress as one of the first leaders of the Communists of the world. It is understood that he will fill an important role on the Comintern Executive ... Messrs. Pollitt, Dutt and Campbell, the British Communists, have been elected to the Comintern Executive Committee.[12]

Since Dimitrov's appointment was made the day after the Congress closed, there were further reports in the *News Chronicle*[13] and *The Times* [14] the next day; these had been preceded by a slightly inaccurate piece in *Reynolds News* on Sunday 18 August:

> POST FOR DIMITROV – TO BE PRESIDENT OF THE
> NEW COMMUNIST INTERNATIONAL.
> George Dimitrov ... is to be appointed president of the Communist International.[15]

The Times correspondent in Riga produced the most colourful picture of the closing session of the Congress

> COMMUNISTS' ORDERS FROM MOSCOW – INTRIGUE
> AMONG FOREIGN TROOPS.
> The Comintern Congress, which opened on July 25 and was attended by 510 delegates from 65 sections of the Communist International, closed in Moscow at 2 o'clock this morning. Twenty members of the International Control Commission were elected ... Among the resolutions unanimously passed were: Instructions for the disintegration of 'Fascist and Imperialist' armies by means of the conspirational elements in them, the spreading of illegal literature, and the holding of secret meetings to intrigue for the dismissal of reactionary officers: also an appeal to the workers of the world to help the Red Army by all means in their power and at any price in order that they might defeat the 'Imperialist' armies in case of war against the Soviet. ... The Congress closed with cries of 'Hail Stalin – Hail the Communist Party – Hail Dimitroff, the steersman'. Dimitroff's speech to the Congress at 1 o'clock this morning was broadcast this evening.[16]

In the *Daily Herald* the only mention of the entire Congress seems to have been made indirectly on Tuesday 22 August in an account of the Executive of the Labour and Socialist International then meeting in Brussels:

> The Executive decided to place on its agenda for the next meeting the question of establishing contact between the Labour and Socialist International and the Communist International with a view to an examination of the conditions for common action in the international sphere in opposition to war and Fascism and in defence of democratic liberty.
> The Secretariat was instructed to submit, as soon as the report and resolutions of the Seventh Congress of the Communist International

are published in full, a written report on the changes which have occurred in the Communist International especially in regard to the appreciation of the importance of the democratic rights and liberties.[17]

From a report in the *Manchester Guardian* on 22 August it appears that this move was initiated by the French Socialists.[18]

Throughout this summer the columns of the press are echoing the rumbling background to the Comintern Congress of fascist and anti-fascist actions – quite apart from the Abyssinian crisis. A cursory glance produces the following;

Lifelong imprisonment for Rakosi. [Hungarian Communist leader][19]

67 Hungarian Communists arrested.[20]

Popular Front from Radicals to Communists in France.[21]

'International' sung in Brest.[22]

Riots in France ... the rank and file of the Communist party is far from united behind the new Stalin policy ... [23]

Terrorism in Germany ... Socialist workman Jaenicke beheaded ... Communist Claus was sentenced to death by beheading ... Thälmann must be considered as being in mortal danger.[24]

The swastika flag of the German liner 'Bremen' was torn down and flung into the River Hudson by anti-Nazi demonstrators in New York yesterday.[25]

End of Freemasonry in Germany.[26]

This survey has covered only some of the national press, although probably the most significant part. The *Daily Herald*'s lack of enthusiasm can be explained if not excused, but also there was no leader comment either in the *News Chronicle* or *Reynolds News*, both 'leftish'. On the other hand the *Manchester Guardian* comment on 31 July has been noted above, and on Wednesday 28 August the following leader appeared under the title THE RED BOGEY:

... It is merely silly to protest because Communist leaders have been saying that the task of British politics is to get rid of the National

Government. Other people besides Communists would also say that ... The speeches at the Moscow Congress show clearly that Communism is on the defensive. It has ceased to promise a world revolution round the corner only (like the British Government) to avert Fascism. ... Even the most suspicious (apart from the British Government) would admit that in the present state of Europe not Communism but something much more evil is the enemy.[27]

The very profusion and diversity of periodicals on the left emphasize the minefield to be negotiated if a united front was to be attained in this country; in particular the nature of the Labour Party posed special problems.

The Scottish Labour Party's weekly *Forward* was published in Glasgow and had a London edition. It is not surprising, in spite of all the rumours and essays towards united action that ran ahead of the Seventh Congress, to find in the June *Forward* an article by Herbert Morrison attacking the Communist Party on precisely this issue.[28] The Scottish Labour Party secretary, Arthur Woodburn, followed in July under the heading 'Futility of the British Communist Party'.[29] In view of the *Daily Herald*'s reticence it is almost a relief to see that on both 31 August and 7 September an advertisement was allowed in *Forward* for a report-back meeting on the Congress with Harry Pollitt and D.F. Springhall at Battersea Town Hall on 8 September.[30] The only comment on the Congress that *Forward* could muster was hardly profound; it appeared on 14 September in Junius Junior's column headlined, HURRAH FOR LABOUR. The last paragraph reads:

How often have we heard from the Communists that the Labour Party is only a Bosses' Party? Worse even than the Tories, and so on. A great change has taken place, for the Communist leader, J.R. Campbell, has written quite recently ... 'The Communist Party is prepared to do all in its power to secure the return of ... a Labour Government.' Hurrah for the next Labour Government! Now I ask you, what next? It is time the Labour enthusiasts looked around a bit. Something is wrong when the *Daily Worker* begins to give its support to us. I suspect the Labour leaders are rapidly going Right Wing or the leaders of the Communist Party would not be so enthusiastic for a Labour Government.[31]

In contrast the Independent Labour Party's weekly *New Leader*, edited by Fenner Brockway, was rather more flexible. As early as May we read in a leading article:

THREE LINES: REFORMIST: COMMUNIST: REVOLUTIONARY SOCIALIST.
Communist Line.

... The Communist Parties are pursuing a tactic which aims at united action by all sections of the working class, including the Reformists, on immediate issues, but which refuses to face up to the conditions necessary to realise the much greater necessity for actual unity among Revolutionary Socialists for the decisive struggle.

They insist that other Revolutionary Socialists must unite with the Communist Parties and must come inside the Communist International.

The hard fact is that the Revolutionary Socialists will not do this. Under the direction of the Communist International the Communist Parties have made so many mistakes in tactics, have been so sectarian in spirit, and have had such a disastrous influence in dividing rather than unifying the working class, the Revolutionary Socialists are not prepared to unite with them or affiliate to their International.[32]

This appeared more than two months before the Seventh Congress was to convene. When it did the *New Leader* on 26 July carried the following report;

'WORLD CONGRESS: COMMUNIST INTERNATIONAL MEETS AT MOSCOW.

We understand that the World Congress of the Communist International is now meeting at Moscow. In view of the international situation the proceedings are not being given general publicity.

It is reported in Continental papers that about 400 delegates are present and that the Congress opened in a Moscow hotel – Hotel Lux – on Sunday. The further proceedings are being held in the Trade Union Palace. The Congress is expected to last three weeks.

The main subject is the growth of Fascism. Dimitrov is opening the discussions. The necessity for a united front with Social-Democratic Parties and Labour Parties is stressed.[33]

A week later, on 2 August, the problem of 'just wars' which the growth of fascism was posing, was dealt with at some length. The argument may be gathered from these extracts.

COMMUNISTS AND THE WAR THREAT.

The main feature of the earlier proceedings of the World Congress ... was a call to unite forces against Hitler's threat of war.

The principal speech ... [by] ... Comrade Pieck ... took the line that the Communists should, under certain circumstances at least, co-operate to defend 'bourgeois democratic' countries against

German Fascism. ... The I.L.P. attitude on this question is stated in the declaration 'Action against War', adopted by the last Annual Conference of the Party:

'The reformist sections of the working class movement in certain countries ... urge that the working class should be ready to support Governments which are 'democratic' – even though they are Capitalist – in a war against 'Fascist countries'.

'Revolutionary Socialists must reject this policy. War is not waged on account of forms of government, but in the interests of Capitalist profit.

' ... For the working class the duty of uncompromising opposition to all Capitalist Governments and the Capitalist League of Nations remains undiminished, despite the change in policy of the Soviet Union.

'Should Soviet Russia be the ally of any Capitalist Government in a future war, it will still be the first duty of the working class to refuse to collaborate with the Capitalist class and win political power and overthrow the Capitalist system in their own countries. In the long run this will be the greatest service to the Soviet Union.'

If the British Government is in any way involved in an attack on the Soviet Union, 'the I.L.P. will urge a General Strike ... and will do all in its power to assist Revolutionary Socialists abroad who take similar action against the Governments of their countries.'[34]

Reading this uncompromising view, one's eye is caught by a nearby headline, so full of portent, GREAT ANTI-FASCIST FRONT IN SPAIN.

A week further on the *New Leader* is reporting a discussion at the ILP Summer School, a debate between William Rust and Fenner Brockway

SOVIET FOREIGN POLICY – SHOULD WORKERS SUPPORT WAR UNDER CAPITALIST GOVERNMENTS?

Rust's central argument was that Soviet Russia had postponed war and given the workers an opportunity to prepare resistance. Brockway replied that the willingness of Soviet Russia to ally itself with Imperialist-Capitalist Governments had the effect of hindering the organisation of the workers for revolutionary resistance to war.

The difference between the Communist Party and the I.L.P. was sharply brought out on the issue as to what should be the attitude of the workers in a Capitalist country allied to the Soviet Union in a war.

Rust replied that in the case of France – which has signed a pact of mutual assistance with Russia – the issue before the workers would be to compel France to fulfil its obligations by entering the war. There would be no point in signing the pact and then saying: 'We only sign up to this point and now draw back'. The slogan should be: 'For the

war! For the defeat of German Fascism!' combined with opposition
to the Imperialist aims of the French Government.

Brockway said that it was the first duty of Revolutionary Socialists
to overthrow any Capitalist Government which took them into war.
Even if allied with Soviet Russia, no Capitalist Government could be
trusted. It would turn on Soviet Russia if victorious. The workers
must seize control of the Government, then they could with
confidence act with Soviet Russia, knowing that they would not be
sacrificed for Imperialism.[35]

James Maxton, MP was, of course, at the Summer School and
on Sunday 4 August spoke urging the Labour Party to be less
rigid in its attitude to a united front;

> In the time at their disposal before the General Election the working
> classes had got to weld out of the elements of the Labour Party, the
> I.L.P., and the Communist Party an intelligent policy and alternative
> to the National Government. That was not going to be achieved by
> the Labour Party and the T.U.C. saying that they were the bosses and
> that the rest of them had to get down on their knees. The I.L.P.
> would respond if the Labour Party came to them or the Communist
> Party saying that they recognised that there was a struggle not of
> party but of the working classes in which all elements of the working
> classes were involved. They were prepared to enter a united front in
> the electoral struggle, just as they had been prepared to enter a united
> front in the struggle against Fascism and war.[36]

In the *New Leader* of 16 August Fenner Brockway accepts that,

> developments of great importance are taking place ... These
> developments are a reflection of the new foreign policy of the Soviet
> Union, which is causing a drastic change in the policy of the various
> Communist Parties.
>
> The Soviet Union is seeking, in view of the War Danger, to create
> the strongest possible front of Governments against Germany and its
> ally Japan. ... The first effect of this policy is to reverse the historical
> revolutionary line of the maintenance of the class struggle within
> Capitalist nations in the event of war. Communist Parties in countries
> allied to Soviet Russia are now asked in time of war to join the ranks
> of 'national unity' and to postpone the revolution until victory has
> been won.
>
> The second effect of this policy is to reverse the revolutionary view
> that the peace machinery of Capitalist Governments cannot
> safeguard peace and is a cloak for Imperialist designs. The
> Communist International and its Parties are now committed to
> support the 'collective system of peace' of the League of Nations as
> an instrument against Germany.

The third effect of this policy is to reverse the revolutionary analysis of Fascism as a natural and inevitable development of Capitalism under certain economic, national and psychological conditions. Capitalist democracy becomes worthy of defence ... against Fascism ... In Britain the prejudices against the Communist Party are so strong in the Labour Party that there has as yet been little response to these developments and Harry Pollitt's speech at Moscow ... has been received coldly ... There must be no cessation of the class struggle in peace or in war. There must be no 'national unity' with the Capitalist class or Capitalist Governments ... The working class must rely on themselves and on their direct revolutionary action.

The new developments may bring the Communist Parties and Social Democrats together. But they will also bring the Revolutionary Socialists together ... [37]

Just before Harry Pollitt's Battersea meeting on the Congress, and as the Abyssinian war slipped ever closer, the *New Leader* produced a firmly sectarian article by R.A. Reynolds of which this is a sample.

SHALL IT BE WAR? – THE UNITED FRONT OF THE IMPERIALISTS, THE LABOUR PARTY, THE CHURCH AND THE COMMUNISTS.

Having received their orders from headquarters, the Communists have also charged madly into the fray with a blind discipline worthy of the Light Brigade.

They are supporting the position of the Labour and Socialist International ... without reservation, and their associated bodies ... have obediently fallen into line, advocating in particular the closing of the Suez Canal ...[38]

Close enough to the ILP but still inside the Labour Party, was the Socialist League, of which Stafford Cripps was a leading member. In June 1935 their National Conference passed a resolution part of which ran:

This Conference ... warns the workers not to be misled into support of a war entered into by a 'National' or capitalist Government in the name of the League of Nations, nor to overestimate the effect of the entry of the U.S.S.R. into the League.

In a speech on the same date Cripps himself called for

... the preparation for *mass resistance to war* by the workers of this country.[39]

In fact the Socialist League, although not without influence, had few working class members.

By 1935 the Socialist Party of Great Britain was to be found mainly in the London area; the purity of its belief in socialism could not be doubted but there was no clear idea of how it could be brought about. Their monthly *Socialist Standard* showed they had no time for united fronts; in July it commented upon,

> ...a piquant situation amongst the 'left-wing' parties [in France] ... That Communists and Socialists can even entertain the idea of forming a Government in coalition with Liberals for the purpose of administering capitalism should be sufficient to disillusion believers in the 'Communist' brand of Communism. And what a 'United Front'![40]

The October number showed the SPGB predictably unmoved by the 67th TUC, let alone the Seventh World Congress,

> Fascism ... is the superficial excuse necessary to render war acceptable ... The paramount issue in the world today is the struggle for Socialism ... [41]

Again,

UNITED FRONT AT LAST.

> The Communists seem to have achieved their hearts' desire, that much-sort-after 'United Front'. And ... on the Italian-Abyssinian dispute they are solidly behind the National Government – or should we say in front of them? 'The League's Covenant must be upheld by all means at our disposal', declared Sir Samuel Hoare ... And he has the solid support of the bulk of the Labour Party, the whole of the Liberal Party, and most certainly the Communist Party ... But their attempts to explain their 'policy' are ludicrous. Lenin's condemnation of the League as a 'Thieves' Kitchen' still holds good for us ... And what has become of their erstwhile boast, to 'turn every imperialist war into a civil war'?[42]

In November there appeared the comment that the ILP lay between the Communist Party and the Labour Party.

> ... although anti-Communist, they are pro-Soviet.[43]

Interestingly there was also the report of a question put by an SPGB member at an ILP meeting in the Memorial Hall on 26 September.

Does the ILP still believe in a United Front?

When the speaker – J. Gaster – replied,

> Yes ... [however] this does not mean suppression of individual differences, but agreement on the immediate objective.

the comment made was,

> So apparently the ultimate end doesn't matter after all![44]

Out here on the frontiers of the left was *The Vanguard* – quarterly journal of the British section of the Militant Socialist International. Their attitude to the Comintern is, perhaps, best shown in an article by Edith Moore in this journal for the fourth quarter of 1935 entitled 'ALL NATIONALISTS NOW!' which starts by quoting Harry Pollitt at Congress, then continues:

> ... Nationalism is one of the strongest bulwarks of modern Capitalism ... so there must be very substantial reasons for socialists to abandon even temporarily their attack upon it. What then ... of the new tactic of the Communist International ... The plain consequence of this attitude is nothing less than the complete abandonment of all the ground that has been slowly won in the development of the spirit of international solidarity in the working class ...
>
> The element of truth contained in the Comintern resolution is that the widespread influence of nationalist feeling is a fact which socialists cannot ignore and that there may be circumstances where it is not wise for socialists to allow the bourgeoisie to exploit this feeling for their own ends ... No one will believe that revolutionary socialists have ... a sentimental affection for the country in which they live. Thus the application of this political line will be interpreted as a trick, a deception to break down isolation ...
>
> The link between the socialist party and the masses ... is forged ... by consistent sincerity in the party propaganda ... a demagogue ... may retain the blind confidence of the masses for a long time. But ... one unmistakeable betrayal, one deliberate and obvious deception of the people, can shatter the confidence which has taken years ... to build up. And for a party to use nationalist slogans whose principles and organisations are well known to be international ... cannot fail to undermine confidence ...
>
> The Communist parties of many countries, and not the least that of Great Britain, have practised insincerity in many ways that have gravely weakened the confidence which they might otherwise have enjoyed. The Third International it seems has still to appreciate this

cause of its isolation. The new tactic ... will not help them out of their isolation in Great Britain ... [45]

In October *The Plebs*, organ of the National Council of Labour Colleges, published an article by their philosophical guru, Edward Conze. As the following extracts show it sums up ultra-left criticism of the new Comintern policy;

THE COMMUNISTS' LAST SOMERSAULT.

The congress had to meet because during the first half of 1935 the Communist parties had completely changed ... to a policy of extreme 'right-wing reformism', which till yesterday was rank heresy and treason ... The new policy was carried through only with difficulty ... In England we saw, for instance, that the Communists were very slow in grasping that they suddenly had to work for a Labour Government. Many of them ... continuing the old speeches on 'Social-fascism' and 'Labour traitors' ... The task of the world congress was to see that such mistakes were avoided in future ...

In Britain ... the *Daily Worker*, to everybody's surprise, also backs sanctions [against Italy] even if they lead to war. But the *Daily Worker* warns us that we should not mistake this for support of the National Government ...

In this vital issue of a war for sanctions the Communists line up with what they used to describe as the right-wing leaders of the Labour Party against the Labour Left, the Socialist League and the I.L.P. That is what I mean when I say that the Communists have moved on to the right wing of the Labour movement ...

How can we explain this amazing change in policy ...? The International, ever since 1923, has suffered from a two-fold contradiction ... On the one hand it tried to square the interests of the Russian Government with those of the workers outside Russia.

On the other hand it attempted to build up a revolutionary mass party in countries outside Russia in a period in which the masses were not revolutionary ...

On the one hand, the Communists had the duty of defending the Soviet Union. On the other hand, they had the duty of defeating their own Governments. What shall they do now if their Governments are allies of the Soviet Union? Shall they strike at their own Governments and thereby jeopardise Russia's military chances? ...

During recent years, the struggle between the imperialist powers developed more and more openly into a struggle between the satisfied Empires like Great Britain and France on the one hand, and the unsatisfied Empires, like Italy, Germany and Japan on the other. What stand did the Soviet Union take in this struggle? It allied itself with one of the satisfied Empires – France. From then on the

Communist revolutionary regards it as his sacred duty to fight for the 'status quo' …

This new policy has led to the bankruptcy of the Communist Parties. In their tortuous attempts to square Leninism and the desire for peace with the support of a war waged by a capitalist League of Nations, the English Communists have lost both self-respect and the respect of others …

The Communist Parties were further faced with the contradictory task of building up a revolutionary mass movement with non-revolutionary masses. They had a double way of trying to solve this contradiction. On the one hand, they could sacrifice their mass influence and adhere to a strictly revolutionary policy, preserving themselves as a small but revolutionary party for the time of revolution. That is what they tried first. The result was that the masses left them, and that no revolutionary mass party exists in any capitalist country …

The fact has gradually penetrated into the brains of the Communists that the masses follow the 'reformist leaders' because the masses want reform. The Communist International now tries to adapt itself to the 'reformist masses', and in this way win them over – to what? To reform.

This calculation is mistaken. The Communists have overlooked the vital fact that now there is no room for them. There is no reason to duplicate the work of the Labour Party. What is the use of having two 'reformist' parties? …

In consequence there is now no party in Western Europe which even claims to train its members to make use of a crisis. And, if another great war comes … and the tide of revolution rises high, the working class in Western Europe will have no suitable leaders, unless they come from outside the Communist parties.[46]

When the war did come Conze, whose forecast of the demise of the Communist Parties was premature, embraced Buddhist pacifism.

On more substantial ground it is worth scanning the *New Statesman and Nation* for 1935. Here one catches sight of Intourist advertisements – these appeared widely in the liberal and left press at the time – but on 3 August there was an advertisement for the *Fascist Quarterly*![47] However the main comments on the Seventh Congress seem *Statesman*-like enough: on Saturday 10 August in the 'Comments' column:

BETTER LATE THAN NEVER

The Congress of the Comintern shows that Communists are like other human beings – they are capable of learning from experience (if it is tragic enough), but only to do so very, very slowly. The Congress came to a very sensible, if belated decision. In future each national Communist Party must take more responsibility for its own policy and expect guidance instead of orders from Moscow ... Apparently they are to attack their potential friends less vehemently and to make more efforts at genuine co-operation with all other anti-Fascist forces. ... There is at least a possibility that if the Communist Party had reached its present point of view four years ago Hitler would never have triumphed.

The lesson has been learned in France, where the working alliance of the parties of the Left is one of the most encouraging features in the European situation. ... In this country it is comic but satisfactory to see the *Daily Worker* demanding sanctions against Italy. Hitherto it has always denounced the League as a bourgeois sham, whose only purpose was to plot a capitalist war against Russia.[48]

On 17 August, while the Congress was still in session, we find the following, again in the 'Comments' section;

... The evidence of the past fortnight shows that the discontent in France with the financiers' hold over the Government is deep and widespread, and suggests that most of the harvest is being reaped by the *front populaire* and not by the Fascist and semi-Fascist groups on the Right ... [49]

Following the news of President Roosevelt's warning to the Soviet Union over possible Comintern interference in US internal affairs, the *New Statesman* on 31 August remarked;

... If the Soviet Government is to be held responsible for what the Comintern says, as well as for what it does, diplomatic relations are hardly possible between America and the U.S.S.R. But the path of wisdom is to ignore the Comintern talk – which is no longer of more than theoretical importance. The realistic thing would be to congratulate the Soviet Government on a change of policy which makes international co-operation possible.[50]

In the spirit of this periodical's famous 'This England' corner which bravely found a little humour in those darkening days, we note from its own columns the suggestion by Alderman Hoare of Derby that the 'Italo-Abyssinian conflict' should be settled by a game of cricket.[51] The Comintern, it seems, was not the only body that had underestimated fascism!

NOTES

1. *Manchester Guardian*, 17 July 1935, p. 11.
2. *The Times*, 17 July 1935, p. 13. O. Woods and J. Bishop, *The Story of 'The Times'*, London 1983, p. 295.
3. *News Chronicle*, 26 July 1935, p. 2.
4. *The Times*, 27 July 1935, p. 11 – From Riga.
5. *Manchester Guardian*, 29 July 1935, p. 12.
6. *The Times*, 31 July 1935, p. 11.
7. *Manchester Guardian*, 31 July 1935, p. 8.
8. Ibid., 8 August 1935, p. 13.
9. *News Chronicle*, 9 August 1935, p. 2.
10. *Manchester Guardian*, 9 August 1935, p. 9.
11. *Reynolds' News*, 11 August 1935, p. 4.
12. *News Chronicle*, 22 August 1935, p. 11.
13. Ibid., 23 August 1935, p. 7.
14. *The Times*, 23 August 1935, p. 9.
15. *Reynolds' News*, 18 August 1935, p. 4.
16. *The Times*, 22 August 1935, p. 11.
17. *Daily Herald*, 20 August 1935, p. 4.
18. *Manchester Guardian*, 22 August 1935, p. 5.
19. Ibid., 16 July 1935, p. 11.
20. Ibid., 7 August 1935, p. 4.
21. Ibid., 8 August 1935, p. 13.
22. Ibid., 9 August 1935, p. 9.
23. Ibid., 10 August 1935.
24. Ibid., 12 August 1935, p. 8.
25. *Reynolds' News*, 28 July 1935, p. 3.
26. Ibid., 18 August 1935, p. 7.
27. *Manchester Guardian*, 28 August 1935, p. 8. cf. *The Times*, 28 August 1935, p. 10.
28. *Forward*, London Edition, 22 June 1935, p. 1.
29. Ibid., 6 July 1935, p. 4.
30. Ibid., 31 August 1935-7 September 1935 pp. 12. Also *Reynolds' News*, 1 September 1935-8 September 1935 pp. 23 and 17.
31. *Forward* London Edition, 14 September 1935, p. 12.
32. *New Leader*, 17 May 1935, p. 2.
33. Ibid., 26 July 1935, p. 3.
34. Ibid., 2 August 1935, p. 3.
35. Ibid., 9 August 1935, p. 3.
36. *The Times*, 5 August 1935, p. 12.
37. *New Leader*, 16 August 1935, p. 2.
38. Ibid., 6 September 1935, p. 2.
39. Socialist League, *Fight Now Against War*, (Pamphlet) 10 June 1935.
40. *Socialist Standard*, July 1935, p. 166.

41. Ibid., October 1935, p. 210.
42. Ibid., October 1935, p. 213.
43. Ibid., November 1935, p. 235.
44. Ibid., November 1935, p. 336.
45. *The Vanguard*, Vol. I No. 8 1935, pp. 197-204.
46. *The Plebs*, October 1935, pp. 240-3.
47. *New Statesman and Nation*, 3 August 1935, p. 170.
48. Ibid., 10 August 1935, pp. 181-3.
49. Ibid., 17 August 1935, p. 210.
50. Ibid., 31 August 1935, p. 266.
51. Ibid., 27 September 1935, p. 407.

Collective Security and The Origins of The People's Front

GEOFF ROBERTS

The years separating the advent of fascism in Germany and the outbreak of the Second World War form a distinctive period in the history of Soviet foreign policy. During this period it was based on a strategy of collective security. The catch-phrase of this novel strategy was 'peace is indivisible'; its aim the creation of an international peace front:

> a firm and stable combination of great and small powers striving for the maintenance of peace within the framework of the League of Nations and their friendly co-operation to avert war up to the point of applying the most extreme measures in the case of necessity.[1]

Collective security emerged in 1933-35 in response to the political and military threats posed by Nazi Germany, Fascist Italy and Imperial Japan. The USSR took its first major step along the road to collective security in December 1933 when the CPSU Central Committee and Politbureau approved proposals for a collective security programme in Europe.[2] These decisions paved the way for a series of prolonged and ultimately unsuccessful negotiations for a regional security agreement in Eastern Europe. But in May 1935 the USSR did succeed in concluding mutual assistance pacts with France and Czechoslovakia and in September 1934 had joined the League of Nations.[3]

By the time of the Seventh Congress of the Communist International, the Soviet Union was fully committed to the pursuit of collective security. Indeed, the convening of the Congress in July 1935 coincided with the peak of Soviet successes in the collective security field. The pacts with France and Czechoslovakia had just been signed. Litvinov was beginning to make an impact in the League of Nations, preparing the ground for the unprecedented League decision to impose economic sanctions against Italy when Mussolini launched his invasion of Abyssinia later that year. Soviet relations with Britain had never been better, following Eden's meeting with Stalin in Moscow in March 1935. Perhaps most encouraging for the collective security project was the relative diplomatic isolation of Nazi Germany and, so Soviet leaders believed, Hitler's continuing domestic difficulties, particularly on the economic front.

The Seventh Congress was, of course, a tremendous boost to the collective security drive. The policy of people's, or popular, fronts adopted by the congress intersected with Soviet foreign policy at a number of points. People's fronts against fascism and war added to the mass pressure on Western governments to adopt collective security policies themselves and, crucially, helped stem the fascist tide which was running high in a number of European countries. People's front agitation and propaganda reinforced Litivinov's efforts to mobilise international opinion against the 'aggressor states'. In turn, the international role of the Soviet Union in the resistance to aggression – notably during the Spanish Civil War and at the time of Munich – was an inspiration to national struggles for peace.

Soviet Policy and Comintern Policy 1928-35
The congruity of Soviet and Comintern policy in the era of the people's front was in sharp contrast to the divergence of strategies evident during the so-called 'Third Period'. In that period, between 1928 and 1933, Comintern policy was based on the idea that capitalism's post-First World War stabilisation was coming to an end and revolutionary upsurges, similar in magnitude to those which had followed in the wake of the Russian Revolution, were imminent.[4]

Soviet foreign policy, on the other hand, was premised, at least in practice, on the continuation of capitalism for some time to come. Its overriding objective was to maintain the relatively stable pattern of relations with the capitalist world established during the 1920s. While the Comintern plotted revolution, Soviet diplomats charted the businesslike relations that existed between the USSR and most Western capitalist states.

Despite the transparent contradictions between Soviet foreign policy and Comintern policy during the Third Period, there is still a widespread view that changes in Comintern strategies and tactics can be largely explained in terms of shifts in Soviet foreign policy. One of the most oft-quoted examples in this respect is the

Comintern's adoption of the people's front policy which is said to be largely the product of the Soviet turn to collective security.[5] Recent research, however, indicates that this was not the case.[6] While the compatibility of people's front policies with the Soviet collective security strategy undoubtedly facilitated their emergence, that does not explain their genesis. To explain the origins of the people's front it is necessary, first of all, to review the disastrous effect on the Comintern of the policies of the Third Period.

Despite the world economic crisis sparked off by the Wall Street crash of 1929, there was no revolutionary crisis. All the Comintern sections succeeded in doing was further isolating themselves within their respective national labour movements. Comintern membership slumped from 445,300 in 1928 to 328,716 in 1931,[7] while social democracy retained its political leadership of the bulk of the European working class.

For most Communist parties the ultra-leftism of the Third Period was simply a bad mistake from which they subsequently recovered. For the German Communist Party (KPD), however, it led to catastrophe, a historic reversal from which there was no recovery short of the Red Army's storming of Berlin in 1945.

Blinded by hostility to social democracy (the 'social-fascists') and a belief that Germany was in a pre-revolutionary period, the KPD failed to recognise in time the dire threat posed by Hitler and the Nazis. Indeed, it was only in March 1933 – *after* the formation of Hitler's cabinet, *after* the Reichstag fire, *after* decrees dissolving the KPD and expelling its deputies from the Reichstag, and *after* the beginning of mass arrests of communists in Germany – that the KPD made its first unequivocal and unqualified appeal to the Social Democrats for a united front against the fascists.[8] It was to no avail. Within weeks the jewel in the Comintern's crown – the largest Communist party in the capitalist world with 360,000 members, 6,000,000 voters and almost 100 parliamentary deputies – had been completely shattered. In the immediate aftermath of this disaster neither the KPD nor the Comintern revised their basic estimates of the political situation in Germany. On 1 April 1933 the Comintern Presidium made the foolish prediction that:

> The establishment of an open fascist dictatorship which destroys all democratic illusions among the masses and frees them from the influence of the social-democrats, will hasten Germany's progress towards the proletarian revolution.[9]

Later that year, in November and December, the Executive Committee of the International held its Thirteenth Plenum. The plenum was almost wholly devoted to the German question and the resolution adopted at the end of the session reaffirmed, in general terms, April's estimate of the revolutionary potential in the German situation.

It is important to remember that while the Comintern was sticking to its perspective of a proletarian revolution in Germany, the Soviet state was actively preparing for the containment of Nazi aggression and expansion. The decisions of the Soviet party in December 1933 have already been mentioned. In line with these decisions Litvinov, speaking at the end of December, denounced German foreign policy, referring to Hitler's idea of 'by fire and sword to cut a road for expansion to the East ... and to enslave the Soviet peoples'.[10] The movement in Soviet foreign policy toward collective security was well underway by the end of 1933. A concomitant shift in Comintern policy did not take place until the following year. The primary cause of this change in policy was not adherence to collective security, but the combined impact of:

a) an upsurge of anti-fascist unity and activity across Europe;
b) a successful political struggle by Dimitrov, Manuilsky and other Comintern leaders to reverse the sectarian Third Period policy; and
c) the pioneering role of the French Communist Party (PCF) in the development and practical implementation of popular front politics.

Origins of the People's Front Policy

The storm-centre of Comintern politics in 1934 was France. It was in Paris in February 1934 that the first united action between French Socialists and Communists since 1928 took place. The occasion was a general strike called by the Communist- and Socialist-led trade unions in response to fascist riots a few days earlier. Four and a half million workers are reported to have joined the strike, including 150,000 who marched in Paris and heard speeches from the Socialist and Communist leaders, Blum and Cachin.

The PCF's initial response to these developments was to welcome the manifestations of grassroots anti-fascism, but at the same time resist any move toward a negotiated political agreement with the Socialist leadership on meeting the fascist challenge in France. Meanwhile, however, the infrastructure of an anti-fascist alliance (the precursor to the French Popular Front) was already being created as local anti-fascist committees and other organisations were set up all over the country. It was this pressure from below combined with the ascendency of Dimitrov and his supporters within the Comintern that led to a reversal of the PCF's opposition to a 'united front from above'. In June 1934, at a PCF national conference called to discuss the question of a united front, Thorez embraced the idea of an alliance with the Socialists against the fascists. A few weeks later, on 27 July, a Unity of Action pact was signed with the French Socialists.

The French unity pact was followed in August by a similar agreement between Italian Socialists and Communists and, in September, by the decision of the Spanish Communist Party to join the Socialist-sponsored trade union-based 'workers' alliances'. In Britain the first mass anti-Mosley demonstrations had already taken place.

Counter-balancing these positive developments in the anti-fascist struggle were two major defeats for the European labour movement at the hands of fascist or semi-fascist forces. The first was the crushing of the Austrian Social Democrats in February 1934. Fascist attacks on socialist premises and headquarters were met with a general strike and an armed revolt in Vienna. The revolt ended in defeat after four days of fierce street fighting. The second, in October, was suppression of the Asturias uprising in Spain, sparked off by the entry of extremist right-wingers into the government. Armed miners and others seized control of the province's capital. Thousands died in the ensuing armed conflict.

One person impressed by these events, particularly those in Austria and France, was Georgi Dimitrov, who was to play a pivotal role in Comintern affairs in the period leading up to the 1935 World Congress.

Dimitrov, leader of the Bulgarian Communist movement in the 1920s, was head of the Berlin-based West European Bureau of the Comintern. Shortly after Hitler became Chancellor of Germany he was arrested and charged with responsibility for the Reichstag fire. The trial, which began in Leipzig in September 1933, captured the public imagination. Overnight Dimitrov became the Comintern's most famous personality. The trial ended with his acquittal and, following considerable pressure on the Hitler government from the Soviet Embassy in Berlin, his departure for the USSR in February 1934.[11]

In early April 1934, following a period of recuperation in Moscow, Dimitrov was invited to a meeting of the Soviet Politbureau. At that meeting he apparently told Stalin that the lack of mass support for communism in the European labour movement was the result of an erroneous approach by Communist parties to the workers, especially social democratic workers.[12] A couple of weeks later, at Stalin's suggestion, Dimitrov joined the Political Secretariat of the Comintern Executive Committee and subsequently became a member of the Executive Committee's Praesidium. It was in these capacities and as Director of the Central European section that Dimitrov met PCF leader Maurice Thorez in Moscow on 11 May. Dimitrov told Thorez the February events in France demonstrated that Communist supporters wanted unity with their social democratic counterparts and, moreover, that:

> Every common action of Communist workers, social democrats and others against the bourgeoisie always works for us, even if at first it does not go exactly in accordance with our slogans.[13]

It seems clear that in spring 1934 Dimitrov was moving toward a radical reassessment of the sectarian policy of the Third Period. Perhaps the most critical step in Dimitrov's political evolution in this period was his appointment as head of a commission preparing a report on the question of the struggle against fascism for the forthcoming Seventh Congress. Dimitrov submitted an outline report to the commission on 1 July. In a letter accompanying his proposals, and in the outline report itself, he challenged all the shibboleths that had informed Comintern politics for the previous five years. He questioned the characterisation of social democracy as social fascism and posed the need to win social democrats – leaders, cadres, trade unionists and rank-and-file members – to revolutionary positions. This could only be achieved, he argued, through unity in action against fascism and through the formation of united fronts from above, i.e. with social democratic organisations and leaders as well as below, i.e. with the mass of social democratic supporters. Communist leadership of the working class, according to Dimitrov's report, had to be won in struggle, not imposed or declared by abstract slogans. He argued as well for a new, concrete analysis of the fascist phenomenan and for a critical reassessment of the Comintern's failure to establish an anti-fascist united front in Germany. These proposals were discussed by the commission the next day. In his own contribution to the discussion Dimitrov stressed the centrality of the anti-fascist struggle in the current period:

> It seems to me that the fundamental political problem that stands before the Communist International ... is the problem of the proletarian united front in the struggle against the offensive of fascism ... the Communist International must boldly undertake in its whole line and in its initiative on every front, the task of creating the necessary unity of the working class against the offensive of fascism, against the danger of war, in the struggle against capitalism.

To do this, Dimitrov concluded, the Comintern had 'to review and change certain formulations, tactical lines and, possibly, certain positions which are not altogether clear'.[14] Dimitrov was not alone in his efforts to effect a change in the Comintern's political line. At an earlier meeting, called to discuss a proposed congress report on the activities of the Comintern Executive Committee, one of the Soviet representatives on the EC, Manuilsky, and the Finnish representative Kuusinen spoke in a similar spirit. Manuilsky, it appears, was particularly forthright:

> It seems to me that our slogans, even the dictatorship of the proletariat slogans, were too abstract ... We must have a more concrete programme of struggle: not proletarian dictatorship, not socialism, but one which involves the masses in the struggle for the dictatorship of the proletariat and socialism.

A programme which would aim to go 'beyond the limits of capitalism', but which was not the same as socialism.[15] Ranged against the Dimitrov-Kuusinen-Manuilsky alliance was another important group of Comintern functionaries who steadfastly resisted the proposed new course. The standard Soviet history of the Comintern describes the intervention of this second group in the following terms:

> Various points of view were expressed in the course of the discussion. Some of the committee members – Bela Kun, Lozovsky, Knorin and Wang Ming – at first defended the obsolete guidelines and only agreed to certain changes in tactics. They demanded a higher assessment of the maturity of the revolutionary upsurge, involving the Comintern in unrealistic forecasts. They maintained at first that the social democrats should still be regarded as the mainstay of the bourgeoisie, that the right deviation still remained the chief danger in

the international communist movement, that the Communist revolutionary trade unions should be kept independent, and so on. In the course of intensive discussions, however, these views were gradually overcome and their adherents themselves admitted the need for their revision.[16]

Crucial to the process of overcoming this hard line opposition in Moscow were the reverberations of inner-Comintern struggles in Paris. It may be that as early as December 1933 Manuilsky was dropping hints to Thorez about the need to change the political course of the PCF.[17] Certainly, this was the import of Dimitrov's remarks to Thorez on 11 May. And in relation to the February events in France, Manuilsky, at a meeting of the Comintern Presidium on 16 May, had this to say about the actions of the PCF:

I think that the Central Committee should seize on the first opportunity to mobilise the masses in the struggle against fascism, and above all against fascist meetings. When the fascists call a meeting address an appeal to the social democratic Central Committee saying that on that basis we are ready to engage in common struggle against the fascist threat to the working class. But when you make these proposals, do not elevate these problems on *to a general plane, on the contrary stick to concrete demands.*[18]

Further guidance for the PCF came in a letter from the Comintern to the party just prior to its June conference on the united front:

You should treat the task of creation of a united front more broadly than *any other* party or organisation whatever in the French working class. The whole force of mass actions of the working class should be concentrated against fascism. In order to create an anti-fascist front it is indispensible to work out a programme of demands which would be supported by the broadest masses ... It is indispensible to make an end of declarations which are often met with in the party press or in the pronouncements of party organs that the party fights to abolish bourgeois democracy. Such empty and completely one-sided declarations are politically erroneous.[19]

In line with this perspective the PCF conference marked a decisive shift toward an anti-fascist unity policy. Thorez, particularly in his closing speech to the conference, held out an open hand to the Socialists:

We want above all unity with socialist workers against fascism: we want above all to work towards workers' unity within a single trade union federation ... we want to enlist the middle classes in the breaking down of fascist demagogy.[20]

It has been claimed that this greater willingness for unity with the Socialists, expressed in the closing stages of the Congress, was the result of a telegram from Comintern headquarters.[21] But published minutes of the PCF Political Bureau meeting of 30 June suggest that the telegram was received *after* the conference[22] and was in any case incomplete.[23] It certainly seems more likely that the PCF was developing the united front policy on its own initiative, especially as over the next few months it exhibited a growing autonomy in relation to the Comintern leadership in Moscow. It was, after all, Thorez who first proclaimed the Popular Front – at Nantes in October 1934 – and against the advice of a high-powered Comintern delegation (including Togliatti).

Before Thorez's famous Nantes speech the PCF and Comintern perspective was still limited to working-class unity, of alliance between Socialist and Communist parties and organisations. At Nantes, on the eve of the Radical Party conference, Thorez called for a broader, people's alliance embracing the middle classes. The Comintern leadership had no objection in principle to a popular front but was concerned about the effects of what they considered to be a premature initiative on unity with the Socialists. Thorez nevertheless went ahead with his planned statement and the policy of the popular front was born.[24]

In December 1934, at an extended meeting of the Comintern Executive Committee's Presidium, the popular front policy of the PCF was endorsed. This decision to back the PCF represented a major defeat for the hardline opposition to a political reorientation of the Comintern. Dimitrov's report to the Seventh Congress a few months later drew together all the threads of the discussion that had raged in the higher circles of the Comintern in the latter half of 1934. The Congress marked the beginning of a political tendency in the Communist movement that was to find its most recent expression in the Eurocommunist phenomenon of the 1970s and 80s.

The origins of this tendency in the failure of the ultra-left Third-Period line, in the experience of anti-fascist unity in a number of countries and in the successful political struggles of Dimitrov and his allies demonstrates that although Comintern policy was made in Moscow, it was not necessarily made by the Soviet Politbureau. In the case of the people's front policy Soviet leaders played a relatively passive role, preferring instead to let the debates run their course. Indeed, the Soviet representatives in the Comintern were themselves split politically, though when the Politbureau did take hand in Comintern affairs – the appointment of Dimitrov, the go ahead to prepare for the Seventh Congress, the endorsement of the proposed reports – its actions favoured the innovators, rather than the sectarians. A reflection no doubt in part, of the government's concerns in the foreign policy sphere.

Soviet-Comintern Relations

It is more fruitful, nevertheless, to view the Comintern as a relatively autonomous institution whose leaders and member parties played an important role in its political evolution and functioning than as an agent of Soviet foreign policy. True, the Soviet leadership's influence in the Comintern – exercised through its political representation in the Comintern apparatus, the material dependence of the Comintern on its resources, personal links and, above all, its ideological leadership – was the most powerful single factor in its history. But that power was not all pervasive, nor was the traffic all one way. Later events in France and Spain were to demonstrate that it was possible for the Comintern to both deviate from and influence the course of Soviet foreign policy. Indeed, at the Seventh Congress Togliatti openly espoused the thesis of 'non-coincidence between the positions of the party of the proletariat in various countries', including the USSR:

> For us it is absolutely indisputable that there is a complete identity of aim between the peace policy of the Soviet Union and the policy of the working class and Communist Parties of the capitalist countries. There is not, and cannot be, any doubt in our ranks on this subject. We not only defend the Soviet Union in general, we defend concretely its whole policy and each of its actions. But this identity of aim by no means signifies that at every given moment there must be a complete coincidence in all acts and on all questions between the tactics of the proletariat and Communist Parties that are still struggling for power and the concrete tactical measure of the Soviet proletariat and the CPSU, which already have power in their hands in the Soviet Union.[25]

The particular example Togliatti had in mind concerned the position of the PCF on defence spending. The problem arose from a communiqué issued by France and the Soviet Union in May 1935 which stated that

> Comrade Stalin expressed complete understanding and approval of the national defence policy pursued by France with the object of maintaining its armed forces at a level consistent with its security requirements.[26]

The PCF, on the other hand, maintained its opposition to French rearmament and continued to do so until after the election of Blum's popular front government in July 1936.[27] In actual fact the contradiction was more apparent than real, for the Russians viewed their new ally with as much suspicion as the French Communists. Hence, Soviet policy toward France was purposeful in terms of the overall strategy of collective security, but in execution was hesitant, contradictory and fluctuating. In the space that existed between the aims of Soviet policy and its implementation there was plenty of room for manoeuvre by parties like the PCF and, indeed, for an independent role on the part of the Comintern.

The most striking example of Comintern influence on Soviet policy occurred during the Spanish Civil War. The initial response of the Soviet Union to the beginning of civil war in Spain was to support French and British-sponsored proposals for non-intervention by outside powers. A declaration to this effect was made by the Soviet Government on 23 August 1936 and in September the USSR joined an international Non-Intervention Committee which met for the first time in London on the 9 September. E.H. Carr argued in his posthumously-published book on the Spanish events that the main motive for this action was a desire to keep in step with Britain and France and to secure the diplomatic isolation of Germany and Italy (who were already supplying Franco's forces).[28]

In the meantime, however, pressure was building up within the international Communist movement and, subsequently in the Comintern and the Russian party itself for military and financial aid to the Spanish Republic. Although it was not until 23 October that the USSR stated it would not, in view of Italian and German intervention, be bound by the non-intervention agreement, the first shiploads of supplies to Spain had in fact left Russian ports earlier that month. Soviet and Comintern volunteers were already filtering into Spain and on 12 October the Comintern had decided to establish the International Brigade.[29]

The Soviet Union remained a member of the Non-Intervention Committee until March 1939, maintaining throughout the intervening period its aid to Spain. Of course, the USSR had its own reasons of state for supporting the Spanish Republic. A fascist victory in Spain would leave France exposed to attack from the South as well as in the East and also give the Axis powers a commanding position in the Mediterranean. Soviet diplomats also believed that a firm stand in Spain would deter further aggression by the fascist states. But the Soviet government had other options too, including the maintenance of unity with Britain and France in the interests of the wider collective security strategy. The fact that the Soviet leadership chose the course of defending Republican Spain – a position it maintained to the end – was in no small part due to Comintern pressure for involvement in the civil war.

There was also another side to the Comintern and Soviet role in the Spanish events. Arms, medical aid, military advisers and volunteers were not the only things transported to Spain. Then came the politics of the 'Great Terror'. Ironically this projection of Stalin's domestic policy, with its successive purges of Soviet and Comintern military and political personnel, into the civil war damaged the Republican war effort which Soviet and Communist aid was helping to sustain.[30]

Paradoxically, the major exception to the general pattern of Comintern's semi-autonomy in relation to Soviet foreign policy was one in which the Comintern served no essential purpose as an agency of Soviet policy. When the Soviet Union finally abandoned collective security in August 1939 and opted for a pact with Nazi Germany, the Comintern abandoned the people's front policy. There was, in effect, a return to pre-1934 political analyses and practices, though not to the extreme sectarianism of the Third Period. The Comintern accepted the Soviet analysis of the war between Britain and France and Germany as an 'imperialist' war in which the working class had no interest. Communist parties were mobilised in support of Hitler's peace offers to the West following the conquest of Poland – a stance which the Soviet government, as part of its political agreements with Germany, also adopted.[31]

Yet there was no intrinsic reason why the USSR could not have continued on its course of a diplomatic accommodation with Germany while at the same time the Comintern continued with the struggle for the people's front. There was, after all, a long tradition in Soviet diplomacy of disavowing the actions of the Comintern. The Comintern contributed little to the Soviet policy of winning time and space in which to prepare for war with Hitler and, in so far as it did anything to undermine the Western war effort, effectively worked against Moscow's interests. But the Comintern's volte-face in 1939 bears little resemblance to the change in policy in 1934-35. The ditching of the people's front policy followed a dramatic and decisive turn in Soviet foreign policy and happened in the context of a European war – a situation which, from the Soviet point of view, demanded the total subordination of Comintern interests to the security of the USSR; whereas collective security emerged gradually and, in policy terms, on an *ad hoc* basis, in response to threats to Soviet security of a lesser order (at least in the short term). The Comintern was thus able to find its own way to the people's front policy. Whether or not the Soviet leadership could have imposed its own solution had the Comintern not been able to do so, is a question that cannot be answered. It is doubtful, however, whether this solution would have wrought the transformations in Communist politics set in motion by the Seventh Congress. The policy of the people's front was, after all, much more than a defensive anti-fascist tactic. It was also an offensive, socialist strategy aimed at the development of broad political and social alliances – a strategic lever to open the road to socialism in the capitalist democracies of the West.

NOTES

1. Ivan Maisky; Soviet Ambassador to Britain. Address published by the Anglo-Russian Parliamentary Commission, March 1936.
2. *Dokumenty Vneshnei Politiki SSSR*, Vol.16; Moscow 1970, pp. 876-7 n. 321; *Istoriya Vtoroi Mirovoi Voiny 1939-1945*, Vol.1, Moscow 1973, p. 283; V. Ya. Sipols, *Vneshnyaya Politika Sovetskogo Souza 1933-1935*, Moscow 1980, p. 150.
3. These events are documented in 'The Struggle for Collective Security in Europe During 1933-1935', *International Affairs* (Moscow), June, July, August and September 1963. A highly-recommended book on the origins and development of Soviet foreign policy during the collective security period is J. Haslam, *The Soviet Union and the Struggle for Collective Security in Europe 1933-39*, London 1984.
4. A useful documentary survey of Comintern policies in the Third Period is given by H. Gruber (ed.), *Soviet Russia Masters the Comintern*, New York 1974. The evolution of the key Third Period concept of 'social fascism' is

examined by J.M. Cammett, 'Communist Theories of Fascism 1920-1935', *Science and Society*, No.2, 1967. See also E.H. Carr; *Foundations of a Planned Economy 1926-1929*, Vol. 3-1, London 1976, Chapters 70 and 72.

5. e.g. F. Claudín; *The Communist Movement: From Comintern to Cominform*, London 1975; see especially pp. 171-210.

6. E.H. Carr, *The Twilight of Comintern, 1930-1935*, London 1982; J. Haslam, 'The Comintern and the Origins of the Popular Front 1934-1935', *The Historical Journal*, No. 3, 1979; B.M. Liebzon and K.K. Shirinya; *Povorot v Politike Kominterna*, Moscow 1975; K.K. Shirinya; *Strategiya i Taktika Kominterna v Borbe Protiv Fashizma i Voiny (1934-1939)*, Moscow 1979 and *VII Kongress Kominterna i Borba za Sozdaniye Narodnogo Fronta*, Moscow 1977. Of older vintage are L. Derfler, 'Unity and the French Left: Some Views of the Popular Front', *Science & Society*, No. 1, 1971 and *Outline History of the Communist International*, London 1971. Much of the information in the text derives from these sources. On the whole I have omitted specific references, but due acknowledgement is made to the authors of these works.

7. O.A. Narkiewicz, *Marxism and the Reality of Power 1919-1980*, London 1981, p. 43.

8. Carr, op.cit., p. 85. The KPD initiative was made in response to a statement by the Comintern on the German situation issued on 5 March. The statement called for a united front between Communists and social democrats against fascism, but it was very much on the Comintern's own terms and in the Third Period mould. See J. Degras (ed.), *The Communist International 1919-1943: Documents*, Vol. 3, London 1971, pp. 254-63.

9. Cited by Carr, ibid., p. 90.

10. Degras (ed.), *Soviet Documents on Foreign Policy*, Vol. 3 (1933-1941), Oxford 1953, p. 55.

11. On Dimitrov's background and the events leading to his imprisonment and trial see Haslam, op.cit., p. 677 and Carr; op.cit. pp. 101-2. The Soviet Embassy's efforts to secure his release and deportation to the USSR is documented in 'Documents: The Power of Proletarian Internationalism', *International Affairs* (Moscow), May 1969.

12. Diary entry of Dimitrov cited by Shirinya, op.cit., pp. 37-8.

13. Bulgarian party archives cited by Shirinya, ibid., p. 38.

14. Dimitrov's outline report, introductory letter and discussion contribution were published in *Voprosy Istorii KPSS* in 1965. English translation in *Marxism Today*, July 1972.

15. CPSU archives cited by Shirinya, op.cit., p. 41.

16. *Outline History*, op.cit., p. 359.

17. C. and A. Vassart, 'The Moscow Origins of the French "Popular Front" ' in M.M. Drachkovitch and B. Lazitch (eds), *The Comintern: Historical Highlights*, New York 1966, pp. 240-1.

18. The quotation comes from an extract from Manuilsky's intervention at the Presidium meeting published in *Cahiers d'Histoire*, No. 18, 1984 pp. 73-4. The journal is published by the L'Institut de Recherches Marxistes – a research body of the PCF.

19. Cited by Carr, op.cit., p. 143.

20. *Cahiers d'Histoire*, op.cit., p. 45.

21. The source of these speculations is Vassart, op.cit. Albert Vassart was the PCF representative in Moscow in 1934-1935. Vassart, who died in 1958,

later left the party. The article cited above was based on a manuscript by his wife Celie Vassart, which was in turn based on notes left by her husband.

22. *Cahiers d'Histoire*, op.cit., p. 46, n. 33.
23. Ibid., p. 20.
24. On Thorez's Nantes speech see Haslam, op.cit., pp. 688-9 and Carr, op.cit., pp. 198-201. According to Carr (p. 200) the first published use of the term 'popular front' was in an article by Cachin published in *L'Humanité* on 24 October 1934.
25. Report of the Seventh World Congress, Modern Books 1936. Togliatti's report on 'The Fight Against War and Fascism', p. 45.
26. Degras, op.cit., p. 132.
27. Haslam, *The Soviet Union and the Struggle* ... , pp. 84-5, 87-9 and 102-3.
28. E.H. Carr, *The Comintern and the Spanish Civil War*, London 1984, p. 17. The Soviet role in the Non-Intervention Committee is related in detail by Ivan Maisky in his *Spanish Notebooks*, London 1966.
29. Haslam, op.cit., pp. 107-15.
30. Carr, op.cit., and Haslam, ibid., chapters 7 and 8.
31. On the change in Comintern policy in 1939, see J. Attfield and S. Williams (eds), *1939: The Communist Party and the War*, London 1984 and J. Haslam, 'The Policy of the Communist International from August 1939 to June 1941', unpublished discussion paper for the University of Birmingham, Centre for Russian and East European Studies.

Trotsky and the People's Front

MONTY JOHNSTONE

Throughout the second half of the 1930s Leon Trotsky conducted an increasingly bitter and strident polemic against the people's front, which he regarded as a betrayal of revolution. His attacks on its theory and practice laid the foundations for a major part of the Trotskyist and 'leftist' criticisms of Communist strategy in capitalist countries over the last fifty years. Even whilst the Seventh World Congress of the Comintern was still discussing its new people's front strategy in August 1935, Trotsky was condemning it for 'the liquidation of the programme, principles and tactical methods established by Lenin'.[1] In the *Transitional Programme* of his Fourth International, written in 1938, he proclaimed:

> The conciliatory politics practised by the 'People's Front' dooms the working class to impotence and clears the road for fascism. 'People's Fronts' on the one hand – fascism on the other: these are the last political resources of imperialism in the struggle against the proletarian revolution.[2]

It is in some ways paradoxical that Trotsky should have reacted in such an intemperate manner to the new turn in the Comintern which corrected the serious sectarian mistakes of the 'Third Period', from 1928 to 1934, which he himself had opposed. The anti-fascist people's front strategy flowed in fact from largely the same premises as those on which Trotsky had based his own cogent criticisms of the Comintern's earlier characterisation of social democracy as 'social fascism'[3] and its failure to make a proper distinction between fascism and bourgeois democracy.[4] He had correctly and repeatedly urged the German Communist Party to replace its restrictive policy of the 'united front from below' by a consistent effort to build a united front with the Social Democratic Party and its leadership against the Nazi threat.[5]

89

During the Third Period Trotsky had rejected the Comintern's view that the seizure of power by the proletariat was the immediate task, and urged the German Communists to adopt defensive tactics in working for a united front against fascism to protect workers' organisations and rights in the framework of bourgeois democracy.[6] In the period of the people's front, however, he was more and more sharply to pose the immediate alternative of fascism or proletarian revolution,[7] condemning the slogan of defence of democracy as 'reactionary' and 'hollow'.[8] Moreover, as we shall see, Trotsky's policies in this period implied *in practice* the abandonment of any conception of the united front from either above or below.

Imposed by Stalin?

Already in July 1933 Trotsky called for the foundation of a 'Fourth International'. He had concluded that with Hitler's victory in Germany the Communist International was 'dead for the revolution', having shown its complete political 'bankruptcy' and 'its organic incapacity to learn, to mend its ways, that is, "to reform itself" '.[9] The declaration of the Comintern Presidium on 1 April 1933 that 'the political line and the organisational policy pursued by the Central Committee of the Communist Party of Germany ... was quite correct' in the period before the Nazi coup[10] appeared to give plausibility to his argument. So did the fact that in December 1933 the Comintern Executive still designated social democracy as the main social support of the bourgeoisie even in fully fascist countries and continued to counterpose the tactic of the united front from below to unity from above.[11] Indeed as late as June 1934 L. Magyar, of the Comintern, was attacking Trotsky in *Labour Monthly* for advocating democracy rather than Soviet power as the chief slogan for Germany and for his 'proposal of forming a united front from *above* with the worst of the social-fascists ... ostensibly in order the better to be able to fight against fascism'.[12]

However, the conclusions drawn by Trotsky were at best overhasty and based on an impressionistic rather than a fundamental, analytical approach. In the same way as before 1917 he had turned his back on the Bolsheviks, denouncing their dangerous 'anti-revolutionary features',[13] Trotsky was now writing off the Third International and the world's Communist parties, whose most effective period lay ahead of them.

Already on 5 March 1933 the Executive Committee of the

Communist International had publicly recommended to Communist parties 'to approach the central committees of the social democratic parties belonging to the Labour and Socialist International with proposals regarding joint actions against fascism and against the capitalist offensive'.[14] In 1934, under the influence of Dimitrov and the experiences of united action by Communists and Socialists in France, a struggle was under way in the Comintern leadership to correct the sectarian policies of the preceeding period. We now know that Dimitrov had to battle hard with Stalin to overcome his opposition to a change in the old line for which he held the major responsibility.[15] Even after having been convinced of the need for a united front with the Socialists, it was Stalin who was behind the Comintern Secretariat's demand for caution in initiating any alliance with the Radical Party.[16] Despite its advice to hold back, delivered by Togliatti, Thorez went ahead in October 1934 with a speech calling for a people's front, deemed by the French party leaders to correspond to the needs of the situation in their country.[17]

In coming round to approve the new policy, Stalin was no doubt influenced by the fact that it clearly complemented Soviet proposals for collective security agreements with the Western democracies to check the aggression of the fascist powers. Both policies sprang from the need to combat fascism that threatened on both national and international planes. Their complementarity is however no proof of the usual Trotskyist contention that the people's front was dictated by Stalin to promote 'the diplomacy of the Soviet bureaucracy', to which the Communist parties were allegedly forced to subordinate the class struggle in their countries.[18] In fact, the people's front grew out of the needs and experiences of working class struggle against fascism and finance capital. It can only be assessed by an examination of how far it showed itself to be the most effective means of promoting that end under the specific circumstances prevailing in the countries where it was applied. 'What is most important, that which constitutes the very gist, the living soul, of Marxism [is] a concrete analysis of a concrete situation,' insisted Lenin.[19]

It is interesting to find Trotsky himself telling C.L.R. James (Johnson) in a private interview in April 1939 that 'you cannot think of the Comintern as being merely an instrument of Stalin's foreign policy.' And he went on:

In France in 1934 the Communist Party had declined from 80,000 to 30,000. It was necessary to have a new policy. We do not know the archives of the Comintern, what correspondence passed, etc. At the same time Stalin was seeking a new foreign policy. From one side and the other we have these tendencies which go to make the new turn. They are different sides of the same process ... The French Communist Party is not only an agency of Moscow, but a national organisation with members of parliament, etc.[20]

Such statements as these, made privately to a leading Trotskyist of the time, completely contradict his public pronouncements that the people's front was a 'criminal policy dictated by Moscow', that 'the Politbureaus of the Communist Parties all consist of paid agents of the GPU' and that the Comintern had become 'a completely submissive apparatus in the service of Soviet foreign policy, ready at any time for any zigzag whatever'.[21]

Seventh World Congress

To have made a serious and responsible critique of the strategy of the people's front Trotsky would have had to proceed from an analysis of the argumentation of the Seventh World Congress, and in the first instance of Dimitrov's report and reply to discussion. In fact, Trotsky never realised his declared intention of drawing up in a special pamphlet or series of articles the 'theoretical and political balances' of this crucial congress.[22] Indeed his windily dismissive references to Dimitrov's extremely rich report as 'wordy and unsubstantial' make it doubtful whether he ever bothered to study it properly, as does his quite extraordinary statement that the call for elected committees of action as the mass support for the people's front was 'perhaps the only progressive idea in the entire resolution' on Dimitrov's report.[23] In a private letter to Jean Rous, then a French Trotskyist leader, on 17 September 1935, Trotsky urged his French supporters to utilise the demand for such committees to secure 'the more or less total elimination of the Radicals or even the right-wing Socialists'.[24]

Dimitrov started from a recognition that the

accession to power of fascism is not an *ordinary succession* of one bourgeois government by another, but a *substitution* of one state form of class domination of the bourgeoisie – bourgeois democracy – by another form – open terrorist dictatorship.[25]

The Communists' attitude to bourgeois democracy could not be the same under all circumstances. In the revolutionary upsurge of 1917-20 they had fought under the banner of proletarian dictatorship, whilst the forces of counter-revolution had gathered around the standard of bourgeois democracy for the defence of capitalism. The situation was quite different in the thirties. 'Now,' said Dimitrov,

> the fascist counter-revolution is attacking bourgeois democracy in an effort to establish the most barbaric regime of exploitation and suppression of the toiling masses. Now the toiling masses of the capitalist countries are faced with the necessity of making a *definite* choice, and of making it today, not between proletarian dictatorship and bourgeois democracy, but between bourgeois democracy and fascism.[26]

The first thing that had to be done was to establish a united front of the working class parties and organisations without conditions except that it be '*directed against fascism, against the offensive of capital, against the threat of war, against the class enemy*'.[27]

Alliance with Middle Strata
Whilst the '*main and immediate task*' was seen as such a workers' united front, the resolution on Dimitrov's report declared:

> In striving to unite, under the leadership of the proletariat, the struggle of the toiling peasants, the urban petty bourgeoisie and the toiling masses of the oppressed nationalities, the Communists must seek to bring about the establishment of a wide *anti-fascist* people's front on the basis of the proletarian united front, supporting all those specific demands of these sections of the toilers which are in line with the fundamental interests of the proletariat.[28]

Maurice Thorez in his speech had especially emphasised the need for a correct approach to these strata:

> The masses of the people in town and country, the middle classes, and the peasants in particular, play a very important historic role. But this role is never an independent one; they either fall under the influence of the big bourgeoisie, of capital, and become the tool of its policy, or they ally themselves with the working class.[29]

This was, of course, a fundamental Marxist tenet that Trotsky himself often proclaimed.[30] But, as in his controversies with

Lenin before 1917 about Russian perspectives,[31] he opposed the conception of such an alliance taking the form of an *agreement between parties* and possibly culminating in a coalition government of them.

Hitherto the Communist International had only envisaged such an alliance of proletarian with democratic bourgeois and petty bourgeois parties in countries which had not yet completed their bourgeois democratic revolutions. In other countries, where the Communists had seen struggle for the destruction of capitalism as 'their immediate mission',[32] there had been no basis for an alliance with non-socialist parties, which did not share this aim. There it had been a question of working to win the middle strata directly to support the workers' parties.

The rise of fascism, however, created a new situation. Already at the beginning of the 1930s Trotsky had correctly appreciated that the immediate task was a defensive struggle against the fascist threat to democratic rights.[33] Explaining the need for a united front of Communist and social democratic parties he had demonstrated, by implication, the basis for a still wider anti-fascist front, including democratic bourgeois and petty bourgeois parties. 'Unless one plays with words,' he had written,

> fascism is certainly not common to all bourgeois parties; the fascist party is a *special* bourgeois party, which is geared to special conditions and tasks and is sharply opposed to other bourgeois parties.

Admittedly the mutual hostility of bourgeois parties was very relative. However,

> the fact that all bourgeois parties from fascism to the Social Democratic Party place the defence of bourgeois domination above their programmatic differences neither does away with their specific characteristics, nor their struggle against each other, *nor our task of taking advantage of this struggle.*[34]

For the first fifteen years of their existence the Communist parties in countries like France and Spain had been unable to obtain any significant success in winning the peasantry of their countries for an alliance with the working class on the basis of an immediate programme of Soviet power. Their experiences certainly did not lend support to Trotsky's assertion in 1935 that the only solution was for the proletariat to 'speak the *language of revolution to the peasants*'.[35] Where the peasants and urban middle strata did not give their support to right-wing parties, they voted in the main for left-wing bourgeois parties like the French Radicals and the Spanish Republican Left. In the mid-1930s an agreement with these parties was the condition for any anti-fascist alliance of the working class and middle strata, who still formed the majority of the population and constituted a potential mass basis for fascism, as had actually been the case in Germany. Marxists had to recognise, as Dimitrov pointed out, that 'these masses must be taken as they are, and not as we should like to have them', with a view to raising their consciousness in the course of a united struggle against fascism.[36]

Opposing the Popular Front when it came into existence in France, Trotsky claimed that 'the first step to an alliance with the petty bourgeoisie is the breaking up of the bloc with the bourgeois Radicals.'[37] This approach was at the very best open to the same objection that he had himself made to the pre-1933 policy of the German Communist Party of unrealistically calling for a united front of the working class without and against the leaders of the Social Democratic Party that the bulk of them followed.[38]

Particularly unjustified was Trotsky's representation of this class alliance between the parties based on the working class and those supported by the democratic petty bourgeoisie as 'the political alliance between the proletariat and the bourgeoisie'.[39] In fact, the Popular Front was directed precisely against the most powerful and dangerous sections of the bourgeoisie, constituted in France by the 'two hundred families' (the financial oligarchy holding the controlling levers of wealth and power) and in Spain by the financial oligarchy that was allied to the big landowners. In both countries the bulk of the bourgeoisie opposed the Popular Front with the utmost virulence, doing everything possible to undermine and defeat it in France and carrying things in Spain to the point of backing Franco's fascist rebellion against it.

United Front in France
The basis for the French Popular Front was laid by the great extra-parliamentary struggles of the French workers from February 1934 which led to the Unity of Action Pact signed in July of that year by the Communist and Socialist parties.

The kind of united front against fascism that Trotsky had for years been advocating had come into being in France. Now, however, he was to shift his ground, denouncing 'the one-sided, almost maniacal (sic) programme of immediate demands' on which the united front was based.[40] What was required, he argued in October 1934, was 'a programme of revolution'. No real improvement in the situation was conceivable 'without the revolutionary invasion of the right of capitalist property'. He insisted that

> the political campaign of the united front must base itself upon a well elaborated *transition programme*, i.e. on a system of measures which with a workers' and peasants' government can assure the transition from capitalism to socialism ... If the revolutionary proletariat does not take power, fascism will inevitably take it![41]

The Pact had laid down steps for 'the self-defence of workers' meetings, demonstrations, organisations and workers' leaders' and mutual assistance against fascist attacks.[42] Trotsky decided to go one better and raise the slogan 'Arm the proletariat and the revolutionary peasants!'[43] which was not only quite unacceptable to the Socialists, but was also highly provocative in the circumstances prevailing in France at that time.

When the Comintern had first developed its policy of the united front in 1921-22 it had made it clear that what was entailed was 'a common fight for the immediate and urgent needs of the proletariat' on which agreement could be reached with the reformist organisations.[44] Lenin argued that in preparatory negotiations with the representatives of the Second and the 'Two-and-a-Half' Internationals, the Comintern should put forward

> only questions that have a direct bearing on practical joint action by the working masses and touching on matters that are recognised as indisputable in the official press statement of each of the three participants.[45]

Trotsky himself had emphasised at this time that 'unity of front presupposes our readiness, within certain limits and on specific issues, to correlate in practice our actions with those of reformist organisations'.[46]

The offensive revolutionary programme that Trotsky put forward for the united front from the autumn of 1934 – whilst accepting that 'the proletariat finds itself in a defensive situation'[47] – was something very different. It could only have led to the break-up of the united front so recently concluded in

France. It had not the slightest chance of being accepted by either the leaders or the membership of the French Socialist Party, which he was to describe as 'not a revolutionary party [nor] even a proletarian party. It is petty bourgeois, not only in its policies but also in its social composition'.[48] Indeed Trotsky's French followers, who had entered the Socialist Party as a faction in the autumn of 1934, obtained out of the 3,000 votes cast at that party's Mulhouse congress the next June only 105 for their policy, and thereafter withdrew or were expelled.[49]

The proletarian united front should therefore not be seen as Trotsky's alternative to the Popular Front, since the advanced demands on which he insisted were in fact incompatible with either. Finally in June 1936 he envisaged the French working class being 'drawn into the impending conflict not only *without* the leadership of its traditional organisations' 'but also *against* these organisations[50], a scenario which quite explicitly excluded any kind of united front.[51]

Joining with the Radicals

The Popular Front, in which the Radicals joined with the traditional workers' parties from July 1935, was not a repetition of the old parliamentary 'cartel' of Socialists and Radicals. Far from '*putting a brake* upon the mass movement',[52] it greatly stimulated it, as the Communists sought to give it a solid extra-parliamentary basis by 'covering the country with an immense network of committees' elected in towns and villages, in factories and in the army.[53] The prospect of electoral success that the Popular Front afforded was a powerful factor in generating widespread support and activity.

Such a prospect was only made possible by the alliance with the Radical Party, which Trotsky predicted was about to 'disappear from the scene' having outlived itself.[54] In fact, whilst the Radicals were to lose half a million votes in the 1936 general election, the one and a half million votes that they received (as many as the Communist Party) showed that they were still a force to be reckoned with. There was no contradiction between encouraging the current of democratic, anti-fascist opinion among the Radicals, which was to bring them into the Popular Front, and at the same time winning hundreds of thousands of their supporters from Radicalism to socialism, as was to happen in the period culminating in the elections of April/May 1936 which reflected this.[55]

As these elections approached, alarm mounted on the right, which desperately sought to avert a Popular Front victory. An article in *International Socialism* correctly describes the position:

> Between them the workers' parties and the Radicals had a 'natural majority' ... The right's only hope was to split off the Radicals, or at least a major section of them.[56]

The policies urged by Trotsky would, of course, have given the right what it sought, but the readiness of the Communists to compromise thwarted the reactionaries' plans. A limited programme of anti-fascist, democratic, social and economic measures, realisable within the framework of capitalism, was agreed on[57]. Candidates of the Popular Front parties arranged in the second ballot, provided by the French electoral system, to withdraw in favour of whichever candidate of the allied parties was in the lead. Trotsky opposed this and expressed his regret that 'revolutionary working class candidates' had not been 'run in all electoral districts in which the Communists and Socialists withdrew in favour of the Radicals',[58] although this would probably have led to the election of more reactionaries.

The elections brought the expected Popular Front victory. Whereas between them the Socialists and Communists obtained only 218 out of 618 seats, the Popular Front as a whole won an absolute majority in the Chamber of Deputies with 378 seats, so that a Popular Front government could be formed by the Socialist Blum.

'The French Revolution has Begun!'

Few historians would agree with Trotsky's picture of the Popular Front 'lulling the workers and peasants with parliamentary illusions [and] paralysing their will to struggle'.[59] The *International Socialism* article quoted above recognises that it 'both responded to and encouraged a rising wave of class struggle'.[60] Encouraged by their victory at the polls, workers all over France embarked in May and June 1936 on their great sit-in strikes, in which Communist trade unionists played a leading part and the Communist Party gave its full support. They were demanding improved wages and working conditions, a forty-hour week, paid holidays, trade union rights and shop stewards, and the negotiation of agreements on both an industry and a factory basis.

Having stated the previous year that 'one would hardly expect a spontaneous strike wave in France',[61] Trotsky now proclaimed from his Norwegian exile: 'The French Revolution has Begun!'[62] This was the sort of 'infatuation with the revolutionary phrase' with which Lenin had again and again reproached Trotsky. The sit-in strikes of May and June 1936 represented a striking growth of working class militancy, initiative and organisation. But Trotsky offered not a morsel of evidence to back his claim that they 'revealed the whole-hearted readiness of the proletariat to overthrow the capitalist system'.[63]

Even if all the two million workers who struck during this period for their immediate demands could have been led to follow a Communist call to revolution, would they have been able to carry with them the other four million or so industrial workers? And could they have obtained the support of the majority of the peasantry, still the largest section of the French people?[64] What serious evidence was there of the readiness of the middle strata 'to support a bold revolutionary initiative on the part of the proletariat', which in its turn would have needed to have been ready 'to venture upon the most heroic efforts and sacrifices' to establish the 'political premises of a revolution', as set out by Trotsky himself?[65]

Supposing that Trotsky was right that the majority who voted Communist was thereby saying 'we want you to do the same as the Bolsheviks in their country in October 1917',[66] would they have been able to command a majority in the country, which Trotsky, following Lenin, had indicated was necessary for a successful revolution?[67]

The French Communist Party did not think so. That is why, after the strike movement had obtained important concessions from the employers in the Matignon agreements of 7 June, Thorez was to declare:

> There is no question of taking power at the present time … If the aim at the present moment is to obtain satisfaction for the economic demands whilst progressively raising the consciousness and organisation of the mass movement, then we need to know how to end the strike as soon as satisfaction has been obtained.[68]

This was no more a 'betrayal', as the Trotskyists have never ceased to declaim, than was the action of Lenin and the Bolsheviks who in June and July 1917 'held back and shaped into a peaceful demonstration' the 'spontaneous excitement' of the Petrograd masses, since they could not at that time count on the support of the peasantry and 'consequently could not have the majority of the people' behind them.[69]

The 'Real Will' of the Masses

In June 1936 Trotsky had correctly appreciated the revolutionary mood of the most militant sections of the French workers. But, as Lenin had cautioned,

> revolutionary tactics cannot be built on a revolutionary mood alone. Tactics must be based on a sober and strictly objective appraisal of *all* the class forces in a particular state (and of the states that surround it, and of all states the world over).[70]

A crucial element for such an appraisal was at hand in the results of the general election which had just been held in France.

Marxists should not, of course, look at election results statically and formalistically. They need to be analysed dynamically in their social context to assess trends and revolutionary potential. Nevertheless 'universal suffrage is an index of the maturity of the various classes in the understanding of their problems', as Lenin wrote. 'It shows how the various classes are *disposed* to solve their problems.'[71] For Trotsky, however, the election results were not' what they seemed. Faced with the victory at the polls of 'the strikebreaking conspiracy of the People's Front',[72] he commented curiously: 'The voter has expressed his will – so far as he can in the straitjacket of parliamentarianism – not in favour of the People's Front but against it'! And he proceeded, disdaining any attempt at substantiation, to pronounce that if the Socialists and Communists had broken up the Popular Front alliance with the Radicals 'they would have received many more votes'. The 'real will' of the masses (a metaphysical entity corresponding to Trotsky's preconceived notion of their striving for revolution) had been distorted by an unholy alliance of

> the Radical bourgeoisie, the Socialist businessmen and careerists (and) the Soviet diplomats and their 'Communist' lackeys ... to dupe and rob [them] politically.[73]

In the elections the Communist Party – which Trotsky had been describing in the previous period as 'diminishing', 'disintegrating', and 'de-composing'[74] – had doubled its poll with nearly one and a half million votes. This was, however, only 12.45

per cent of the total. Even assuming against all the evidence that the Socialists with 16.92 per cent had been prepared to join with the Communists in proceeding 'from the very first day of the strike' to establish 'a régime of dual power',[75] would they have had a reasonable chance, with under 30 per cent of the votes between them, of carrying the majority of the people with them?[76] Was it not simply wishful thinking to believe that millions who had registered their support for bourgeois parties at the ballot box one week would have transferred it to the workers' parties on the barricades the next? And, indeed, if these millions were really capable of such volatility and illogicality, is it not just as probable that they would have veered back again to the right when things became difficult the week after?

Had the workers' parties as a minority attempted 'the conquest of power by the proletariat', which Trotsky deemed 'possible only on the road of armed insurrection against the state apparatus of the bourgeoisie',[77] the likelihood is that they would have driven a significant part of the one and a half million Radical voters into the arms of the Right, which was looking for a pretext to crush the 'Bolshevik menace' particularly if the Trotskyist historian Tom Kemp is right that 'during the summer [of 1936], under the influence of the strikes and the concessions made to the workers, the middle class moved to the right.'[78] Colonel de la Rocque and his fascist *Croix de Feu* – with an estimated 300,000 supporters trained for civil war by 60,000 officers of the reserve – would have had a field day.

Nor should one neglect the international context, and its attendant dangers. Across the Rhine stood Nazi Germany allied to Fascist Italy in the south-east – both getting ready to help Franco smash Republican Spain, whilst the British bankers used every form of pressure to give them a free hand to do so. The possibility of a fascist intervention in France could not be excluded in the case of a premature proletarian uprising.

The Spanish Civil War

The bankruptcy of Trotsky's opposition to the people's front policy shows itself most clearly in Spain. Here there was not just a fascist danger but, from July 1936, an actual fascist uprising led by Franco and his fellow-generals on behalf of the landowning aristocracy and the monopoly capitalists. In February the Popular Front – an alliance of Socialists, Communists and middle-class republicans – had beaten the right and centre parties. They won 269 out of 480 seats in the Cortes (parliament) and a Popular Front government took office. This victory, which the workers' parties were not strong enough to have won on their own, unleashed a great explosion of militancy and initiative among the working people – contradicting Trotsky's assertion that the people's front was 'lulling the workers and peasants with parliamentary illusions' and 'paralysing their will to struggle'.[79] Workers occupied factories and peasants and agricultural workers took land from the big landowners. The Communists helped to spread grass-roots Popular Front Committees throughout the country, whilst demanding actions against the generals plotting against the Republic.

When the fascists started their insurrection against the Popular Front government in July 1936, on the initiative of the Communist Party and other sections of the left and in face of hesitation from the government, workers' militias were formed to fight against Franco's forces. Thanks to the direct action of the armed workers, the fascist rising was crushed in most of the main towns in the first fortnight of the war. It was now that Franco turned to fascist Germany and Italy, which proceeded to give him the decisive assistance in arms, planes and personnel to continue the offensive against the Spanish Republic. To smash this threat from the ruthless forces of domestic and foreign fascism was the most urgent task of the moment. How could it best be achieved?

On 30 July 1936, we find Trotsky writing that the socialist revolution was on the order of the day as the only means to defeat fascism. 'The victory of the people means the end of the Popular Front and the beginning of Soviet Spain.'[80] The result of pursuing the course urged by Trotsky in the circumstances of the Spanish Civil War would have been to narrow down the alliance against fascism by breaking the unity of the workers' parties with the peasants and the middle strata who supported the republican parties. Naturally Trotsky wanted such unity – but only 'from below', without the parties and party leaders that they still followed.

Trotsky called the Spanish Popular Front an 'alliance with the bourgeoisie's shadow', since the bourgeoisie itself was with Franco, and asserted that the Left Republicans 'represented no one but themselves'.[81] It would be difficult to imagine a cruder parody of historical materialism. Trotsky here dismisses the Marxist concept of the relative autonomy of ideas and institutions in favour of a dogmatic presumption that either a party directly represents one of the two main classes of society – or it represents no one.[82] The millions of Spanish working people, opposed to fascism but not yet Socialists or Communists, who had returned the 162 republican and other non-socialist left MPs within the framework of the Popular Front, counted for nothing. Those to whom they gave their votes ... 'represented no one'!

To have overthrown the parliament just elected by the people by a revolution for the establishment of Soviet power would have confirmed the precise allegations against the 'Reds' made by the fascists from the summer of 1936.[83] If the workers' organisations had in reality tried to seize power in this way, they might well have enjoyed *temporary* success in the industrial towns, but at the cost of alienating the wider support at home and abroad. This was crucial if they were to stand a chance of crushing the forces of fascism with their substantial material assistance from Hitler and Mussolini.

Therefore the Communists devoted themselves to consolidating and extending the anti-fascist unity of the People's Front and achieving the predominance of the working-class within it. Things advanced here much further than in France. The leftward swing in the country was reflected in a new People's Front government in September, under the left Socialist Caballero, with a majority of workers' representatives and including two Communist ministers and (from November) four Anarchists. Important measures of nationalisation and state control were carried out.[84] Extensive democratic transformations, involving the creation of a new popular state apparatus, were undertaken.

Winning Peasants

To preserve the Popular Front alliance with the Republican parties under these circumstances did not mean 'to subordinate the proletariat to the leadership of the bourgeoisie'.[85] On the contrary, it meant detaching sections of the liberal bourgeoisie from the main force of the class enemy supporting Franco and drawing them and, above all, their millions of peasant and middle-class followers into struggle under the hegemony of the working-class.

Of special importance was the decree passed in October 1936 on the initiative of the Communist Minister of Agriculture, which effectively expropriated the big landowners. And Dolores Ibarruri was to emphasise:

The peasants all over Spain – note that, all over Spain, and not only in the part that now happens to be in our hands – will have the land which was turned over to them by the decree of the Ministry of Agriculture of October 7, 1936.[86]

Yet Trotsky alleged – from what special intelligence he does not make clear – that 'The Spanish peasants ... say: "With Franco and with Caballero, it is the same thing" ', and added with touching solicitude: 'I am with this primitive Spanish peasant.'[87]

If the overall policy of the Spanish Communist Party in the Civil War was correct, many mistakes were nevertheless made. Great harm was done by the way in which, at the height of the Stalinist purges in the Soviet Union, NKVD (Soviet State Security) agents were sent into Spain and carried out measures of repression against honest revolutionaries, such as Andrés Nin, the leader of the leftist POUM.[88] Far from being linked to the Popular Front conception, such actions worked in precisely the opposite direction.

The party's strategy, which must be assessed politically, was to achieve the widest possible unity for the defeat of Franco, whilst at the same time defending and extending the social gains won in the democratic, anti-feudal, anti-monopoly-capitalist revolution.[89] It was, therefore, a complete distortion for Trotsky repeatedly to allege that 'the Comintern declared with regard to Spain that the social reforms will come after the victory.'[90]

Trotsky's statements on the Spanish Civil War often contradicted each other. At times we find him emphasising the need 'to draw a distinction between the fighting camps in Spain'[91] and writing (in September 1937):

> The Stalin-Negrín government [i.e. the Spanish Republican government of the time] is a quasi-democratic obstacle on the road to socialism; but it is also an obstacle ... on the road to fascism. Tomorrow or the day after tomorrow the Spanish proletariat may perhaps be able to break through this obstacle and seize power. But if it sided, even passively, in tearing it down today, *it would only serve fascism.*[92]

At other times however he was asserting that '*without the proletarian revolution the victory of "democracy" would only mean a round-about path to the very same fascism*', and concluding that it was 'necessary to openly and boldly mobilise the masses against the Popular Front government'.[93] Proceeding from this latter view he even went so far as explicitly to champion civil war and an 'uprising of the proletariat' in the rear of Republican Spain at a time when it was waging a life-and-death struggle against the forces of Franco, Hitler and Mussolini.[94]

At the beginning of May 1937 an armed uprising did in fact take place in the Republican city of Barcelona. Interviewed shortly afterwards by Associated Press, Trotsky characterised it as 'a more or less spontaneous movement' and noted correctly that such uprisings were 'all to the advantage of the fascists'.[95] However this did not prevent him from declaring elsewhere his support for the insurrection, whilst expressing his criticism that it was not carried through to the end. 'If the Catalan proletariat had seized power in May 1937,' he asserted, as usual without the slightest attempt at substantiation,

> they would have found support throughout Spain ... In the territory occupied by Franco not only the workers but also the peasants would have turned toward the Catalan proletariat, would have isolated the fascist army and brought about its irresistible disintegration.[96]

At the time the rebels called off their action – Trotsky was to emphasise that he had been disquieted by the news of an "armistice" in Barcelona'[97] – it has been estimated that as many as 950 people had been killed and 3,000 wounded.[98] To seek and support civil war behind the Republican lines when there was already a civil war going on against the fascists, who occupied a considerable part of the country, was *objectively* to play into their hands. The fascists understood this very clearly. That is why they used their agents to stir into revolt the perfectly genuine and sincere Anarchist 'Friends of Durriti', members of the leftist POUM and such few direct supporters as Trotsky had in Barcelona, as emerges from the information given by Franco's brother, Nicolas, to the German ambassador, Faupel, on 7 May 1937.[99]

Serious weaknesses there certainly were on the side of the Popular Front, but Franco's victory was due above all to his decisive superiority in military might as a result of the substantial German and Italian war supplies and armed intervention in the air, on the ground and at sea, and the cruel charade of 'non-intervention' performed by Britain and France.[100] Trotsky denied the overriding significance of these factors in explaining the Republic's defeat,[101] and spoke of 'all the conditions for victory [having been] at hand'.[102] This was like disputing that the military preponderance of the Versailles forces in May 1871 –

thanks to the Prussian assistance in releasing their French POWs to them – was the crucial element in the defeat of the Paris Commune, as Marx and Engels had shown.

Conception of Revolution

Trotsky's writings on the popular front show his conception of revolution in the West, to which most of his followers attach the greatest contemporary significance, to be the weakest part of his legacy. He viewed the prospects for such revolutions through the prism of the October Revolution, believing that they must of necessity take the same form of Soviets, insurrection and civil war. Even when in the 1930s the new phenomenon of fascism threatened to atomise the working class movement, as he had clearly recognised, his conception of the forms of alliance needed to defeat it was frozen in the experience of 1917 and the line of the first four Congresses of the Comintern (1919-22), to which he urged a return.

When the Comintern and the Communist parties of France and Spain from the mid-1930s extended the conception of the united front of workers' parties to a wider people's front of all anti-fascist parties, including bourgeois and petty-bourgeois left republicans, his condemnation was backward-looking and eschewed the Marxist method of analysing what was required in the current specific situation. Thus he compared the Popular Front to the bloc of Mensheviks and Socialist Revolutionaries for waging the imperialist war in the totally different conditions of Russia in 1917, and wrote: 'Apart from the question of whether the policy of the "People's Front" is good or bad, it happens to be the traditional policy of Menshevism against which Lenin fought all his life.'[103]

As the Bolshevik leader Lunacharsky showed in his sympathetic profile of Trotsky in the early period of Soviet power, Trotsky's 'path to revolution ... followed a straight line'. When history disproved his prognoses or ushered in new and unforeseen situations, he lacked Lenin's 'sense of reality which leads one now and then to alter one's tactics' and the 'tremendous sensitivity to the demands of the time' that prompted Lenin 'at one moment to sharpen both edges of his sword, at another to place it in its sheath'.[104]

Despite the high regard that Krupskaya, like Lenin, had for the role that Trotsky had played in the October Revolution, she noted in 1924:

When he speaks of Bulgaria or Germany, he occupies himself but little with the correct estimate of the moment. If we regard events through Comrade Trotsky's spectacles, it appears exceedingly simple to guide events. Marxist analysis was never Comrade Trotsky's strong point.[105]

Trotsky's writings on Spain and France twelve years later provide a most eloquent and pathetic confirmation of these words of Lenin's widow. On 30 July 1936, he produced his simple formula guaranteed to bring results within a day. 'The Spanish revolution,' he wrote,

> can even take the army away from its reactionary officers. To accomplish this, it is only necessary to seriously and courageously advance the programme of socialist revolution ... The fascist army could not resist the influence of such a programme for twenty-four hours; the soldiers would tie their officers hand and foot and turn them over to the nearest headquarters of the workers' militia.[106]

On what information did he base this extraordinary claim? Just over two weeks later he was to write to the representative of the Trotskyist movement in Barcelona about the situation there: 'The level of information reaching me stands at zero'![107] It was from the same position of isolation in his 'distant village in Norway' with only a radio to rely on that he had proclaimed on 9 June 1936: 'The French Revolution has Begun!' and given his recipe for how it could secure victory on the basis of the slogan 'Soviets Everywhere!'[108]

Political Basis of Voluntarism
There is, I believe, an underlying political basis for such voluntarism, which flowed from Trotsky's assumption that spontaneously the 'multi-millioned masses again and again enter the road of revolution'. When such revolutions failed to come off, he deduced quite logically from his unwarranted and unproven premise that this could only be because 'each time they are blocked by their own conservative bureaucratic machines'. These allegedly included the Communist parties which had definitively gone over 'to the side of the bourgeois order' and played a 'cynically counter-revolutionary role throughout the world'.[109] His simplistic claim that 'the historical crisis of mankind is *reduced* to the crisis of the revolutionary leadership'[110] stands in marked contrast to Lenin's understanding of revolution as 'a profound, difficult and complex science'.[111]

It is not surprising that from such premises Trotsky failed adequately to face up to and draw practical conclusions from the profound differences in social structure, institutions, culture, traditions and outlook between Russia before the October Revolution and the bourgeois democracies of the West. Lenin had begun to pose the problem in 1920 when he called on Communists to 'seek out, investigate, predict and grasp that which is nationally specific and nationally distinctive',[112] and approved in 1922 the slogan of workers' governments as a possible *form of transition* to the dictatorship of the proletariat in countries like Germany.[113] Although Lenin did not have a chance before his final illness to think out this question further, Gramsci was to develop his conception of 'a war of position' as 'the only form possible in the West', criticising Trotsky who, he wrote, 'in one way or another can be considered the political theorist of frontal attack in a period in which it only leads to defeats'.[114]

The people's front strategy and experience represented an important advance towards this type of approach. Far from signalling their 'renunciation of the proletarian revolution in favour of conservative bourgeois democracy', as Trotsky alleged,[115] the people's front was conceived by the communists as a class alliance under the growing hegemony of the working class for the defence and extension of democratic rights, which afforded possibilities for a move to the left and transition to the next stage of proletarian revolution, although unfavourable circumstances did not allow this to take place in the 1930s. In both his criticisms of Bolshevism before 1917 and his later criticisms of the people's front, Trotsky failed to see that in both cases the democratic stage could serve as a *bridge* to the socialist stage rather than an obstacle to it.

NOTES

1. 'The Comintern's Liquidation Congress' (23 August 1935), in *Writings of Leon Trotsky*, hereafter noted as *Writings, 1935-36*, p. 8.
2. *The Death Agony of Capitalism* (Transitional Programme of the Fourth International), London 1970, pp. 13-4.
3. Stalin's formula of 1924 that 'Social Democracy is objectively the moderate wing of fascism' (J. Stalin, *Works*, Moscow, 1953, Vol. 6, p. 294) was widely quoted and followed by Communist Parties in this period. (See, for example, *Communist Review*, London, July 1931, p. 241; *Die Internationale*, Berlin, February 1932, p. 67). See also Stalin's report to Sixteenth C.P.S.U. Congress (1930) on the need for an 'uncompromising struggle' against the 'social-fascists'. (ibid, vol. 12, pp. 260-1.)

4. The Eleventh Plenum of the Comintern Executive in 1931 stated that it was necessary to stop drawing a line 'between fascism and bourgeois democracy, and between the parliamentary form of the dictatorship of the bourgeoisie and its open fascist form.' (Quoted in A.I. Sobolev *et al.*, *Outline History of the Communist International*, Moscow 1971, p. 313.) Trotsky criticised this thesis in his *What Next? Vital Questions for the German Proletariat* (1932), which is included in Trotsky, *The Struggle against Fascism in Germany*, New York 1972, hereafter *Struggle against Fascism*, pp. 154-62.

5. The Comintern's 'Third Period' mistakes are acknowledged and criticised in Sobolev, op.cit., pp. 280, 291, 309-13, 325, 328-30, 334, 339. Unfortunately, however, the fact that similar criticisms were made *at the time* by Trotsky (see *Struggle against Fascism, passim*) and others like the Brandlerites and the Sozialistische Arbeiterpartei (SAP) is not mentioned.

6. *Struggle against Fascism*, pp. 157-9, 72, 367-8.

7. See particularly his writings opposing the Popular Front in his *Whither France?* (various English language editions published in New York, Colombo and London) and *The Spanish Revolution* (1931-39), New York 1973, Part III.

8. 'The Tragedy of Spain' (February 1939), in *The Spanish Revolution*, op.cit., p. 331.

9. 'It is impossible to remain in the same International' (July 1933), *Writings* (1933-34), p. 22.

10. O. Piatnitsky, *The Present Situation in Germany*, London 1933, Appendix, p. 44.

11. Sobolev, op.cit., p. 339. Trotsky criticised this in 'Are there no limits to the fall?' (January 1934), *Writings* (1933-34), pp. 211-2.

12. L. Magyar, 'The Bankruptcy of Trotskyism', *Labour Monthly*, June 1934, p. 369. Emphasis in original.'

13. Trotsky, *The Permanent Revolution*, New York 1965, p. 112.

14. *Labour Monthly*, April 1933, p. 268.

15. J. Mérot, *Dimitrov: un révolutionnaire de notre temps*, Paris, 1972 pp. 184-7. Mérot used detailed information obtained from the Institute of History of the Bulgarian Communist Party.

16. G. Ceretti, *A l'Ombre des Deux T*, Paris 1973, pp. 158-61, where the author quotes what Togliatti told him at the time.

17. Ibid. Ceretti was present at the discussion between Thorez, Duclos and the Comintern's representatives. See also M. Thorez, *Fils du Peuple*, Paris 1960, pp. 95-102; Duclos, *Mémoires*, Paris 1968, Vol. 1, pp. 420-1. The idea that Communist Parties should also start talks with petty bourgeois and peasant parties had already been mooted in a committee meeting apparently in August or September 1934 by Manuilsky, who alone among the Comintern leaders present had supported Dimitrov in his discussion with Stalin. (Sobolev, op.cit., p. 359; Mérot, op.cit., pp. 186-7.) Later Stalin was to congratulate Thorez for the Popular Front initiative. (Thorez, op.cit., p. 102.)

18. See, for example, Mandel, *From Stalinism to Eurocommunism* London, 1978, pp. 17-8.

19. V.I. Lenin *'Kommunismus'* (June 1920), in his *Collected Works*, Moscow and London, 1963-70 hereafter *CW*, Vol. 31, p. 166.

20. *Writings* (1938-39), p. 62. My emphasis.

21. *Whither France?*, Colombo 1961, p. 117; *The Case of Leon Trotsky*, London 1937, p. 195; *The Revolution Betrayed*, London 1957, pp. 186-7.

22. 'The Stalinist Turn' (September 1935), *Writings 1935-36)*, p. 13.

23. 'The Comintern's Liquidation Congress' (August 1935), ibid., p. 11; *Whither France?*, p. 117. His statement about the resolution is all the more ridiculous in that many points are made in it similar to those which he himself had been urging on the Comintern up to 1934!

24. Quoted by J.-P. Joubert, 'Trotsky et le Front Populaire', *Cahiers Léon Trotsky* (Grenoble), 9 January 1982, with the permission of Houghton Library, Harvard University, which holds the Trotsky Archives. This correspondence is in the previously closed section, which was opened in 1980.

25. G. Dimitrov, *The United Front*, London 1938, p. 12. Emphasis in original.

26. Ibid., p. 110. Emphasis in original.

27. Ibid., p. 32. Emphasis in original.

28. *Resolutions of the Seventh World Congress of the Communist International*, London 1935, pp. 7, 11. Emphasis in original.

29. M. Thorez, *The Successes of the Anti-Fascist United Front*, London 1935, p. 23.

30. See for example, *Whither France?*, pp. 10-11.

31. Trotsky, presenting in 1929 an account of these controversies, states quite correctly that 'the theoretical as well as the political dispute among us was not over the collaboration of the workers and peasants as such, but over the programme of this collaboration, its party forms and political methods.' (*The Permanent Revolution*, op.cit., p. 66.) However, in trying to minimise his disagreement with Lenin, he downplays the significance of this. See also Lenin, *CW*, Vol. 15, pp. 370-4.

32. Theses on Tactics adopted by Third Comintern Congress (July 1921), in J. Degras (ed.), *The Communist International (1919-1943)*, Documents, London 1956, Vol. 1, p. 248.

33. See, for example, *Struggle against Fascism*, p. 72.

34. Trotsky, *Die österreichische Krise*, Vienna 1929, p. 11. My emphasis.

35. *Whither France?* p. 94. Emphasis in original.

36. *The United Front*, p. 25.

37. 'The New Revolutionary Upsurge and the Tasks of the Fourth International' (July 1936), *Writings (1935-36)*, p. 33.

38. *Struggle against Fascism*, pp. 165-70.

39. Trotsky, *The Spanish Revolution*, op.cit., p. 309.

40. *Whither France?*, pp. 55-56.

41. Ibid., pp. 39-40.

42. *Labour Monthly*, October 1934, p. 624, which carries the text of the Pact.

43. *Whither France?*, p. 29.

44. ECCI-RILU Manifesto on the United Front, in Degras (ed.), op.cit., pp. 316-9.

45. Lenin to Bukharin and Zinoviev, 1 February 1922, *CW*, Vol. 42, p. 393.

46. Trotsky, *The First Five Years of the Communist International*, New York 1953, Vol. 2, p. 95.

47. *Whither France?*, p. 75.

48. 'A New Turn is Necessary' (June 1935), *Writings (1934-35)*, p. 317. But cf the French Trotskyist OCI's *Quelques Enseignements de notre Histoire*, Paris 1970, p. 13: 'The Socialist Party's social composition in 1934 was largely working class.'

49. J. Rabaut, *Tout est possible! Les 'gauchistes' français, 1929-1944*, Paris 1974, pp. 164, 180-1.

50. *Whither France?*, p. 162. Emphasis in original.

51. In Spain Trotsky's demands were such that he was aware that they did not even provide a basis for unity with his old comrade Nin and the bulk of the semi-Trotskyist POUM. Therefore, he wrote, 'the revolutionists must turn to the workers, to the depths, against the vacillations and waverings of Nin. Unity of the proletarian front does not mean capitulation to the centrists.' ('Is Victory Possible in Spain?', April 1937, *The Spanish Revolution*, p. 259.)

52. *Whither France?*, p. 131. Emphasis in original.

53. *Les Cahiers du bolchévisme*, 15 December 1935, quoted in G. Lefranc, *Juin 36*, Paris 1966, p. 80; M. Thorez, Report to Eighth Congress of French Communist Party (January 1936), *Oeuvres de Maurice Thorez*, Book 3, Vol. 11, pp. 106-7.

54. *Whither France?*, pp. 12-13, 15. Trotsky was failing to appreciate that 'we must *not* regard what is obsolete *to us* as something obsolete *to a class, to the masses*.' (Lenin, *Left Wing Communism, an Infantile Disorder*, 1920. *CW*, Vol. 31, p. 58. Emphasis in original).

55. The great demonstration organised by the Communist and Socialist Parties on 24 May 1936, in memory of the Paris Communards showed that the Popular Front created favourable conditions for independent socialist activity and propaganda. Yet for Trotsky the demonstration was 'the most convincing and most unalterable disavowal of the People's Front policy by working class Paris'! (*Whither France?*, p. 145).

56. R. Kirkwood, 'The fire last time: France 1936', *International Socialism*, No. 56, March 1973, p. 15.

57. See M. Thorez, *France Today and the People's Front*, London 1936, pp. 192-200.

58. *Whither France?*, p. 145.

59. 'The New Revolutionary Upsurge' (July 1936), *Writings* (1935-36), p. 35.

60. Kirkwood, loc.cit.

61. *Whither France?*, p. 64.

62. Ibid., p. 150.

63. *The Death Agony of Capitalism*, op.cit., p. 13.

64. Around 1930 the total population of France was 42 million of whom 14 million belonged to the peasantry, 12 million to the petty bourgeoisie and 13 million to the working class, including 9 million factory workers and their families (C. Willard *et al*, *Le Front populaire*, Paris 1972, p. 18.)

65. Trotsky, *The History of the Russian Revolution*, London 1936, p. 1024.

66. *Whither France?*, p. 143. This proposition is more than dubious, since the Communists fought the election on the basis of a militant struggle to implement the People's Front programme, not to carry through a socialist insurrection.

67. Trotsky, *Ecrits*, Paris, 1959. Vol. 3, p. 471. cf. Lenin (October 1917): 'If the revolutionary party has not a majority among the front ranks of the revolutionary classes *and in the country generally*, there can be no question of insurrection.' (*Selected Works*, Moscow/London, n.d. – 1937? – Vol. 6, p. 293. My emphasis.)

68 *Fils du Peuple*, p. 127.

69. Lenin, Letter to Comrades (October 1917). *CW*, Vol. 26, p. 210. Trotsky made the same point on these events: *History of the Russian Revolution*,

pp. 593-4.

70. *'Left-wing' Communism, CW*, Vol. 31, p. 63, emphasis in original.

71. 'The Constituent Assembly Elections' (December 1919), *Polnoe Sobranie Sochineniy*, Moscow 1963, Vol. 40, pp. 20-21. Emphasis in original. (For another translation see *CW*, Vol. 30, pp. 271-2.) See also Lenin, *CW*, Vol. 26, pp. 80, 183-4 & 195; also Trotsky himself, *The First Five Years of the Communist International*, Vol. 2, pp 350-1, for the importance of election results in 1917 for showing that the Bolsheviks could count on a majority supporting them.

72. *Whither France?*, p. 138.

73. Ibid., p. 144.

74. *Writings* (1933-34), pp. 27, 89, 213.

75. 'The New Revolutionary Upsurge' (July 1936), *Writings (1935-36)*, p. 34.

76. Contrast this with the results of the elections to the Constituent Assembly in Russia in November 1917. To the 24-25 per cent Bolshevik vote should be added the majority of those who voted for the Socialist-Revolutionaries, who topped the poll but split into two parties. The Left S.R.s, commanding the greater popular support, backed the October Revolution and formed a coalition government with the Bolsheviks. Felix Morrow, in the Trotskyist classic *Revolution and Counter-revolution in Spain*, London 1963, is therefore wrong in asserting that 'by the present Stalinist criterion (of majority support in the country – M.J.), one could condemn the Russian Revolution' (p. 138).

77. Trotsky, op.cit., p. 35. It is not clear how Trotsky reconciled this statement with his claim on the previous page of the same article that it would have been possible to 'have overthrown the bourgeoisie in June, almost without civil war, with the minimum of disturbance and of sacrifices.' (Ibid., p. 34).

78. T. Kemp, 'Betrayals of 1936-37', *Workers Press*, 25 March 1970.

79. Trotsky, *The Spanish Revolution 1931-1938*, New York, 1973, p. 229 (July 1936).

80. 'The Lesson of Spain', *Spanish Revolution*, pp. 234-9, cf. ibid., pp. 324-5: 'Only the socialist revolution is capable of crushing fascism ... Victory will go either to the socialist revolution or to fascism.' (December 1937).

81. *Spanish Revolution*, pp. 309-10 (December 1937).

82. Contrast this with Marx's treatment in his *Eighteenth Brumaire* of the ideological factors involved in the formation of separate parties of the same class and of the character of the French Social Democratic Party of the time as a coalition of two classes (Marx-Engels, *Selected Works*, Moscow/London, 1950, Vol. 1, esp. pp. 233-4, 247-50.) However when criticising Stalin's equally crude party model in relation to the Soviet Union, Trotsky sheds his own dogmatism. (See his *Revolution Betrayed*, pp. 266-8.)

83. They cited three forged documents purporting to reveal general instructions for a revolution and the installation of left Socialists and Communists as a 'Soviet'. (See H. Thomas, *The Spanish Civil War*, 1968, p. 150.)

84. In its programme of December 18, 1936, *The Eight Conditions for Victory*, the Spanish Communist Party proposed the nationalisation of the basic industries and the setting up of a Co-ordinating Council for industry and the Economy.

85. *Spanish Revolution*, p. 309 (December 1937).

86. *Speeches and Articles*, p. 234. cf. ibid., p. 101: 'Our party is a consistent

advocate of collective labour, including labour in agriculture, because collective labour makes it possible to utilise machinery, fertilisers and irrigation on a large scale, thus ensuring an increase in produce and lightening the labour of the peasants. But collectivisation, work in common, must follow from a clear expression of the will of the peasants and must never be imposed on them by force.'

87. *The Case of Leon Trotsky*, London 1937, p. 294.
88. This is the view of Santiago Carrillo, formerly General Secretary of the Spanish Communist Party. He denies that the majority of Communist leaders knew about Nin's assassination. (S. Carrillo, *Le Communisme malgré tout*, Paris 1984, pp 16-7.)
89. cf. Trotsky in April 1936: 'The October Revolution has vigorously demonstrated that the socialist revolution cannot be carried out within the framework of democracy. The "democratic" revolution and the socialist revolution are on opposite sides of the barricades. The Third International theoretically confirmed this experience. The "democratic" revolution in Spain has already been carried out. The Popular Front is renewing it ...' (*Spanish Revolution*, p. 213.)
90. *The Case of Leon Trotsky*, p. 294. See, also, *Spanish Revolution*, pp 243, 320.
91. *Death Agony*, p. 55.
92. *Spanish Revolution*, p. 296. My emphasis.
93. 'Is Victory Possible in Spain?' (April 1937), *Spanish Revolution*, pp 258-9. Emphasis in original.
94. *Spanish Revolution*, p. 261 (April 1937), pp. 323-4 (December 1937).
95. Trotsky, *Writings, 1937-8*, p. 84 (1 June 1937).
96. *Spanish Revolution*, p. 279 (August 1937).
97. *Spanish Revolution*, p. 302 (October 1937).
98. I. Maisky, *Spanish Notebooks*, London, 1966, p. 136.
99. *Akten zur Deutschen Auswärtigen Politik. 1918-1945. Aus dem Archiv des Deutschen Auswärtigen Amtes*, Baden-Baden 1951, Vol. 111, Series D (1937-1945). *Deutschland und der Spanischer Bürgerkrieg. 1936-1939*, p. 243 (Document 254).
100. The closing of France's frontier with Republican Spain for deliveries of arms also made even more difficult the transportation of Soviet military aid at a time when the fascists were attacking and sinking ships suspected of carrying cargo from Soviet ports to Republican Spain. (See 'Solidarity with the Spanish Republic from 1936 to 1939', *Soviet News*, 14 November 1972; I. Maisky, *Spanish Notebooks*, pp. 48-9, 116-7.)
101. *Spanish Revolution*, p.341 (March 1939).
102. Ibid., p. 331. (February 1939).
103. *Writings, 1937-38*, p. 171. (December 1937.)
104. A.V. Lunacharsky, *Revolutionary Silhouettes*, London 1967, p. 67.
105. N. Krupskaya, 'The Lessons of October', in *The Errors of Trotskyism*, London 1925, p. 336.
106. *Spanish Revolution*, p. 235.
107. Ibid., p. 240.
108. *Whither France?*, pp. 150-6.
109. *The Death Agony*, p. 13.
110. Ibid., p. 12. My emphasis.
111. Lenin, Reply to Debate on Peace (March 1918), *C W*, Vol. 27, p. 198.

112. '*Left-wing' Communism, C W*, Vol. 31, p. 92.
113. See Sobolev, op.cit., pp. 161-4; A. Reisberg, *Lenins Beziehungen zur deutschen Arbeiterbewegung*, Berlin, 1970, pp. 452-4.
114. A. Gramsci, *Selections from the Prison Notebooks* London 1973, pp. 237-8. In considering Trotskyist presentations of the people's front as simply dictated by Stalin to promote conservative diplomatic ends, it is worth noting that at the beginning of the 1930s Gramsci in his fascist jail was counterposing to the Comintern's 'Third Period' line a strategy of common action with other Italian anti-fascist parties for intermediate, democratic objectives. See G. Fiori, *Antonio Gramsci: Life of a Revolutionary*, London 1970, pp. 255-7.
115. 'Does Soviet Government still follow Principles?' (January 1938), *Writings* (1937-38), p. 171.

Myths From Right and Left

NOREEN BRANSON

It is sad to reflect on how often people have failed to learn the lessons of history. When it comes to a subject like the world Communist movement in the 1930s, the failure is not surprising, for since that time, those hostile to Communists have been hard at work, trying to bury the truth, or to distort those truths that cannot be totally obliterated.

Ideas Promoted from the Right

The general impression created by Thatcher's friends is that the Second World War broke out because, instead of rearming and so building up Britain's strength, Prime Minister Neville Chamberlain went in for 'appeasement' of the enemy. 'Appeasement' was in part a response to pressure for disarmament from the labour movement which wanted peace at any price. Conservative Winston Churchill was the leader of those opposed to 'appeasement', and in the end he became Prime Minister during the war and led the nation to victory.

This picture is arrived at by the elimination of many facts and the misrepresentation of others; as a result it bears little resemblance to reality. Below are listed some of the facts needed to put the record straight:

1) What the labour movement (including the Communists) stood for in the 1930s was *not* appeasement of the fascist powers, but collective action against the aggressors under the auspices of the League of Nations. It is true there was a large anti-war movement and this took a pacifist form in the case of the Peace Pledge Union (formed in 1934); the Women's Co-operative Guilds also adopted a pacifist stand. But the pacifist influence was never the dominant one within the labour movement which stood for collective security under the League of Nations; this meant collective imposition of economic sanctions and, if necessary,

115

military sanctions to stop any nation attacking another. The International Peace Campaign, founded in Brussels in 1936, which had much support in the labour movement but also had among its leading figures Conservative Viscount Cecil and a number of Liberal MPs, always opposed appeasement and consistently argued for action by the League. Unfortunately the Conservatives as a whole, led first by Baldwin and then by Chamberlain, were resolutely opposed to any such action by the League, and persistently sabotaged moves for such action by other League members.

2)   It was Communists who, at their Seventh World Congress in 1935, accurately identified the fascist powers as the chief instigators of war, and who, in a resolution, described the plan of the German Nazis as 'a war of revenge against France, dismemberment of Czechoslovakia, annexation of Austria, destruction of the independence of the Baltic states, which they are striving to convert into a base for attack on the Soviet Union, and the wresting of the Soviet Ukraine from the USSR'.[1] During the ensuing years, this analysis of Hitler's aims was to be proved true in every particular.

3)   The one thing that might have deterred Hitler would have been for Britain to have joined in the mutual assistance pacts drawn up in accordance with the Covenant of the League of Nations and signed by France, the Soviet Union and Czechoslovakia in 1935. It was Communists who led the campaign for Britain to join such pacts which laid down that if one of the signatories was the victim of unprovoked aggression the others would go to its aid.

4)   Chamberlain not only refused to be a party to any such pact; in 1938 he went to Munich and persuaded France to abandon its pact with the Czechs, and forced through an agreement that large parts of Czechoslovakia be handed over to Hitler, including the famous Skoda arms works. Only one MP opposed Chamberlain's plan for the dismemberment of Czechoslovakia. It was not Churchill, but William Gallacher, Communist MP for West Fife.[2]

5)   Much of the pressure on Chamberlain to do a deal with Hitler came from sources like the 'Cliveden set'. Cliveden was the home of Lord Astor, chairman of *The Times*; his brother owned the *Observer*; both these newspapers were openly pro-German and wanted a deal with the fascist powers. It was the Communists who consistently exposed the manoeuvres of the 'Cliveden set' and pro-Nazi organisations like the Anglo-German Fellowship.

6) It is true that Communists opposed the massive rearmament programme launched by the British government and criticised the decision of the Parliamentary Labour Party in 1937 to abandon its opposition to this. The Communist Party was against the rearmament programme because the government 'uses armaments only in support of fascism, of imperialist war, of reaction and of colonial suppression'.[3] As Harry Pollitt, general secretary of the Communist Party put it:

> We are perfectly willing to support any measures necessary to defend Britain from fascism either from British or foreign sources. But we are ruled today by a government which prepares the way for the advance of fascism in Britain, and supports fascist aggression abroad ... The question of defence is not only a question of guns. It is also a question of who controls them.[4]

Chamberlain's main motive for bowing to Hitler's demands was anti-Communism. Alec Douglas-Home, Chamberlain's PPS at Munich, and Conservative Prime Minister in the 1960s, said in retrospect:

> I think the main thing to grasp is that Chamberlain, like many others, saw communism as the major long-term danger. He hated Hitler and German fascism, but he felt that Europe in general and Britain in particular were in even greater danger from communism. Hitler was an evil man but in the short term one should – and possibly could – do a deal with him, and after that he could be controlled.[5]

Hitler and Chamberlain both regarded the Soviet Union as the enemy, and Thatcher is following in their footsteps. So it is not surprising that the role of the Soviet Union in the war that followed Chamberlain's appeasement of Hitler is seldom talked about. From 1941-45 the Soviet Union was Britain's ally and, as Churchill himself admitted, it was the Russians who, in the end, 'tore the guts out of the German army' and so ensured victory over the Nazis. Thatcher and her friends prefer not to be reminded of this embarrassing truth, as was revealed early in 1985, when the Government showed marked unwillingness to celebrate the anniversary of VE day because it would necessitate some recognition of the Soviet Union's contribution to victory.

Myths from the Left
From an angle opposite to that of the Thatcherite right an equally distorted picture is presented. It emanates originally from

Trotsky, but has since been embraced, not only by those who believe themselves to be followers of Trotsky, but by certain professional historians who would certainly make no claim to be Marxists. For them the story is roughly as follows: At its Seventh World Congress in 1935 the Communist International made an about-turn and, on the pretext of the need for anti-fascist struggle, abandoned its former aim of world revolution. In the years 1935-39, Communist parties throughout the world tried to damp down the class struggle and, with it, movements for colonial freedom; socialist propaganda was soft-pedalled in order to build up a 'popular front' not only with Labour Party 'reformists' but also with middle class liberals; internationalism was discarded so as to tune in with Stalin's aim of an alliance with Western imperialist powers. In short, from 1935, the Comintern performed a counter-revolutionary role.

To appreciate the distortions and, indeed, total untruths contained in the above, it is necessary to recall some of the events leading to the 1935 Congress. The Communist International, which was a world Communist party, had been founded after the Russian revolution of 1917. Until 1933, it had always been assumed that the next great proletarian revolution would be in Germany. This was because the German Communist Party was much the largest outside the Soviet Union, commanding the support of millions of German people. But the disunity between the German Communists and Social Democrats enabled Hitler to come to power in 1933; under this fascist dictatorship, not only the German Communist Party but all other political parties were smashed.

The Seventh World Congress in 1935 was the outcome of two years' discussion among Communists of all countries as to what had gone wrong and why. It had to be recognised that the policies of the 'class against class' period from 1928-32, had been based on a faulty analysis of the situation and had, moreover, served to isolate Communist parties from the workers they aimed to lead. It was also realised that, if the world working class was to go forward to socialism, fascism had to be defeated in the countries where it was already in power, and prevented from developing elsewhere. While these discussions went on, Communist parties were, to an increasing extent, involved in actions that foreshadowed the policies finally adopted by the Congress, which was no sudden 'about-turn', but on the contrary served as the expression of policy changes long since in operation. The new attitude did not signify any abandonment of fundamental aims. As Dimitrov pointed out, German fascism was acting as the 'spearhead of international counter-revolution'.[6]

Two special characteristics of fascism were identified and discussed at the Congress. Firstly, it was stressed that fascism aimed to smash democratic gains previously made by the workers, and to abolish hard-won rights. The fight to protect those rights did *not* involve 'abandoning the class struggle' – it was part of the class struggle. Secondly, the fascist powers were identified as the leading warmongers. A major responsibility of the world movement was to expose their plans and build up opposition to them.

The Results: Class Struggles in the Workplace
Did the new analysis made by Communists at the Seventh World Congress result in attempts to 'damp down' the class struggle? Did it mean, as Trotsky argued at the time, and his followers have alleged since, that the Communist movement ceased to play an anti-capitalist role? If the activities of the Communist Party of Great Britain are examined, it becomes clear that these allegations have no basis whatsoever.

The party in Britain was very small; it had only 7,700 members at the time of the Seventh World Congress, though it was to grow to almost 18,000 by 1939. Yet during those years, the party was to make a contribution to the struggle against the class enemy out of all proportion to its size. This becomes clear if its activities in the industrial sphere are examined.

For Communists, the workplace had always been regarded as the most important area for political activity since it was here that the confrontation between capitalist and worker could emerge in its most direct form. There was a growing number of industrial struggles in the second half of the 1930s, and in nearly all of them Communists played a leading part. For example, in South Wales, Communists were in the forefront of the fight against company unionism which culminated in the stay-down strikes in the autumn of 1935, after which the coal owners gave in.[7] Communists played a similar role in the Harworth dispute of 1936-37 which led to the defeat of company unionism among the Nottinghamshire miners. Mick Kane, a well-known Communist and president of the Harworth branch of the miners' union was given a two-year prison sentence for his part in this dispute; widespread protests led to his release a year later.[8]

In the engineering industry, the party made a major contribution towards the growth of the shop stewards movement. The aim was not only to build up workshop floor organisation, but to establish links between stewards in different factories. The most spectacular success was in the aircraft industry. Following a strike in 1935 at Hawker Aircraft, an Aircraft Shop Stewards' National Council was established with representatives from a number of factories. Its organ, the *New Propellor*, had, by 1937, achieved a circulation of 14,000 spread around 49 factories.[9] As a secret Home Office memorandum was to complain early on in the war: 'in industry the Communist Party has obtained a representation among Shop Stewards out of all proportion to the strength of the Party in the factories.'[10]

Recognition by right-wing trade union leaders that Communists were undermining their authority was demonstrated in the case of the London busmen. In 1932, Communists had initiated a London busmen's rank and file movement, which had as its journal the *Busman's Punch*. In 1937, the busmen came out on official strike for shorter hours. Bevin and Deakin, the two right-wing leaders of the Transport and General Workers' Union, ordered the men back to work and laid down that the rank and file movement was a subversive body to which no union member could belong. The leading Communists involved were all expelled or debarred from holding office in the union, though some time later they secured reinstatement.

Those trade union leaders who believed in class collaboration and wanted a docile membership were in no doubt as to who offered the main challenge to their supremacy. 'Trade Unions cannot enter into collective bargaining without accepting responsibility for carrying out their agreements,' asserted a statement issued by the TUC General Council in 1936. It went on:

On numerous occasions, however, the Executives of Unions have been faced with unofficial strikes, deliberately fomented by Communists and directed not so much against the employers as against executive authority and the unions themselves.[11]

It is clear from the above examples (and many others could be given) that neither the employers nor the right-wing trade union leaders thought that Communists were trying to 'damp down the class struggle' – on the contrary. It is noticeable that Hugo Dewar in his book *Communist Politics in Britain* avoids mentioning any of these activities of the Communist Party in industry. Obviously they contradict his often repeated statement that for the Communist Party after 1935 'the class struggle was suspended'.

Communists were never in doubt about the ultimate object of these activities. J.R. Campbell, a long-standing member of the Communist Party's Central Committee, said at the party's 1937 Congress that members who were elected to trade union positions

> must see that their task is not merely to raise the level of wages, but to raise the level of class consciousness, is not only to make the workers see that their interests are opposed to the interests of the capitalists, but to make them see that the capitalist system is a menace to the whole human race. Therefore we must make the trade union machine not merely a machine for raising wages but one which organises the workers for the great historic tasks of overthrowing capitalism by mass action.[12]

Action against the class enemy was not confined to the industrial sphere. The late 1930s saw the development of huge tenants' movements, the formation of tenants' defence leagues. There were massive rent strikes against the private landlords in East London; the first major struggle took place in Bethnal Green, and was organised by Communist Bob Graves; it was followed by strike after strike in Stepney – here the tenants' defence league had three full-time elected officials who were all Communists: 'Tubby' Rosen, secretary, and Ella Donovan and Harry Conn, organisers. The strike movement spread to other parts of London and to other towns. In Birmingham there was a rent strike of 40,000 council tenants who waged a successful battle against their Tory Council's decision to increase rents. Secretary of the Birmingham Municipal Tenants Association was Communist Jessie Eden.

Meanwhile, Elsy Borders and her husband Jim, both members of the Communist Party, led a movement of owner-occupiers of 'jerry-built' houses against the building societies; 3,000 such owner-occupiers went on mortgage strike.

Though these movements frequently hit the headlines in the *Daily Worker* of those years (and indeed in other newspapers as well) they receive no mention whatever in Dewar's book; again, to give them any notice would contradict his theory that in the later 1930s the class struggle was abandoned by the party.

Colonial Liberation no Longer an Aim?
It has been alleged that at the Seventh World Congress,

movements for colonial freedom were treated as a side issue, and that after the Congress, Communists aimed to damp down colonial liberation struggles so as not to put pressure on governments who might be won for the popular front policy. This allegation is totally without foundation. Support for it is, regretably, to be found in E.H. Carr's book, *The Twilight of Comintern 1930-1935*. Carr was a remarkable scholar whose work on the history of Soviet Russia has rightly commanded much respect. But in this particular volume there are many factual errors, and the facts, when accurate, are frequently misinterpreted. Thus, what happened on the colonial question at the Seventh World Congress is described by Carr as follows:

> Care was taken not to ruffle the susceptibilities of those imperialist powers whose support Comintern was seeking to woo for the anti-fascist front. The records fail to reveal the presence of any Indian or Indonesian delegate at the congress. Delegates of Syria and of Indo-China addressed it; but the brief published records of their speeches do not refer to the suffering of their peoples under French imperialist rule. The question was avoided by all the delegates from countries possessing colonies except the Netherlands delegate ... The call in the resolution on Dimitrov's report for a struggle 'against the increasing imperialist exploitation, against cruel enslavement, for the expulsion of the imperialists for national independence' was routine business. This was the year of the liquidation of the long-moribund League against Imperialism.[13]

The following points must be made in answer to these accusations:

1) It is not true that no Indian or Indonesian delegates were present. The speech of Tambe on behalf of the Indian party was reported in the English-language edition of *International Press Correspondence* (known as *Inprecorr*, available weekly at 2d a copy). Tambe said of the Indian Communist Party that it was 'still young and for the time being illegal. British imperialism and the Indian bourgeoisie persecute it with terrorist measures. A large number of comrades are lying in jail.'[14] It is true that Tambe was the only Indian party speaker, but this was because the other Indian delegates had been arrested before they could leave their country. Roestam Effeni started his speech on behalf of the Indonesian party by saying 'in spite of growing exploitation whereby Dutch imperialism is trying to find a way out of the crisis at the cost of the oppressed peoples' ...[15]

2) It is not true that the colonial question was avoided by delegates from countries possessing colonies. For example, Thorez, who represented the French party, said that they were fighting with great energy 'for the independence of the colonial peoples of Northern Africa and Indo-China whom we support with all our strength in their struggles against the yoke of French imperialism'.[16] Harry Pollitt, representing the British party, spoke of the need to assist the Indian, African, Egyptian and Irish peoples in their 'revolutionary struggle for complete liberation from British imperialism'.[17]

3) It is not true that the call for national independence was treated as 'routine business'; there was a long discussion introduced by Wang Ming of the Chinese Party on 'the revolutionary movement in the colonial countries'.[18]

4) It is not true that the League Against Imperialism was liquidated in 1935; the reasons for its demise two years later are examined below.

What really happened? The Congress discussed and adopted a new approach which, it was believed, would strengthen and accelerate the struggle for colonial liberation. It was recognised that the 'class against class' policies of the Sixth World Congress, i.e. calls for an immediate revolution and denunciation of all possible allies – had proved as counter-productive in colonial countries as in Europe. Thus, the Sixth World Congress had laid it down that in India 'the Communists must unmask the national reformism of the Indian National Congress'.[19] But at the Seventh World Congress it was recognised that this sectarian approach had been a mistake and Indian Communists were urged to participate actively in anti-imperialist movements already in existence; as Wang Ming put it:

> Both within and without the National Congress the Indian Communists must consolidate all the genuine anti-imperialist forces of the country, broadening and leading the struggle of the masses against the imperialist oppressors.[20]

Soon afterwards, the Indian Party and, indeed the Communist Party in Britain, developed close links with the left-wing socialists within the Indian National Congress, in particular Jawaharlal Nehru and Krishna Menon.

It is within this context that decisions concerning the League Against Imperialism must be viewed. The League had been established on the initiative of the Comintern in 1927 with its international headquarters in Berlin. In 1933, after Hitler had come to power, its headquarters were transferred to London. This was an appropriate move since Britain ruled over an empire far larger than that of any other imperialist power, and the British section of the League had always been among its liveliest. Reginald Bridgeman was its international secretary, and Ben Bradley, who had served four years in an Indian jail during the notorious Meerut conspiracy case, was secretary of its British section.

The difficulty was that the Labour Party had, in 1933, declared the League to be part of the 'Communist Solar System', and ruled that it was a proscribed organisation, which meant that no member of the Labour Party could belong to it or even appear on its platform at meetings. The result was, as Ben Bradley put it, that the small group of people interested in the colonial struggle were 'seriously restricted in their activities because of their association with a banned organisation'. He wanted to advance from this position and 'activise the working class organisations and peace societies, especially the youth sections of whose growing interest in colonial questions we are aware'. It was for this reason, that the decision was taken in May 1937 to disband the organisation.[21] In its place the Communist Party concentrated on developing activity around various broad organisations which were not banned – for example, the India League and the China Campaign Committee. For this purpose, the party established its own Colonial Information Bureau and issued a fortnightly *Colonial Information Bulletin*.

The Fight Against New Wars for Colonial Conquest

Another factor recognised at the Seventh World Congress was that it was the fascist powers and their allies – Italy, Germany, Japan – who were engaged in or preparing for new wars of colonial conquest; therefore there was a link between the anti-fascist struggle and that for colonial liberation. This was exemplified in the invasion of Abyssinia by Italy which began just after the Congress ended. Communist parties called for the League of Nations to impose sanctions against Italy but, fully aware that the matter could not be left to the League, also called for direct action against Italy. As a result, dockers in France and elsewhere refused to load ships bound for Italy. However, when the Executive Committee of the Comintern approached the Labour and Socialist International urging joint direct action, the

LSI refused, mainly as a result of opposition from the representatives of the British Labour Party.[22]

A similar situation arose when, in August 1937, Japan launched an all-out offensive on China. The Labour Party officially called on the government to impose sanctions on Japan, and urged British citizens to boycott Japanese goods. It immediately became clear that the British government would not only refuse to impose sanctions on Japan; it would try to block any efforts to get the League of Nations to impose sanctions. In this situation the Communist Party urged direct action to stop both the import of goods from Japan and the export to that country of war materials. Commenting on the Labour Party's proposed boycott by British citizens, it said:

> These things will not materialise unless the British working class act now by refusing to load or unload Japanese ships calling in British ports. One ship stopped is worth scores of resolutions. All ships stopped would be the greatest victory for peace in our generation ... We therefore ask all our comrades and sympathisers working in ports to watch the movements of Japanese vessels and prepare the workers for action. We ask them to carry on agitation against the loading of any vessel whatsoever for Japan.[23]

This call did not go unheeded. In December 1937 dockers in Southampton, where there was a lively Communist Party group, refused to unload a Japanese cargo; their action was followed in Middlesbrough, and later in London, where stevedores refused to load a Japanese ship – the *Haruna Maru* – with pig-iron, and it was obliged to sail away empty.

The British Labour Party and trade union leaders denounced these actions and all those who were supporting them, and successfully blocked moves for an embargo on Japanese goods by the International Transport Workers' Federation.

Anti-Fascist Movements a Diversion?

From the Seventh World Congress onwards, the anti-fascist struggle was regarded as a primary aim by all Communist parties. Did this mean (as Hugo Dewar alleges[24]) that the party had been 'converted to Liberalism'? On the contrary, the fight for the preservation of democratic rights was seen as a crucial element in the struggle for the overthrow of capitalism. In support of this approach, Dimitrov had at the Congress reinforced his argument with a quotation from Lenin, who once said:

It would be a fundamental mistake to suppose that the struggle for democracy can divert the proletariat from the socialist revolution, or obscure, or overshadow it ... the proletariat will be unable to prepare for victory over the bourgeoisie unless it wages a many-sided, consistent and revolutionary struggle for democracy.[25]

In Britain, a major concentration was to stop Oswald Mosley and his British Union of Fascists from gathering support. In October, 1936, the Communist Party together with the ILP, the local ex-servicemen's association and East London Jewish organisations, issued a call to block Mosley's march through East London. Despite the fact that the Labour leaders begged everyone to stay away, over a quarter of a million people responded and forced Mosley to march west instead of east. The following year, the same thing happened in South London when Mosley planned to march through Bermondsey. Again, despite pleas from the Labour leaders, hundreds of thousands participated in a counter-demonstration called for by the Communist Party, and Mosley was forced to take another route. As a result, Mosley's organisation began to disintegrate.

The most important anti-fascist struggle was in Spain where, in July 1936, army officers led by General Franco staged a revolt against the Popular Front government. The revolt could have been quickly quelled were it not for the intervention of fascist Germany and Italy who sent arms, troops and aircraft to fight on Franco's side. Meanwhile the British government declared a policy of 'non-intervention' which meant that the democratically-elected Spanish government was denied the right to buy arms to defend itself against the fascist attack. The Labour leaders, initially, supported this non-intervention policy. It was the Communist Party which opposed it from the very beginning; moreover it did not confine itself to taking up a position, but went into action, collecting for medical aid and food for Republican Spain. Above all, it organised the British Battalion of the International Brigade, whereby almost 2,500 British volunteers went to Spain to fight against Franco. Altogether, between 1936-38, some 40,000 volunteers from 54 countries served with the International Brigades which were set up as a result of an agreement between representatives of the Comintern and Caballero, the Socialist Prime Minister of the Spanish Government.

It was one of the most outstanding demonstrations of international solidarity ever made by the world Communist movement or by any other. Despite this, it has been quoted by followers of Trotsky as an example of the 'abandonment of internationalism', since they believed that it was the task of Communists *not* to help the Spanish government's forces to fight Franco, but to organise a revolution against that very government. Indeed some of Trotsky's former followers in Spain, who were members of an ultra-left party known as the POUM, actually tried to stage a revolt against the Popular Front government behind the lines, though it was obvious that such attempts to split the anti-Franco forces could only help the fascists.

J.R. Campbell answered those who alleged that support for the Spanish government meant abandonment of the aim of revolution as follows:

> Victory in the Civil War means the extension of the Popular Revolution in Spain. Defeat in the civil war means the liquidation of the Popular Revolution in Spain. The war and the Revolution are indivisible. The Communist Party has declared that victory in the war and the Revolution demands the maintenance of the unity of the People's Front, on the basis of defence of the democratic Republic. Remember that we are talking about a democratic republic of a new type – where the land has been taken from the landlords, where the factories and the banks are controlled by the People's Front Government, where a new educational regime is being developed. It is this regime that the Trotskyists and the near Trotskyists designate as 'counter-revolutionary'. According to these gentlemen, the struggle in Spain is between the counter-revolutionary governments.[26]

In this movement against fascism, Communists sought to establish the broadest possible unity among all anti-fascists, primarily, of course those in the trade union and labour movement, but also people from outside the labour movement. This did *not* mean that the party helped to create an atmosphere favourable to a 'non-class view of the social conflict' (as alleged by Dewar[27]). What Communist parties all over the world, including that in Britain, had begun to understand was that if you can lead people into action on some issue on which they feel strongly, the very experience itself can bring about a change in their ideas, can open their minds to the need for a new kind of society, whereas you seldom convert anyone to socialism by preaching from the sidelines.

At the Fifteenth Congress of CPGB held in September 1938, Harry Pollitt made answer to criticisms by those who opposed broad movements: 'Don't let us be sidetracked by the opponents of unity,' he said. 'Liberalism is one of their bogies. No one is proposing a love match or permanent marriage with Liberalism or any other creed whose basic principles differ from our own.' But he went on to say:

> The ruling class in Britain has always carried through the policy of 'divide and conquer'. Once again, the most reactionary sections of Monopoly Capital are trying to carry through this policy in order to gradually establish Fascism in Britain. The chief task of the moment is to put an end to the policy of the Chamberlain clique.[28]

Can War be Prevented?

Communists in Britain had for long been exposing Hitler's aggressive intentions at a time when others preferred to look the other way. The party argued that, if Hitler's plans were to be foiled, Britain must cease to act as Hitler's friend and should, on the contrary, join the mutual assistance pact between France and the Soviet Union. Such a grouping, it was believed, would be powerful enough to make Hitler hesitate, would deter him from putting his plans into operation. The opposite happened. In September 1938, when Hitler was threatening Czechoslovakia, Chamberlain persuaded the French to withdraw all support for the Czechs and at a meeting in Munich arranged for the dismemberment of Czechoslovakia.

The Communist Party, and initially, the Labour Party, campaigned against the proposed carve-up, and vast 'Stand by the Czechs' meetings were held but, as war tension mounted, the Labour leaders panicked, and it was left to the Communist *Daily Worker* to continue to promote the 'Chamberlain must go' campaign. As mentioned above, Communist MP William Gallacher was the only one in the House to protest against Chamberlain's projected visit to Munich.

The facts about this Munich betrayal are usually avoided by those who present Communist policy as designed to 'tune in with Stalin's desire for alliances with imperialist powers.' The truth is that if the campaign to oust Hitler's friend Chamberlain from office had succeeded, the Second World War could have been postponed, might even have been prevented. And if, nevertheless, it had taken place, it would have been fought in circumstances far more disadvantageous to Hitler. As J.R. Campbell pointed out at the time:

> While it is true to say that war is inevitable under the capitalist system, it does not follow that it is inevitable at any given moment. Whether war comes is determined by the struggle between the forces making for peace and the forces making for war.[29]

The Outcome

E.H. Carr's book is entitled *The Twilight of Comintern 1930-1935*. Not a very appropriate metaphor. 'Out of the shadows into the sunlight' would fit much better. For it was during these years that the Comintern finally rid itself of the illusions of the 'class-against-class' period, when it was believed, quite wrongly, that a 'revolutionary upsurge' was imminent. Instead, Communists in every country began to face reality, something that all those who claim to be Marxists have to do if they are going to take people forward to socialism. Moreover, they at last began to learn the lesson which Lenin had tried to drive home when he wrote *Left-Wing Communism: An Infantile Disorder*: 'the task devolving on Communists is to *convince* the backward elements, to work *among* them and not to *fence themselves off* from them by artificial and childishly "left" slogans.'[30]

The lesson of the years that followed the 1935 Congress is not that Communists betrayed the cause of socialism, but that despite their efforts, the friends of fascism, including the Chamberlain clique, were able to 'divide and conquer'. The outcome was the Second World War.

NOTES

1. 'The Tasks of the Communist International in Connection with the Preparations of the Imperialists for a New World War', Resolution on Report of Ercoli, *Report of the Seventh World Congress*, published by Modern Books, London 1936.
2. *Hansard*, 28 September 1938.
3. Statement issued 10 August 1937. See Report of Central Committee to 15th Party Congress, in *For Peace and Plenty*, Report of 15th Congress, p. 6.
4. *For Peace and Plenty*, p. 33.
5. Interview with Kenneth Harris, *Observer*, 16 September 1962.
6. Dimitrov's report on The Working Class Against Fascism, *Report of the Seventh World Congress*, p. 6.
7. See Hywel Francis and David Smith, *The Fed*, London 1980, pp. 278ff.

8. See R. Page Arnot, *The Miners in Crisis and War*, London 1961, Chapter 5.
9. For further information about Communist activities in engineering see Edmund and Ruth Frow, *Engineering Struggles*, Manchester 1982 and Richard Croucher, *Engineers at War*, London 1982.
10. PRO Cab 98/18. Memorandum from the Home Secretary C.A.(41) 4.
11. Report of the 68th Annual Trades Union Congress, 1936, p. 227.
12. *It Can Be Done*, Report of 14th Party Congress, pp. 114-5.
13. E.H. Carr, *The Twilight of Comintern 1930-1935*, London 1982, pp. 419-420.
14. *International Press Correspondence* (referred to hereafter as *Inprecorr*), 17 August 1935.
15. *Inprecorr*, 2 December 1935.
16. Speech by Maurice Thorez on 'The Successes of the Anti-Fascist United Front', *Report of the Seventh World Congress*.
17. Speech by Harry Pollitt on 'Unity against the National Government', ibid.
18. Report delivered by Wang Ming, ibid. See also *Inprecorr*, 17 August 1935.
19. *Inprecorr*, 12 December 1928.
20. Wang Ming, loc.cit. See also *Inprecorr*, 17 August 1935.
21. The quotations are taken from the informative note on the League Against Imperialism written by John Saville which appears in Volume VII of the *Dictionary of Labour Biography*. See also *Inprecorr*, 17 August 1935.
22. *Daily Worker*, 16 November 1935. See also *Inprecorr*, 12 October and 9 November 1935.
23. Statement issued on 2 October 1937, reprinted in Report of the Central Committee to the 15th Party Congress, p. 88.
24. Hugo Dewar, *Communist Politics in Britain: The CPGB from its Origins to the Second World War*, London 1976, p. 123.
25. Dimitrov's speech in reply to the Discussion, *Report of the Seventh World Congress*, p. 17.
26. J.R. Campbell, *Questions and Answers on Communism*, London 1938, pp. 92-3.
27. Dewar, op.cit., p. 109.
28. *For Peace and Plenty*. Report of the 15th Congress of the CPGB pp. 120-1.
29. Campbell, op.cit., pp. 34-6.
30. Lenin, *Collected Works*, Vol. 31, p. 54.

Women Against War and Fascism: Communism, Feminism and the People's Front

SUE BRULEY

From its inception, the Communist Party of Great Britain (CPGB or CP) held the view that it was the capitalist system which was responsible for the oppression of women, and that only by the abolition of this system could women achieve justice and equal rights with men. This point of view was summarised in *Communist Training*, published in 1927 which said:

> The emancipation of the women from slavery and inequality depends upon the victory of Communism. The Communist women's movement is not a feminist movement. Communist women are co-workers in the common struggle ... Revolutionary Marxism knows no specific woman question and no specific woman's movement. Communism will be achieved not by the united efforts of all women of different classes, but the by the united struggle of all the exploited.[1]

This attitude had its origin in a resolution passed by the Third Congress of the Communist International in 1921. Clara Zetkin, the veteran German Communist, was largely responsible for drawing up the resolution which stated that 'There is no specific "woman question" and no specific women's movement.' The resolution did not deny that sexual inequality was a feature of capitalist society, but rejected the view that this provided the basis for an autonomous women's movement. It held that women's status in society was primarily determined by her social class. The feminist movement was characterised as 'bourgeois feminism' and seen as a 'diversion' for working class women. Zetkin proposed that the strategy for women's emancipation lay not in an autonomous movement for 'bourgeois rights' but a proletarian women's movement under the direction of the

Communist party. At each level of the party structure women's committees or sections would be created to conduct agitational work amongst women.[2]

As the prospect of revolution in Western Europe declined there was a distinct lessening of the Comintern's interest in the women's movement. At the same time there was a marked decline in the women's movement generally in the early 1920s. The Comintern did, however, establish an International Women's Secretariat (IWS) to encourage the growth of women's sections in the individual Communist parties. Clara Zetkin was the head of this organisation and, when she retired, she was replaced by another German, Hertha Stürm.

The need for such women's sections found a place in the Report in 1922 of a Commission set up by the CPGB to review party organisation. Six of its pages devoted to work among women stressed the importance of work in the trade unions for certain specific demands: for the admission of women on equal terms with men, for equal pay for equal work, for equal privileges and responsibilities, for the focusing of the attention of the unions on the needs and better organisation of their women members and upon the necessity to organise them. It urged Communists to work in the Women's Co-operative Guilds (these Guilds met in the afternoon and consisted solely of housewives); it emphasied the need for contact with unemployed women, speaking of 'the abominable treatment meted out to women at the Exchanges'. It proposed a structure of women's sections and committees within the party.

However, the party was rather slow to follow this up and did not begin serious work until 1924 when a women's conference was held and Beth Turner was elected National Women's Organiser. Efforts were made to establish Women's Sections in all party branches.[3] It was hoped to draw in women from the Co-operative Women's Guilds, trade union branches and Labour Party Women's Sections.[4] This policy was a failure. Many branches did not establish Women's Sections and those that did get underway proved to be isolated and ineffective. Women members who were full-time housewives gravitated towards these groups, which often met in the afternoon, whilst women industrial workers largely ignored Women's Sections. In March 1926 the *Woman Worker* (later the *Working Woman*) was launched. It ran for 36 monthly issues and was discontinued in 1929 due to its failure to make any impact and the declining fortunes of the party as a whole. Significant gains were made during the General Strike and miners' lock-out but these women recruits were not retained.

The party's failure to make real gains among women during the 1920s contrasts very strongly with the phenomenal growth of Labour Party Women's Sections in these years. It seems very likely that the reluctence of the party to take up any issues relevant to women, such as the young women's vote and access to birth control facilities, must have played an important part. The party condemned family endowment (or allowances) as an employers' trick to reduce wages.[5]

The extreme sectarianism of the Third Period, which was officially announced in the middle of 1928, was a disaster for the party. As membership rapidly dwindled women comrades were fully occupied in trying to keep 'mainstream' party work going and were even less inclined than before to conduct work specifically aimed at women. As a result many Women's Sections disappeared. An outburst of militancy among women textile workers, however, forced the party to reassess its attitude. Very large numbers of women were involved in the Yorkshire woollen strike of 1930. Following that the movement of weavers against the 'More Loom system' in the Lancashire cotton industry resulted in a prolonged period of strike activity ending in the county lock-out of 1932. Women were in a majority in the weavers' union. During these years women textile workers were at the forefront of the class struggle, and since a great proportion of the male membership was unemployed it became vital to make women recruits from this sector. The party realised that it had little hope of success among such women unless it stressed issues such as the married women's right to work, equality in unemployment benefit and the campaign for improved maternity and infant welfare services. For a brief period, therefore, the party did make some attempt to end the isolation of 'women's work' and to integrate work among women into its 'mainstream' activity.[6] Some gains were made, but recruitment was very modest.

From 1933 it was the menace of fascism which gripped the attention of the party before all else and, as a result, the Comintern swung from its ultra-left 'class against class' policy to an attempt to create a broadly based anti-fascist movement. This people's front policy was the theme of the Seventh World Congress in July and August 1935. The sectarian and isolationist policies of the past were denounced and instead maximum collaboration with socialists, trade union bodies, co-operatives and even religious and petty bourgeois organisations was called for. The slogan of 'Workers' Revolutionary Governments' was abandoned in favour of a 'United Front against Fascism and War'.

The people's front policy had important implications for the relationship between Communist parties and the women's movement. This was apparent for over a year before the Seventh Congress. In August 1934 the World Congress of Women Against War and Fascism was held in Paris. The gathering of nearly 1,200 delegates took place under the auspices of the *World Committee Against War and Fascism* which had emerged in 1932, as a result of initiatives taken by Willi Münzenberg of Germany, who was responsible for the formation of many of the Comintern's organisations in the mid-1930s.[7] According to the publicity for the Congress, Communist women were in a minority among Socialist, Pacifist, Christian and Liberal women delegates. To what extent this was true is difficult to judge. H.M. Wicks, one of the few historians of the Comintern to mention the 1934 women's congress, states that over 30 of the 40 women in the American delegation were Communists.[8] There were 56 delegates from England, including Mrs Carmel Haden Guest, who was prominent in the anti-war movement and not a Communist. It is clear, however, that many of the other delegates, Marjorie Pollitt and Katie Loeber (neé Kant, as she was also known) for example, were well known Communists.

At this time Hilda Vernon was working in the office of the National Unemployed Workers' Movement. She attended the Paris Congress as a delegate of the NUWM. She told me about the enormous impact that the Congress made on her.

> There was an atmosphere which I still couldn't put into words, that was entirely different from anything I'd ever known, after all I'd been to plenty of conferences and meetings and goodness knows what. It was all women. They created an atmosphere of some sort of spirit ... they were so much more expressive ... They were sort of willing to talk and reveal themselves much more. And I was very impressed with it, and that was what made me willing, when we came back, and I was asked to take over the secretaryship of the British section that I agreed to do so.[9]

I asked Hilda Vernon why it was necessary to organise a separate women's section. After all, women were already involved in the main movement and Isabel Brown was the leading power behind the Relief Committee for the Victims of Fascism. She explained that the anti-war movement had been able to make contacts, via the women's movement, in many countries, for example Italy, in which it would have otherwise been unable to organise. Beyond this tactical reason, she felt that there was a much deeper justification for making a special appeal to women,

> During the 1930s everybody in this country knew war was coming, and the people who knew it most were mothers ... We had lived through the First World War, our generation. We knew something of war and, it was not a theoretical question for us ... they knew what war would mean. They knew that their men would be called up and killed and that there would be another generation of widows. They knew that with modern warfare their children might be killed as well as themselves.[10]

Preparations for the World Congress of Women Against War and Fascism began well before the event. In Britain an Organising Committee was launched, with Hannah Laurie as the 'Provisional Hon. Sec.' and Sylvia Pankhurst as the Treasurer,[11] neither of whom were Communist party members. The committee contacted women's organisations and asked them to sponsor delegates to the World Congress. A public meeting was held in Caxton Hall London, a month before the Congress, to publicise the event, and Dr Maude Royden, the Christian feminist, Sylvia Pankhurst and Marjorie Pollitt were billed as the main speakers. The World Congress was described as 'organised on a non-party basis' and efforts were made to obtain a very broadly based group of women delegates.[12] After the Paris Congress the Organising Committee stepped up its work and formed itself into the British Section of the Women's World Committee Against War and Fascism with Hilda Vernon as its full-time Secretary.

The Women's Committee Against War and Fascism (WCAWF) aimed to work through existing women's organisations, rather than to build up a mass membership of its own. It secured affiliations from the National Union of Women Teachers (NUWT), the Association of Women Clerks and Secretaries and the Six Point Group (which was against all protective legislation for women). Its headed notepaper contained an impressive list of non-CP sponsors, including Vera Brittain, Mrs Lilla Brockway, Jennie Lee, Ellen Wilkinson, Sybil Thorndike, Dr Maud Royden and the Countess of Warwick. There were also some well known CP members and sympathisers on the list: Mrs Despard, Joan Beauchamp, Mrs Tom Mann and Marjorie Pollitt.

The Committee gradually intensified its activity. It issued pamphlets, and members of the National Committee (consisting of representatives from affiliated organisations) spoke at public meetings on the themes of 'Against War and Fascism' and 'Defence of Mother and Child'. Public meetings, marches and other events were organised for International Women's Day in 1935 and subsequent years.[13]

The Committee was not just against war and fascism; its founding manifesto placed its campaign in a socialist and feminist context. The Women's Charter proclaimed,

> We recognise that women cannot achieve freedom and equality under capitalism. We demand complete social, economic and legal equality.[14]

This was followed by a list of sixteen demands, which were extremely wide-ranging. For women workers it called for a seven hour day, the right of married women to work and equal rights for women in the trade unions. The demands also included the repeal of the Anomalies Act and the Means Test. On the welfare side, they asked for free maternity hospitals, for the legalisation of abortion and for the 'Release of all women who have been imprisoned for abortion'.[15] These last two demands were highly controversial and represented the first occasion on which CP women were involved in the demand for the decriminalisation of abortion.

On the surface it appeared that the WCAWF members, be they socialist, Communist, pacifist or independent feminists, worked together harmoniously and were united by their overiding commitment to oppose war and fascism. In fact this was far from the case, and tensions sprang up from an early stage, particularly between Communist and non-Communist women. Hannah Laurie, who was also active in the Catholic Crusade, wanted to make the campaign appeal to 'all classes'.[16] It is likely that she was opposed by Communist women (and possibly the Labour women) who also sought to make a broad appeal, but retained a particular interest in attracting working class women. In addition Laurie felt that some of the CP women and their supporters were sectarian and manipulative.[17]

Laurie particularly resented the treatment of Sylvia Pankhurst by the rest of the Committee. In a letter to Maud Brown she stated that Pankhurst had worked hard for the Committee, 'despite the many efforts to discredit her and ignore her efforts'.[18]

Laurie referred to the fact that Pankhurst had produced the first draft of the *Women's Charter* and wrote,

> but since that time no serious attempts seem to have been made to co-operate with her in this matter ... She was a member of the Committee, elected to carry out this work – she *had* put down her views – and she *ought* to have been included in the ensuing deliberations.[19]

It appears that, although the WCAWF consisted of a very wide variety of women, the Communist women were very much to the fore and probably exerted a controlling influence. They encouraged prominent non-party women to be publicly associated with the Committee, but did not expect them to take much part in policy-making. There was long-standing suspicion between Pankhurst and the Communists. She had been a member at the foundation of the party but had quarrelled with it as she rejected parliamentary action or unity with the Labour Party and wanted to keep her own journal, *The Workers' Dreadnought*. Both she and Laurie dropped from the scene in 1935.[20] There is reason to believe that this was linked with their disagreements with the CP women and their inability to influence committee decisions. The fact that Laurie was replaced as Secretary by Hilda Vernon, who was closer to the CP and joined it soon afterwards indicates that the party's influence on the Committee was, if anything, increasing. Pankhurst was an international personality and widely acclaimed as a champion of women's rights. To lose a person of such stature was undoubtedly a great loss to the WCAWF, but we should not overlook the fact that many non-party women continued to be involved with the committee. The very presence of Communist women in such a broadly based organisation was a radical change for the CP. By the time of the Seventh Congress the new policy had been established and the popular front was a familiar feature of Comintern politics.

Unlike earlier CI Congresses, the 1935 meeting did not include among its 43 sittings one devoted entirely to work among women. The only hint of the Comintern Women's Department is a speech by Kirsanova, a Soviet woman from the IWS, among the 41 speeches, in six sessions, which were made in the discussion of the 'Ercoli' (Togliatti, leader of the underground Italian CP) report on 'The Fight Against War and Fascism'.

According to the *Inprecorr* report Kirsanova was given an 'enthusiastic reception' when she took the platform to make her speech on the international movement of women against war and fascism.[21] But she was placed in a session with five other speakers, sandwiched between the Japanese and Korean delegates, neither of whom mentioned this subject. It was a token gesture, and, after appearing in *Inprecorr* even that was omitted from the published congress reports. The 1939 Moscow edition even goes so far as to say that only the major speeches have been included, 'eliminating everything that is no longer of actual interest'![22]

The International Women's Secretariat had only a minimal presence at the Congress. By this time Clara Zetkin was dead and the IWS had declined in prestige and influence. Articles in *Inprecorr* on 'The Proletarian Women's Movement' appeared less and less frequently. Nevertheless, it was clear that women had an important part to play in the people's front. The idea of a separate Communist women's organisation, which could attract large numbers of working class women, was abandoned. In one of the major speeches of the Seventh Congress, 'Ercoli' dealt with this question. He announced that comrades conducting women's work had

> replaced broad mass work in the existing organisations by the creation of a narrow and sectarian Communist women's organis-ation.[23]

The only correct strategy for reaching the 'masses of women who are not under our influence' was to make direct contact with them in the organisations to which they belonged. But, unlike previously,

> we must by no means endeavour to destroy such organisations.[24]

In another speech at the 1935 Congress, Pollitt also referred to this question. In a section on 'Women and the United Front', he laid down that in order to build a united front among women, Communist parties need not orientate themselves exclusively to women of the working class. He urged comrades to

> make it all embracing in such a way that it can win to its support, not only the organised workers, but every democrat and lover of peace, all sections of the petty bourgeoisie.[25]

The way was opened for Communist women to end their isolation and make contact with independent feminist groups. Even direct collaboration was possible, providing there was a shared commitment to oppose war and fascism

The Women's World Committee Against War and Fascism remained based in Paris and its French section grew into a very large organisation. Through its Spanish section it developed relief work in Barcelona and Valencia with refugee women and children. One of its representatives, Agnes Dumay, was killed whilst working for the World Committee in Spain.

The British section of the Women's World Committee continued to operate as a women's pressure group in the peace movement and to campaign for women's advance generally. This fusion of anti-war and feminist aims appears to have been successful and the Committee's activities were gradually extended. Hilda Vernon, the secretary, told me about their work:

> There were air raid shelters and so on which we knew were quite inadequate and we had a big campaign on that ... We wrote pamphlets which we sold in large numbers ... we were responsible for organising the International Women's Day meetings. We always organised a poster parade around the centre of London on Armistice Day ... We organised a quarterly conference on issues affecting women.[26]

The international aspect of the Committee's work was always prominent. They were the first to organise relief work for Spain and also initiated meetings for British women to express support for the women of Republican Spain. Maud Brown and Charlotte Haldane took a special interest in China and the former organised an adoption scheme for the child victims, 'warphans' as she called them, of the Japanese attack. A boycott of Japanese goods was initiated. Work on the Abyssinian question was also conducted. One of the most important aspects of the Committee's international work was the efforts which were made to obtain the release of women in German concentration camps. Hilda Vernon told me how this work was carried out:

> We sent delegations, we went over to Germany and insisted on trying to see some of the women we knew were in concentration camps ... One of them, Edith Weiss says she knows that she owed me her life to this intervention. Because, one of the things we found, we discovered in dealing with this petition that if you could show that there was an outside interest, then it sometimes stayed the hand of the executioner.[27]

In September 1936 the Committee launched a monthly paper, *Woman Today*, which was edited firstly by Magda Gellan and later by Charlotte Haldane. It was an attractively produced and readable paper which aimed to be 'a forum for all progressive women'; the material in *Woman Today* was certainly very wide-ranging and not at all restricted to the peace movement at home and abroad.

The paper had a very strong feminist orientation and promoted 'full social, political and economic rights and liberties for women'. Various problems of women workers were discussed and articles by members of the National Union of Women Teachers, the Association of Women Clerks and Secretaries and other women trade unionists were published. There were articles on the history of the women's movement, including an occasional series by Joan Beauchamp on her experiences as a pre-war suffragette. There were contributions on birth control and even abortion and the aims of the Family Planning Association were supported.

The Women's Committee developed important links with the feminist movement. Eleanor Rathbone, who led the movement for family endowment and sat as an Independent MP, became a supporter.[28] From the end of 1937 *Woman Today* gave increasing support to many individual women's organisations such as the Spinsters' Pension Association, the Over 30 Association, the Married Women's Association and the Nursery Schools Association. A diary page in the paper enabled these bodies to publicise their activities.

Throughout the 1920s the CPGB had been hostile to feminism. The party's unceasing message to women was 'Class war was not Sex War'. Consequently, feminists much as Stella Browne, the birth control activist, left the party.[29] With few exceptions politically able Communist women did not show much enthusiasm for party work on women's issues during these years. This area of work was seen by many women cadres as something of a ghetto which detracted from 'mainstream' party work.[30] The introduction of the people's front policy resulted in a subsidence of much of the party's traditional antagonism to feminism. For the first time in its history there was a partial breakdown of the polarisation of communism and feminism as mutually exclusive ideologies.

This enabled the emergence of a new type of Communist woman activist. Feminist cadres, as I shall call them, were politically developed and articulate women who chose to orientate their party work towards socialist-feminist issues and were happy to work with non-party feminist organisations. These women wanted their political work to reflect their identity as women rather than to detract from it as previous women cadres had sought to do. They directed their energies towards achieving a kind of socialism which would radically transform women's lives.

Nan MacMillan is a good example of this new type of party woman. She taught in London from 1926 and joined the CP in 1929. Nan MacMillan chose to be active in the National Union of Women Teachers rather than the NUT because she did not feel that the latter was doing enough to advance the cause of equal pay. The NUWT campaigned under the slogan of 'No Pay for Friday' as women teachers were currently receiving only four-fifths of the men's rate.

She also felt strongly about another issue:

> I came into the profession when you couldn't marry. Now this was another thing that incensed me, and I felt was wicked ... All my generation was barren, because we couldn't marry at the time when we should have been marrying and having children.[31]

This was not an abstract political issue for Nan MacMillan but one which deeply affected her own life, as she was forced to live in secret with her partner, who was also a CP member in the teaching, profession:

> If it had got about, we both would have been sacked for immoral conduct. So life was very difficult. I was very keen to get the marriage bar removed.[32]

Nan MacMillan became increasingly influential in the NUWT and in 1934 was elected President of its London Region. She worked successfully with Labour women teachers and other non-aligned women activists. At the end of 1935 the London County Council lifted its ban on married women teachers and this must at least in part be attributed to the campaign by the London movement.

Feminist cadres are evident both at the rank and file as well as the national level. Betty Kane joined the party in Sheffield during the General Strike. She was working in a small tools factory and she did much to recruit her fellow women workers from the machine shop into the Transport and General Workers' Union.[33] She went as a Trades Council representative to the Mothers' Action Group which conducted a campaign for every women to have the right to a hospital bed for her first birth.[34] The work of

Hilda Vernon on the Womens' Committee Against War and Fascism, has already been described. She had been a leading member of the ILP's Revolutionary Policy Group before it split off to join the CP in 1935. Besides her work for the WCAWF she was involved in many other women's questions, including birth control.[35]

The Women's Department of the National Unemployed Workers' Movement was a powerful body within the NUWM and this was largely due to Maud Brown who we could also describe as a feminist cadre. She was remembered to me by one of her surviving comrades as a 'terrific fighter' and 'afraid of nothing and nobody'.[36] Maud Brown led the first women's contingent on the 1930 Hunger March and there were contingents on all the subsequent marches. Contrary to popular belief at the time, Maud Brown was not a member of the Communist Party, although her views appear to be identical to those of the party during this period. Much of the Communist Party's work amongst the unemployed during the 1930s was displaced onto the NUWM and this was particularly true of its work amongst unemployed women. Its Women's Department poured out a formidable volume of propaganda material to be used by its local women's sections. It issued speakers' notes and pamphlets such as Maud Brown's *Stop This Starvation of Mother and Child*. Rising rates of maternal mortality and the evidence of malnutrition amongst unemployed families were vital components of the NUWM's case against the means test. The Department, under Brown's leadership, also agitated against the 1931 Anomalies Act and for an end to discrimination against married women and many other issues involving women. Maud Brown was active in the WCAWF and supplied articles on issues affecting unemployed women to its paper *Woman Today*.

The emergence of feminist cadres was also facilitated by shifts within the feminist movement which made its politics closer to the CP than they had ever been before. The early wave of feminism had concentrated on legal and political rights and during the sharp class conflicts of the 1920s its remnants became known for their anti-socialist and anti-trade union policies.[37] Now the movement was becoming much more diversified. There was an increasing amount of parliamentary lobbying by women's pressure groups, such as the Family Endowment Society, the Children's Minimum Council, and the National Union of Societies for Equal Citizenship (a successor to the suffrage societies). The Maternity Mortality Committee, which was founded in 1927 by May Tennant and Gertrude Tuckwell, had its most active period between 1929 and 1935. Whilst not being committed socialists or Communists, many feminists, in their work to reduce maternal deaths and end malnutrition, made it clear that many of the current social evils were the result of the unequal distribution of wealth in society, and that they were acting on behalf of the underprivileged section of the community. The other issue into which both movements were drawn was, of course, peace. This was particularly apparent after the outbreak of hostilities in Spain in July 1936.

The plight of Republican Spain gripped the imagination of the British public in a remarkable way. The passionate desire to defend the Republic from the Nationalists induced more than 2,000 British men to volunteer for the International Brigades. More than a quarter of these did not return and many others were wounded. It is not generally known that the first Briton to die in Spain was a woman. Felicia Browne, an artist from London and a member of the St Pancras branch of the Communist Party, was shot on 25 August 1936, at the age of 32, on the Aragon front. She was travelling to Barcelona to attend an international sports festival, but the outbreak of the Nationalist revolt intervened. She refused to be evacuated and immediately enrolled in the militia, as did many other Spanish women, who became known as 'milicianas'. An anti-fascist magazine recounted to its British readers how Browne met her death.

> A party of ten volunteers, including Felicia Browne, set out at night to blow up a rebel munition train. Attacked, four to one by a fascist patrol, they retreated. A wounded man had to be left behind. Felicia returned to help him, but rebels riddled them both with bullets.[38]

The 'milicianas' were withdrawn from the Republican side within a few months and no other British woman became directly involved in combat.[39]

Winifred Bates was also in Spain at the time of the military uprising. She and her husband went to Barcelona, where she was asked to make radio broadcasts in English. This soon became a nightly event. Later she took on the task of looking after the British nurses in Spain.

About 100 other British women went out to Spain. The largest number was sent by the Spanish Medical Aid Committee and there was also a strong Quaker contingent. The first Medical Unit left Victoria on 23 August 1935, a reinforcement unit left the following month and other teams were sent in 1937. The women in Medical Aid for Spain were mostly nurses, and there were also two radiographers a physiotherapist, a radiologist, and ten women involved in administration.

Some of the British women were party members, Nan Green, Winifred Bates, Mary Slater and Annie Murray, for example, but by no means all were Communists. A few of the rest were socialists, but on the whole they regarded themselves as anti-fascists, rather than committed left-wingers. Nurse Phyllis Hibbert, on her return to England after fifteen months in Spain, wrote that,

> sixty per cent of the nursing staff had no definite political views, but were merely democrats with a desire to succour the suffering.[40]

The English nurses were highly-trained compared to their Spanish counterparts and were greatly valued for their skilful work and tremendous dedication. Conditions were often appalling, with lice, rats, poor equipment and bad sanitation. They worked excruciatingly long hours which drove them to the point of exhaustion.

Precious leave was often taken up with public meetings and other activities to raise funds for Medical Aid. One of the nurses, Ruth Ormsby, was killed in a fire in Barcelona and two others, Mary Slater and Janet Robertson, caught typhoid. Many of the women were injured by shrapnel. Winifred Bates wrote of one such incident:

> There was one brave little woman who was nursing in a tent during a horrible raid. She quietly put tin soup plates on the faces of the soldiers as they lay in bed, to save them from flying shrapnel. She was wounded herself in the head and arm as she did it.[41]

Bates also recalls some nurses in an ambulance train

> who told me that they could never decided whether it was better to work in the tunnel where the stench was awful, or out in the open where they were exposed to direct hits from the air. For themselves they preferred the fresh air, but for the men they thought the tunnel was best.[42]

Nan Green worked on the Ebro front as secretary to the Chief Medical Officer of the 35th Division. She helped to compile medical statistics, made tea and tried to keep up morale. Along with other 'more or less' sedentary workers, she was asked to give blood: this could occur as frequently as twice in a fortnight.[43]

The International Medical Service in Spain and the evacuation and relief programmes carried out there could only be sustained by a vast amount of aid from outside. Britain played a vital role from the start and kept up a steady flow of funds throughout the civil war and in the period immediately after when vast numbers of refugees were looked after in make-shift camps in France. The peak period was the winter of 1938 and early 1939: during this time 29 foodships were sent from Britain to Spain.

At first existing organisations, such as the Relief Committee for the Victims of Fascism, of which Isabel Brown was secretary, took the initiative in calling public meetings to raise funds. But the response was so great that within weeks a whole network of specialist groups had sprung into existence. Medical Aid for Spain was probably the most well known, but there were many others such as the Milk for Spain Fund, the Spanish Youth Foodship Committee, the Christian Foodship Committee, Foster Parents for Children in Spain and the Labour Party Spain Campaign.

Thirteen MPs from different political parties formed themselves into the Parliamentary Committee for Spain; five of them were women: the Duchess of Atholl (Conservative), Megan Lloyd George (Liberal), Eleanor Rathbone (leader of the National Union of Societies for Equal Citizenship, and an Independent MP), Ellen Wilkinson and Dr Edith Summerskill (both Labour). Wilfred Roberts, a Liberal MP on the committee proposed the formation of a National Joint Committee to co-ordinate the work of all the individual groups. The Committee was launched in January 1937, and met regularly in the largest of the House of Commons Committee Rooms. The Duchess of Atholl became Chairman and the three joint secretaries were MPs from the three major parties. About 150 people attended the Committee meetings, representing all the religious, trade union, co-operative and political bodies, as well as specialist relief organisations engaged in Spanish work. A full time National Organiser, Ernest Brown, husband of Isabel and also a party member, was appointed and a monthly bulletin issued. Many workers were able to give their services free, so costs were kept to a minimum and the Committee made a rule that no more than 5 per cent of the money raised should be spent on administration.[44]

In May 1937 the National Joint Committee took on its heaviest commitment and evacuated 3,840 children from Bilbao after the destruction of Guernica. Leah Manning, who was leader of the NUT and later became an MP competently managed the massive task of arranging for the children to be shipped to Southampton. They were kept for three months (at the government's insistence) in a thirty acre camp in North Stoneham and then dispersed around the country in children's homes especially set up to care for them. The plight of the Basque children made the appeal for funds even more pressing. Fortunately the huge financial resources required were spread very widely; the Catholic Church, the Salvation Army, the Miners' Federation and many local groups each took over responsibility for maintaining a certain number of children.

The Aid for Spain appeals mushroomed into a truly mass movement: about 850 local, regional and affiliated bodies were attached to the National Joint Committee during the peak of activity.[45] The film *The Defence of Madrid* was shown at 400 different venues early in 1937. Labour Party Women's Sections (over 1,600 of them) concentrated on knitting garments and the Duchess of Atholl launched a knitting competition for girls. The Women's Co-operative Guild and other women's organisations boosted the relief work, especially in the collections of food and clothing. The Women's Committee Against War and Fascism and the AEU sent regular lorries of food, while Grimsby fishermen sent frozen cod. The AEU, the Miners' Federation and the London Co-operative Society financed their relief work through voluntary levies of the membership. Groups such as the Manchester Foodship for Spain and the All London Aid Spain Council, which drew in very large sections of the public, were in action across the entire country.

The Communist Party was heavily involved in every aspect of Spanish work. Agitation for the reversal of the government's non-intervention policy was the most urgent political task, but this was done on a very broad basis, appealing to 'all men of goodwill', 'democrats' and 'progressive people'. Overall, however, party members porbably devoted far more time and energy to relief work than to political propaganda and this was especially so for Communist women. Here the humanitarian, rather than the political aspect, was always in the forefront.

Isabel Brown recalls that the National Joint Committee aimed to be a non-political body:

We pledged ourselves that we would never use the platform of the National Joint Committee to further our own political ideal and we stuck to it.[46]

As a result of this policy, party members worked alongside other socialists, liberals, clergymen and even sympathetic conservatives and political differences were never discussed. It was the party's most successful venture into people's front work. Isabel Brown frequently appeared on public platforms with figures such as the Duchess of Atholl and the Earl of Listowel. Her passionate appeals for funds made Brown into the movement's most important orator and earned her the reputation as 'the English Pasionaria'. At the meeting in the Empress Stadium, London, to welcome back the International Brigaders in January 1939, £3,800 was collected in less than twenty minutes after her speech, and other meetings raised sums almost as large. Isabel Brown's appeal was always very emotional and direct – 'ten shillings will buy the life of a Basque child' – but stunningly effective. Not only cash, but wedding rings, broaches and other valuables would be handed down to the platform by members of her spellbound audiences.[47]

The involvement of other Communist women was of a less spectacular but nevertheless important nature. Many participated to some degree in Spanish work and were the mainstay of their local Aid Spain Council or its equivalent. Phyllis Bell worked in Paris from 1936 until 1939 co-ordinating Spanish Aid and helping refugees from Germany. Charlotte Haldane worked clandestinely for three months in Paris in 1937, helping to receive and prepare the British volunteers on their way to Spain. Whilst in London she was secretary of the Dependants Aid Committee until Fred Copeman, an ex-International Brigader, took over from her. She launched a National Memorial Fund, which was supported by Brailsford, Lawther and other public figures. Dora Cox worked at the International Brigade office in Lichfield Street in 1937-38, helping with the paper work connected with the British volunteers, both alive and dead.

Elizabeth Hull of Sheffield remembered organising dinner-dances to raise money for Spain, and apparently the tickets were never difficult to sell. Two of those interviewed, Betty Harrison and Ivy Tribe, were recruited to the party on the strength of its support for Spain. The former, subsequently helped to set up and maintain a Basque children's home in Bradford where she was living.

Evelyn Howley, Lil Price, Nan Green and Rose Kerrigan were

among those who had husbands in Spain. A fifth, Bessie Berry married Sam Wilde, the last commander of the British Battalion, shortly after his return to England. George Green, father of two and husband of Nan Green who, as mentioned previously, was also in Spain, was killed on the Ebro front. Nan did not know for six months whether he was alive or dead. Rose Kerrigan was eight months pregnant with her second child when her husband, Peter, went out to Spain as a political commisssar. Like many other wives, she shared his political commitment and made no attempt to persuade him to change his mind.

Much has been said and written of the bravery of the men who volunteered for the International Brigade. The memories of those who died are rightly cherished by the labour movement, but we should not forget the courage and tenacity of those who were left behind. Many of the volunteers were family men and their wives had to take on the responsibility for bringing home a wage in their absence. Since over 500 died in Spain and some of those that returned were disabled, for many wives being the principal breadwinner became a continuing feature of their lives.

During these years Communist women primarily looked outward, but the position of women inside the party was not neglected. In 1935 the Women's Department at headquarters was quietly and unofficially revived in the form of a central co-ordinating committee. In the late 1930s the Communist Party developed a new orientation towards local government and social welfare issues which made it predictable that the leadership would cast a critical eye in the direction of party work among women. The result was a long and serious resolution submitted to the Fourteenth Congress in May 1937. This was later supplemented by the Central Committee report submitted to the September 1938 Congress and a Central Committee resolution in the spring of 1939.

As in many previous Congress resolutions on this subject, the May 1937 resolution, which was introduced by Rose Smith, declared that this area of work had been 'completely neglected' and called for a 'complete change in the party's attitude to this vital question'. A new feature, however, was the recognition that many of the party's most able women sought to avoid work among women:

> there have also been tendencies among women Party members to be unwilling to devote themselves to this work, regarding it as equivalent to relegation to an inferior part of the Party's work.[48]

The leadership had realised that the full development of people's front work among women was seriously handicapped by the party's long-standing downgrading of women's work and the consequent reluctance of its women cadres to apply themselves to this work. The 1937 resolution sought to overcome this difficulty by impressing upon women members the importance of women's work and instructing that

> While no hard and fast rules should be laid down that all women party members should engage in this work, in the majority of cases it will be found that this is the most fruitful field of specialised activity for women party members, taking this as their special field of work ...[49]

Continuing in this vein of self-criticism the party recognised that its previous work had failed to examine closely the specific demands of women. It was frankly admitted that

> It has been thought sufficient to make a few general agitational appeals to women on the basis of their common interests in the struggle against war, fascism or the rising cost of living.[50]

The 1937 resolution then proceeded to outline a programme to revitalise and extend the party's women's work. In addition to detailed demands in the traditional areas of peace, prices, women in industry and unemployed women, a series of social welfare demands were listed. Most of these are of a very general nature and covered housing, hospitals and clinics, education and measures to combat malnutrition. One new demand which related specifically to women was for the establishment of women's centres, where educational, social and advisory facilities would be provided.

Referring to organisation the resolution called for a revival of a separate structure of women's groups within the party. As before, these were to operate at branch, district and national level.

From this time the central women's department was increasingly evident with a busy routine of co-ordinating women's activities in the party, issuing pamphlets and speakers notes and generally promoting party work around women's issues; Rose Smith was the leading comrade in this area of work during these years. In 1938 it was reported that district women's committees were functioning in several areas and women's sections had been revived in many branches.

Women's sections were involved in a great variety of activities. All of them did Spanish relief work in some form or another. In Lancashire, Leeds and Sheffield Communist women were involved in Maternal Mortality Committees and Tyneside women also started a Mother and Child Health Campaign Committee. The cost of living was a great issue and the 1937 pamphlet *Why Pay More* by Rose Smith was probably the CP's most successful pamphlet aimed at women in the late 1930s. Some branches, Bethnal Green for example, organised petitions against rising food prices and devoted a lot of energy to obtaining housewives' signatures. South Wales and Glasgow organised public meetings on this issue and one area of Glasgow set up a Council for Housewives. In Stockton pressure was exerted for the formation of Food Councils to stop profiteering in food. Women Communists also played an important role in the tenants' movement, which made great advances in the late 1930s, particularly in London and Birmingham where rent strikes were held for rent controls and modernisation programmes.

As the international crisis deepened many Communist Party women's groups became involved in Air Raid Precautions (ARP) and evacuation plans. Communist women held a conference of women's organisations to discuss this issue and party women in general pressed for the provision of bomb proof shelters and democratic control over government plans for the evacuation of women and children.

The enormous emphasis on people's front work meant that most politically active party women spent most of their time trying to build other organisations. There are numerous examples of labour and communist women working together on various local, *ad hoc* groups. The Women's Sub Committee of the Northern Council Against Fascism, which was based in Manchester, was an important example. They worked together harmoniously in Maternal Mortality committees, Aid Spain Groups, and other organisations, along with Women's Co-operative Guild, trade union and other representatives. There are isolated cases of strong local links being forged between the Labour Party and Communist Party Women's Sections but on the whole the Labour Party's opposition to the CP's proposals for unity made any general advancement towards organic links between the two bodies impossible.

The Labour Party women's leadership remained opposed to any sort of joint work and readers of *Labour Woman* were urged not to become involved with Communist women.[51] Despite this cold shoulder, Communist women followed closely the activities of Labour Party women's sections, supporting them wherever possible and providing publicity for their campaigns on the rising cost of living, for nursery education and so on. In June 1937, a Women's Conference on Unity was held in Manchester. 55 women delegates attended and were addressed by Barbara Betts (later Castle), an ex-National Committee member of the Socialist League. This appears to be the only example of any attempt to extend the united front work of the Communist Party, ILP and Socialist League to the work among women in these organisations.

The people's front ambitions of the party reached far beyond the labour and socialist movement. This can be most clearly seen in the Women's Committee Against War and Fascism where there was no specific appeal to working-class women. In fact, the opposite was the case; it gravitated towards well-known personalities and 'women of influence' as can be seen by its letter heading. The Women's Committee promoted women's unity against war and fascism above political affiliation or social class. The WCAWF appeared to be a very broad organisation but underneath the surface it was very closely connected with the Communist Party.

There were far more Communist Party contributors to *Woman Today* than from any other political party, trade union or women's organisation, although their political affiliation was never stated. The full-time positions of secretary and editor of the paper were occupied by party members. There was a good deal of overlap between the Women's Committee and the Women's Department of the party. Many of the personnel were the same and they were involved in identical campaigns. In many situations it was impossible to tell whether an event had been organised by the party or the Women's Committee. This can be most clearly illustrated by the example of the annual International Women's Day campaign, held in the second week of March, which was more successful in the late 1930s than in previous years. In a Central Committee Report of 1938 the party claimed credit for the success of this campaign, but the International Women's Day events had been initiated by the Women's Committee Against War and Fascism which was supposed to be a totally separate entity from the party. These campaigns were an opportunity to make an appeal for some sort of broad women's unity. For the

1938 campaign, the London women were able to gain the support of several women's organisations for its public meetings. Also in 1938, the International Women's Day Manifesto was launched which aimed to draw in non-party supporters. Mrs Corbett Ashby, an important Liberal feminist and peace activist, and Rose Simpson, Secretary of the Co-operative Women's Guild, were among those who signed.

In May, 1938, the second World Congress of Women Against Fascism was held in Marseilles, with Spain as the dominant item on the agenda. Margery Corbett Ashby headed the British delegation. This marked a major breakthrough for the British section of the WCAWF and for the people's front in general, as Mrs Corbett Ashby was an important public figure. Before the war she had been active in the non-militant branch of the women's suffrage movement. She stood as a Liberal parliamentary candidate many times and in 1938 was Vice-President of the Women's Liberal Federation. During the inter-war years she was active in NUSEC and in the Women's International League for Peace and Freedom.[53]

In March 1939, the Women's Committee Against War and Fascism was killed off and in its place the Women's Committee for Peace and Democracy was launched. An attempt to broaden the basis of the organisation yet further was behind the move. Mrs Corbett Ashby was in the chair.[54] At the same time greater links were established with Labour women. Dr Elis Jacobs, a Labour councillor and prospective parliamentary candidate, became Vice-Chairman of the new organisation. Two Labour women MPs, Ellen Wilkinson and Dr Edith Summerskill, wrote articles for *Woman Today* in April and June 1939 respectively. By the outbreak of the war, therefore, the Women's Committee could boast the support of influential women from many different spheres.

The people's front proved to be a success for the party and membership steadily climbed during the 1930s. We have no figures for women members just before the ourbreak of war, but there were about 2,500 women Communists early in 1938 and the number rose steeply after this.[55]

As we have seen, in these years the Comintern, and with it the CPGB, completely changed its attitude towards the women's movement. From outright hostility to feminism it turned to qualified support in an attempt to build a broad alliance with women in the struggle against fascism and war. To this end it gravitated towards leading feminist personalities such as Eleanor Rathbone, Viscountess Rhondda and Margery Corbett Ashby as well as Labour women such as Ellen Wilkinson and Edith Summerskill. In its Spanish Aid work it associated closely with Quaker women, Liberals and even Conservatives such as the Duchess of Atholl. It did not try to recruit such women but to win them to a favourable view of the party and, through them, bring others into a broad anti-fascist movement.

It is also evident that, while much of the people's front work was done publicly, much was also done behind the scenes to make sure that the WCAWF was controlled by the party as much as possible. Mrs Corbett Ashby, for one, did not realise the extent of Communist Party involvement.[56] The CP, and others on the left, have, all too often, seen the packing and manipulation of committees as the way to build and win the leadership of mass movements, and used well known names merely to give an image of broad support. Perhaps one of the lessons of the 1930s is that open political work is the better way to build up united movements and win mass support.

In conclusion, the people's front policy did create much greater possibilities for broadly based work around genuinely women's issues than at any other time in the Comintern's history. In Britain much good work was done around feminist issues by CP women as a result. But this does not mean that the Comintern intended CP work in the late 1930s to be genuinely feminist. It had not absorbed the politics of feminism but rather saw the women's movement as another set of organisations to be subsumed under the people's front umbrella and saw women in terms of the special difficulties they posed for recruitment – to draw them in you needed a special approach. This was still seen as an organisational rather than a political problem.

NOTES

1. CPGB, *Communist Party Training*, revised edition 1927, pp. 86-7
2. *Decisions of the Third Congress of the Communist International*, 1921, Moscow, CPGB, p. 100.
3. Turner was not the first Women's Organiser. Helen Crawford acted in this capacity 1921-22, but her post was axed as part of an economy drive.
4. For details see S. Bruley, 'Socialism and Feminism in the Communist Party of Great Britain, 1920-1939', PhD Thesis, LSE, University of London, 1980. Chapter 3, on women's sections makes extensive use of oral material;

subsequent references to 'Interview' are all to this thesis.

5. R.P. Dutt, *Socialism and the Living Wage*, 1927, CPGB, pp. 120-7.

6. For more details see Bruley, op.cit., Chapter 5.

7. For details see, D. Caute, *The Fellow Travellers*, London 1977.

8. H.M. Wicks, *Eclipse of October*, London 1958, pp. 315-7.

9. Interview, 13 July 1977, London.

10. Ibid.

11. Letter dated 1 June 1934 from H. Laurie to S. Pankhurst, 'If I guarantee to do the donkey work for you would you agree to being our Treasurer.' Subsequent letters indicate that Pankhurst did take up this position. Pankhurst Archive, File No. 94 (64) Institute of Social History, Amsterdam.

12. H.M. Wicks, op.cit., casts doubt on the representative nature of the Congress. It is not known how many of the 56 British delegates were Communists.

13. J. Beauchamp, *Women Who Work*, London 1937, has a photograph of two demonstrations held by the WCAWF for International Women's Day 1935, p. 80.

14. Pankhurst Archive, File No. 94 (64).

15. Ibid.

16. (a) In a letter 12 July 1934 from Laurie to Pankhurst, she referred to the fact that she was Secretary of the Catholic Crusade.
(b) In a letter 'Sunday' from Laurie to Pankhurst, she states, 'Marjorie Pollitt's speech at Fulham indicated willingness to work with *all* classes against war and fascism.' The tone and context of this remark indicates approval as well as surprise. Pankhurst Archive, loc.cit.

17. (a) The letter 'Sunday', ibid., goes on, 'Maud Brown is more sectarian – but she is'nt a Party member.'
(b) Letter 12 August 1934 from H. Laurie to Pankhurst states, 'I have already spoken to Pollitt about the jiggery-pokery work that has gone on.' Since this date is just after the Paris Congress, it is likely that this remark relates to events there.

18. Letter, 11 August 1934 from H. Laurie to Maud Brown. Copy sent to Pankhurst. Pankhurst Archive, loc.cit.

19. Ibid.

20. The File No.94 (64) of the Pankhurst Archive which deals with her involvement with the WCAWF mainly relates to the 1933-4 period. The last date mentioned is 22 May 1935, which is a copy of a letter which Pankhurst sent to Magda Gellan, in which she states that she has been inactive and not present at Committee meetings.

21. *Inprecorr*, 24 August 1935.

22. *VII Congress of the Communist International Abridged Stenographic Report of the Proceedings*, Moscow 1939, Foreword. The *Report of the Seventh World Congress of the Communist International*, Modern Books, London 1936, does not include the Kirsanova speech either. There were only two women in the British delegation, Esther Henrotte of the Co-op and Eva Nutter, a Lancashire textile worker. There were some fifteen men.

23. Ercoli, 'The Fight Against War and Fascism', *Report of the Seventh World Congress of the Communist International*, ibid.

24. Ibid.

25. H. Pollitt, 'Unity Against the National Government', ibid.

26. Interview, loc.cit.

27. Ibid. See also Selina Cooper Papers, Lancashire County Records Office, Preston.

28. Rathbone spoke at a meeting called by the WCAWF in London in January 1937, reported in the *Daily Worker*, 16 January 1937. She also sent messages of support to *Woman Today*, see, for example, the December 1937 issue.

29. For details see Bruley, op.cit., pp. 71-80.

30. See above, note 4.

31. Interview, 26 November 1976 and correspondence 22 April 1979.

32. Ibid.

33. Interview, 28 May 1977, Doncaster.

34. Ibid. Betty Kane did not actually remember this, but she was reminded of it by Frances Moore who was also present.

35. Interview, loc.cit.

36. Interview, 26 April 1977 and 10 May 1977, London.

37. For details of the Women's Guild of Empire, led by ex-suffragette Flora Drummond see Bruley, op.cit., p. 138, and Chapter 4, n.23.

38. *Tomorrow*, December 1936.

39. An amusing incident occurred when Jessica Mitford, a young aristocrat with left-wing sympathies, phoned the CP head office, 'to ask if they needed any women guerilla volunteers.' 'We don't know anything about that here,' a cockney voice had answered firmly. J. Mitford, *Hons and Rebels*, London 1978, p. 95. Mitford did eventually get to Spain. She ran away with her young cousin Esmond Romilly. Their adventures in Bilbao are described in the book. She became involved in Romilly's reporting work and did not do any fighting.

40. *Bulletin*, Spanish Medical Aid Committee, June 1938.

41. Winifred Bates, *A Woman's Work in Wartime*, unpublished typescript, International Brigade Association Archive, Marx Memorial Library.

42. Ibid.

43. Recalled in J. Cook, *Apprentices of Freedom*, London 1979, pp. 133-4.

44. Isabel Brown Interview, Imperial War Museum, Accession No. 884108, p. 37.

45. Interim Report of the National Joint Committee for Spanish Relief, undated but April 1939, p. 1.

46. Isabel Brown, loc.cit., p. 50.

47. Ibid., p. 43.

48. *Resolution on Work Among Women*, Report of the 14th Congress, CPGB, 1937, p. 302.

49. Ibid., pp. 302-3.

50. Ibid., p. 302.

51. For example, see *Labour Woman*, February 1937.

52. Some of the Communist women who wrote for *Woman Today*: Magda Gellan, Hilda Vernon, Rose Smith, Joan Beauchamp, Sylvia Townsend Warner, Nan MacMillan, Irene Paynter, Bessie Dickinson, Kathleen Gibbons, Elsy Borders.

53. *Liberal Year Book*, 1938 and 1939, and Interview, 16 January 1980, Sussex.

54. *Woman Today*, March 1939. Interview, loc.cit. and correspondence, 13 December 1979 and 28 December 1979. Dame Margery Corbett Ashby flatly denied having any connection with any organisation which had any CP

influence, despire documentary evidence to the contrary.

55. Ted Bramley, 'International Women's Day, what it means to us', *Discussion*, February 1938.
56. Interview, loc.cit.

The People's Front and the Intellectuals

MARGOT HEINEMANN

The mid 1930s are rightly seen as the moment when the left in Britain first made a massive contribution to the arts, literature and science, and began to develop something like a culture of its own. For the first time intellectuals, artists and professional people began to come towards the left and to ally themselves with the working class movement, not just as exceptional individuals but in quite large numbers and with wide practical effect. This could not have happened without the initiative of Communists and the change in Communist attitudes which was signalled, though not begun, by the Seventh World Congress and the strategy of the united people's front. The shock of Hitler's coming to power hit intellectuals and professional people as well as the labour movement, and had already created a wide basis and willingness for anti-fascist and anti-war action well before the Seventh Congress met. What the Congress did was to reinforce these attitudes, to condemn the sectarianism and hesitations that still held Communists back from organising united work with other anti-fascists of different beliefs or social class, and to assert, in the strongest terms that ideological and cultural work were not frills but a central part of the work of the Communist parties and of the whole anti-fascist struggle. Dimitrov in his report put this most strongly:

> Many comrades did not believe that so reactionary a variety of bourgeois ideology as the ideology of fascism, which in its stupidity frequently reaches the point of lunacy, was capable of gaining a mass influence at all. This was a great mistake. The putrefaction of capitalism penetrates to the innermost core of its ideology and culture, while the desperate situation of wide masses of the people renders certain sections of them susceptible to infection from the ideological refuse of this putrefaction ... We for our part must develop an extensive ideological struggle based on clear, popular arguments and a correct, well thought out approach to the

peculiarities of the national psychology of the masses of the people.[1]

In particular, he showed the fascists made use of distorted history and legend to appeal to the people:

> The fascists are rummaging through the entire history of every nation so as to be able to pose as the heirs and continuators of all that was exalted and heroic in its past, while all that was degrading or offensive to the national sentiments of the people they make use of as weapons against the enemies of fascism. Hundreds of books are being published in Germany with only one aim – to falsify the history of the German people and give it a fascist complexion ... In these books the greatest figures of the German people of the past are represented as having been fascists, while the great peasant movements are set down as the direct precursors of the fascist movement.[2]

He continued

> Mussolini makes every effort to make capital for himself out of the heroic figure of Garibaldi. The French fascists bring to the fore as their heroine Joan of Arc. The American fascists appeal to the traditions of the American War of Independence, the traditions of Washington and Lincoln.[3]

So:

> Communists who do nothing to enlighten the masses on the past of their people ... in a genuinely Marxist spirit, who do nothing to link up the present struggle with the people's revolutionary traditions and past ... voluntarily hand over to the fascist falsifiers all that is valuable in the historical past of the nation ...[4]

Existing freedom must be shown as something the workers have won by bitter struggle and need to defend now:

> While being upholders of Soviet democracy, we shall defend every inch of the democratic gains which the working class has wrested in the course of years of stubborn struggle, and shall resolutely fight to extend these gains ... How great were the sacrifices of the British working class before it secured the right to strike, a legal status for its trade unions, the right of assembly and freedom of the press, extension of the franchise and other rights! The proletariat of all countries has shed much of its blood to win bourgeois-democratic liberties, and will naturally fight with all its strength to retain them.[5]

The Intellectuals

In these efforts working intellectuals had a crucial role to play. Speaking on the need to win them over, Serafima Gopner (Soviet

Union) said that both economic crisis and fascism were hitting them hard. Cuts in production and social service expenditure meant that 'engineers, architects, doctors, journalists, actors, artists and teachers are seeking for any kind of unskilled work'. Meanwhile in Nazi Germany intellectuals faced 'physical and moral terror' and destruction of all cultural values. Sacking of Jews, burning of the books of world-famous authors, cutbacks in the training and scientific activity of women workers, glorification of war itself as the 'steel bath of renewal' – these were part of a process of 'spiritual counter-revolution'.

All this had led to some leftward swing among intellectuals, for example in the struggles of teachers and civil servants to defend their living standards in Britain as elsewhere, the mobilisation of intellectuals around the Amsterdam-Paris anti-war movement, the campaigns in defence of Dimitrov and Thaelmann, and the 'demonstration of unity between the writers and the proletariat' shown in the attendance of well-known foreign authors at the Soviet Writers' Congress in 1934 and the International Conference for the Defence of Culture in Paris in July 1935. But although *some* were turning directly to Marxism and the Soviet example as the way out of the crisis, this still applied only to an advanced minority. The main work of winning the *broad masses* of intellectuals to the side of the people's anti-fascist front had yet to be done, and its importance was still under-estimated; for the intellectuals had 'tremendous influence' on the workers as well as on the petty bourgeoisie who formed the mass basis of fascism:

> There is a close connection between the underestimation of work among intellectuals and sectarianism, because leftism is expressed in particular in the fact that the comrades who carry on work among intellectuals are regarded in many sections as almost right opportunists. At best, this front is regarded as the last in importance.

There must therefore be an end to the fear of contact with the intellectuals and their representatives, including those of the most varied political, philosophical and artistic trends. The Communists must help them in their fight for a livelihood and the opportunity to do creative work:

> These interests fully coincide with the interests of the proletariat, with the immediate and final aims of the Communists. The intellectuals form a most important link in the united people's anti-fascist front.[6]

Harry Pollitt at the Congress stressed that the fight against unemployment relief cuts had demonstrated how new allies could be won for the working class – especially in South Wales, where not only the miners' lodges, local and divisional Labour parties were drawn into the struggle, but also 'every teacher, doctor and clergyman'.

> Why? Because the teachers and doctors not only feel their fight to be hard enough owing to the existing poverty and malnutrition, but also because the very character of their work brings them into close contact and daily touch with the workers' conditions.

The winning of these, together with all who opposed any restriction of democratic rights and who hated and feared war, was now one of the party's most important political tasks.

The Application in Britain

It is easy now to take all this for granted as mere common sense, to assume that the British party must always have understood the importance of cultural and ideological work and welcomed and encouraged members who were intellectuals to make their special contribution to it, but this was not the case at all. Indeed in the 'class against class' period intellectuals and the cultural skills they brought with them were often regarded with suspicion, as conscious or unconscious carriers of capitalist ideas. They could prove themselves only by cutting themselves off from their middle class connections.

An article on 'Intellectuals and Communism' by R. Palme Dutt, in *Communist Review*, shows in an extreme form how the question could still be seen as late as September 1932. Noting that Marxism of sorts had recently become quite fashionable among intellectuals, Dutt warned that even those who had taken the crucial step of joining the party, accepting its discipline, working in their local branches and selling the *Daily Worker*, unfortunately still longed to work among their own professions as well. They wanted to form party organisations of scientists, historians and so on, in addition to local branches, and even to co-operate with non-party colleagues to discuss questions of philosophy, science and culture. Such projects must be firmly rejected, since

> there is no special work and role for Communists from the bourgeois intellectual strata ... The intellectual who has joined the Communist Party ... *should forget that he is an intellectual* (except in moments of necessary self-criticism) *and remember only that he is a Communist.*

He must work like every other member on the only task of all Communists, to win the *workers*. If he objects that he does not have contact with non-party workers, he must somehow make it.

No one, of course, would actually stop Communists from entering into discussions and polemics in their special field, says Dutt, but this was 'work of the third degree, of the fifth degree, of the tenth degree of importance' – except for those 'physically, morally and constitutionally incapable of fighting in any other field, i.e. incurable professorial types'. Unless the party was vigilant, women who joined it would expect to work among non-party women and intellectuals among non-party intellectuals. One of the worst 'offenders' seems to have been Maurice Dobb – the distinguished economist and, at that time, almost the only economist in the party. He had just published a book explaining and defending Soviet economic developments in language calculated to appeal to 'British bourgeois liberals'. 'To them the book may be welcome – not to the workers', said a scornful review in the same issue of *Communist Review*.

Even those who offered their professional skills directly to win the *workers* were often regarded with hostility. When the chairman of the party's Fleet Street branch suggested, in 1932, that its members who were trained journalists might help by working full- or part-time for the *Daily Worker*, Dutt scornfully rejected the offer in the July *Communist Review*. Such people had nothing important to teach and were likely to bring their ideological poison with them:

> Capitalist journalists – consciously or unconsciously – are *spiritual, ideological* agents of capitalism in the same sense as clergymen. The trade and technique of capitalist journalists, as of capitalist politicians is to lie.

In this atmosphere the party was unlikely to make effective use of the middle-class members it had, let alone win widespread influence among those sections.

The process of painful reappraisal after 1933 began to change such attitudes. William Gallacher was among the first to raise the urgency of the middle class being won for the support rather than the destruction of working-class organisations and, in 1934, told Cambridge Communist students that the party needed good scientists, historians and teachers, and that they should study and become good students, not run away to factories.[7] From such meetings grew a clearer understanding of the relationship between the 'middle sections' and the working class. A real revolutionary from these sections had the duty to bring his/her own people to the side of the working-class movement, not opt out by finding an individual niche inside the working class.

At the party's 1935 congress, held before the Seventh World Congress, Pollitt stressed that 'we must see in these students, intellectuals, authors, doctors, scientists and professors valuable allies who can be won for the working class.' After the Seventh Congress, however, the party gave much greater priority to work among middle-class and professional people. 'There is a new political awakening among them which is going to be a tremendous strength to the working-class movement,' Pollitt told the 1937 congress. Rejecting the 'contemptuous references to the People's Front' frequently made from the so-called 'extreme left', he pointed out that the middle class could no longer feel certain of ensuring their children comfortable and steady jobs. This 'anxious uncertainty for their own position and that of their children' had brought them to a clearer understanding and sympathy for 'the mothers and fathers of South Wales and the North-East Coast, where for the boys and girls of the working-class families there is only the blind alley of unemployment'. The fight for security could bring them into alliance with the working-class movement. And many of them also had wider, non-economic political interests, especially in opposing fascism, which could make them effective allies in the work of the National Council for Civil Liberties and the local peace movements.

By 1938 party membership and influence had grown fast among these sections and the Central Committee reported that more forces were urgently needed at the centre and in the districts or organise and co-ordinate the work. National conferences of delegates from the professional sections had been held in London, district ones in Scotland and Tyneside, with more to follow, which had brought home the importance of this field for the party as a whole and not just for a few 'specialists'.

At the 1938 congress Pollitt reinforced the argument with a striking analysis of the class composition of Britain (even though at that time the manual workers were a much larger proportion than they are today). He pointed out that alongside 12 million workers in leading production and transport industries (with their families some 30 million people), there were 11 million professional and middle-class people, 'ranging from doctors to advertising agents; from clerks to teachers; from artists to writers, to small shopkeepers and businessmen'. All these sections were concerned at the effects of economic crisis, fascism and the war danger. Many were becoming organised for the first time or demanding the right of organisation. Among both Catholics and Protestants there was horror at the fascists' attack on religion. Political ideas were changing too, and the rise of the Left Book Club in the last two years had directly affected the outlook of tens of thousands. The winning of unity in action with these sections was not just *desirable* but *essential* for defeating Chamberlain; he said in reply to the sectarians:

> It is politically very short-sighted not to recognise these developments and to ignore the importance of bringing all these sections of the people and their organisations into co-operation with the labour movement.
>
> It is necessary to recognise that at the present decisive moment, neither the working class alone nor these other sections of the people are able by themselves, with their present divided forces, to bring about the changes in policy that are required and that can lay the sure basis for defeating Chamberlain ...

The question was how the working class could win the support of all these people and of 'the various democratic, peace and religious organisations that so many are identified with' for the common struggle.

Cultural and Trade Union Organisation: Widening Out

A number of left-wing organisations of writers, artists and scientists had already been formed around 1933-34, often on the initiative of Communists inspired by the Soviet example and the various international conferences of the time. The Artists' International was started in 1933, followed in 1934 by the Writers' International. By 1933-34 the Cambridge Scientists' Anti-War Group was actively campaigning against the militarisation of science. But if the *broad masses* of intellectuals were to be won for an alliance with the working class, the appeal had to be less exclusively directed to those already pledged to socialism. Everyone who wanted to oppose fascism, poverty or war should be able to find a place of some kind in the action, even if they disagreed about the causes of these things, or were committed to quite different styles and theories of art and history from those of the Marxists, or were willing at most to sign a petition or a letter to the press. And ways had to be found to bring in the 'non-political' majority, concerned mainly with their own survival and future security as professional people in a harsh economic situation: which meant adding forms of trade union work to the cultural and ideological work already being done.

Organisation of the 'Forces of Culture'

Traditionally professional workers had been largely unorganised. There was a snobbish attitude to trade unions to be overcome. The individualist outlook persisted even in the fields where most professional workers had become employess of some kind. Communists from the mid-1930s therefore spent much of their effort working to build up existing professional unions, notably among teachers and students and to form or revive them where they scarcely existed, as among scientists, architects and film-technicians.

From 1935, for example, student Communists realised that they had to win over those who were mainly concerned to pass their exams and get a job, and who included the poorer students in the red-brick universities. This might mean working in the official student unions and the National Union of Students, which covered all students to bring pressure on the government to expand the social services and provide the fully skilled jobs for which students had been trained.

'Widening-Out' and the Artists' International

What the many-sided process of 'widening out' meant in practice can be seen in the growth of the Artists' International after 1935, when it set out to attract artists who might have been put off by its insistence on a specific commitment by members to a socialist political programme.[8] Its new aims stated 'The Artists' International Association stands for Unity of Artists against Fascism, War and the Suppression of Culture.'

This allowed many older and more established artists to support its aims, and an immensely successful exhibition, Artists Against Fascism and War, was organised, in which Augustus John, Laura Knight and many other traditional painters exhibited alongside 'modernists' such as Henry Moore, Barbara Hepworth, Ben Nicholson, John Piper and Moholy Nagy, as well as the socialist realists who were prominent in the leadership. The exhibition, opened by Aldous Huxley, attracted over 6,000 visitors and, as Montagu Slater shrewdly commented in *Left*

Review for January 1936, 'Those whom art and politics have put asunder, an exhibition against war and fascism has joined together.'

It is important to note that this represented a conscious alliance, not concealment or abandonment by the Communists of their socialist commitment. Nor was there any turn away from theoretical and critical work. In the same year the AIA published *Five on Revolutionary Art*, to which the Communists Francis Klingender, A.L. Lloyd and Alick West contributed critical essays on basic principles alongside Eric Gill (a left-wing Catholic) and Herbert Read (anarchist, pacifist, and supporter of surrealist and abstract modes in art). It was a consciously and deliberately *pluralist* production.

The strengthened AIA now did more directly political work, producing posters, banners and placards for May Day and peace demonstrations, and murals for the Peace Pavilion sponsored by the French Popular Front at the Paris World Fair (1937). By 1937 it was also able to take on something like a trade union role, working out and organising pressure for its members' professional interests. A large British Artists' Congress was held, chaired by Quentin Bell and supported by many of the best-known artists, designers and critics – Duncan Grant, Henry Moore, Eric Ravilious, Herbert Read, Vanessa Bell, McKnight Kauffer – covering every style and aspect of artistic work. It divided into what we would now call 'workshops' to discuss the organisation and funding of art, the reform of art education and teacher training, the need for government finance and patronage, scholarships and work for unemployed artists, as well as discussions on aesthetic questions. The biggest AIA exhibition yet was held – with over 1,000 works – for the first time including abstract and surrealist works on a large scale. On May Day 1938 more than 200 artists marched behind the AIA banners, including surrealist group members dressed as a band of Neville Chamberlains and giving fascist salutes.

Writers and the People's Front

Left-wing writers of the period were never really the 'Auden generation' of later literary legend. Anti-fascist writing ranged from social-realist, historical and working-class novels and documentary reportage to fantastic allegory, dream or nightmare visions of the future, popular songs and anti-Nazi thrillers. As with the AIA, the unifying factor was politics not artistic style.

A focus for Communist and left-wing writers was provided by *Left Review*, founded in October 1934 as the magazine of the Writers' International. Under mainly Communist editors (Montagu Slater, Tom Wintringham, Edgell Rickword and Randall Swingler) it carried reviews of books, art, music, theatre and films, as well as literary and political articles on the people's front and news of national and international cultural conferences.[9] At the same time it published the work of creative writers and poets, anti-fascist but by no means all identified with the party. Alongside already well-known names – Hugh MacDiarmid, Ralph Bates, Winifred Holtby, Sylvia Townsend Warner, Naomi Mitchison, Storm Jameson, Auden, Spender, Day Lewis and Jack Lindsay – much of its space and attention were given to stories and sketches by new worker-writers. Regular competitions were run to encourage such contributions, with established authors such as James Hanley and Arthur Calder-Marshall acting as judges. Among the most telling stories were those of the Indian Mulk Raj Anand and the Irishman Jim Phelan, and Scottish, Welsh and Irish nationalist writers also appeared – a remarkable coverage for any literary magazine at that time. Liveliness and satirical bite were provided by the cartoons and illustrations of 'the three Jameses' – Boswell, Fitton and Holland.

Later came John Lehmann's *New Writing*, with more space for work by anti-fascist authors. Himself a member of the Auden *New Country* group, Lehman linked up through Austrian and German anti-fascist friends with the international writers' network around Henri Barbusse and the various cultural conferences in which the Comintern was concerned. Through *New Writing* outstanding refugee writers like Anna Seghers and many French and Spanish popular front and many Soviet authors first reached English readers, alongside Auden's poems, Isherwood's powerful stories evoking pre-Hitler Berlin and sketches by the miner B.L. Coombes, whose autobiography *These Poor Hands* was among the finest working-class reportage of the time.

If one compares *Left Review* or *New Writing* with the aggressively sectarian *Storm* (1932-33) which preceded them,[10] one sees how the Seventh Congress line had transformed the ideas and the sheer amount and range of left cultural work going on nationally and internationally. *Left Review* became a forum where international discussion could be reported, and differences among contributors and readers – about commitment or detachment in writing, about style, about whether 'difficult' works could be progressive – could be clearly stated and argued out.

Criticism and Cultural Theory

To reclaim the best in past cultural traditions needed a broader and more flexible Marxist approach to history and the arts. What indeed would be the point of defending the cultural heritage against the Nazi book-burners if it contained nothing but illusions and errors? Thorez had told the Seventh Congress that the French Communist Party laid claim to the Enlightenment writers of the eighteenth century, such as Voltaire, whose materialism had laid the basis for the dialectical materialism of Marx and Engels. Similarly the British could look back to 'the noble anger of Milton at tyranny and injustice, the idealism of Shelley, the searing contempt of Byron and Cobbett'.

> Since scientific socialism is the culmination of all historic advance, it would be destroying the basis for its own future advance if it repudiated the past.[11]

There was still a good deal of sectarian thinking around, according to which capitalism in decay is incapable of giving rise to *anything* valuable in art,[12] and even the literature, language and art of its past were dismissed as useless to revolutionaries. Thus the novelist Alec Brown declared in an early *Left Review* discussion: 'Literary English from Caxton to us is an artificial jargon of the ruling class; written English begins with us.' With comparable assurance, Great War poets like Sassoon and Graves were denounced by a *Communist Review* writer as 'intellectual orchids wilting before the savagery and chaos … shrinking into the shell of individualism and aestheticism'.[13]

However, the new theoretical approach was seen in the editorials and review articles of *Left Review*, where a group of Communist journalists and critics including Montagu Slater, Ralph Fox, Douglas Garman, Edgell Rickword, Tom Wintringham and Randall Swingler dealt sympathetically and sharply both with major writers of the past and with the contemporary culture of the left. They emphasised the special importance for the socialist and democratic movements of Milton, the Leveller writers, Hogarth, the English Romantics, Cobbett and Blake, the Chartists and Dickens, and criticised the abstract character of books claiming to be Marxist criticism which gave no sense of the specific historical and formal qualities of the literature they discussed.[14] These pieces laid the basis for the general literary theory of Caudwell's *Illusion and Reality* and Alick West's *Crisis and Criticism* and also for pioneering books on progressive writers, T.A. Jackson's *Dickens: the Progress of a Radical* and Jack Lindsay's *John Bunyan, Maker of Myths*. In 1936 the party in its Peace Library series published a pamphlet by Rickword entitled *War and Culture: the Decline of Culture under Capitalism* which declared:

> Culture is not only music and science and philosophy, it is games and dancing and popular songs, everything that raises our existence above the struggle to keep alive.

But capitalism had made the people into consumers instead of partners in culture and sport, separating the artists and writers from those who did the productive work and making the art itself more unreal. Only an alliance with a united militant working-class movement offered a solution for the intellectuals, and it was now possible to win over 'not only individuals, but an effective majority of those whose specialised mental training can only be fully and freely utilised under socialism'. Against the militarisation and barbarisation of culture by Nazis and British imperialists, the pamphlet called on the people to use '*our* theatre, *our* films, *our* poems and novels against the infectious influence of the warmakers'.

Theatre

The break with self-isolating sectarianism after 1935 enabled left-wing theatre to become an inspiring force in the whole popular movement as well as the main source of new dramatic ideas and forms in the British theatre.

The Workers' Theatre Movement (WTM), under Communist leadership, had already developed a tradition of mobile and street theatre. By the early 1930s, however, it was concentrating rigidly and exclusively on agitprop sketches. Its slogan was 'A Propertyless Theatre for a Propertyless Class'.[15] It regarded most existing plays as useless and any kind of realism or individual characterisation as inherently bourgeois. Its manifesto of 1932 declared that it rejected 'decisively the role of raising the cultural level of the workers through contact with great art, which is the aim of the dramatic organisations of the Labour Party and the ILP. The 'exuberant sectarianism' (nostalgically recalled by some

later historians) of its politics and its bitter antagonism to the
Labour Party are preserved in songs such as the by-election ditty,

> Three candidates of the boss are we,
> Tory, Labour and New Party,
> You can vote as you like for one of us three,
> Candidates of the boss.

However impressive the energy and commitment of the
'cultural shock-brigades' (with names like Red Megaphones and
Workers' Red Radio, borrowed directly from the German
agitprop groups), the crude stereotyping could often make the
shows boring as well as politically disastrous – 'political suicide'
as WTM leader Tom Thomas ruefully admitted later.[16] The
revolutionary propaganda often amounted to slogan-shouting –
'It's coming, coming, the workers' revolution'. The actors were in
practice limited to Communists and the violent anti-Labour
rhetoric was beginning to be felt as a hindrance to real struggle.

The gradual dissolution of the WTM and the formation of
Unity Theatre marked an important change in policy. Just after
the Seventh Congress several London WTM groups, headed by
Hackney's Revel Players, joined to form the broader based Unity
Theatre, which aimed to reach out to trade unionists and labour
people both as audiences and performers. This required a new
programme, higher technical standards and better rehearsed
performances. The new theatre club acquired its own permanent
premises and welcomed the help of professional theatre people
who were now joining or coming close to the CP, among them
André van Gyseghem, Herbert Marshall, John Allen and, later,
Paul Robeson. Unity's aims were to foster the drama on 'the
principle that true art, by effectively presenting and truly
interpreting life as experienced by the majority of the people, can
move the people to work for the betterment of society'. It was to
be a people's theatre and also 'to devise, import and experiment
with new forms of dramatic art'. Comparable successful theatres
grew up in Manchester, Merseyside, Newcastle, Glasgow and
many other centres.

In 1937 more than 300 volunteer trade unionists transformed a
derelict mission hall near Kings Cross into a modern theatre and
cultural centre. Its general council included Labour politicians
Stafford Cripps, G.R. Strauss and Joseph Reeves, theatre
directors Tyrone Guthrie and Michel Saint-Denis and actors Paul

Robeson and Lewis Casson who had recently toured with *Six Men of Dorset*, written by Miles Malleson and the Dorset railwayman, Harry Brookes, about the Tolpuddle Martyrs and sponsored by the TUC.

'Outside' performances by mobile groups were still a central part of Unity's work as was the training of its actors, especially in short sketches and plays for labour movement meetings, from which its sectarian content had largely excluded the WTM.

However, 'propertyless theatre' and German agitprop were no longer the only models. The new movement experimented with a great variety of forms and styles, from poetic drama to 'living newspapers', mass declamations, satirical pantomime and historical pageants. Realistic drama was now admitted as one possible form because it was still one of the most familiar and appealing to real working-class audiences. Other groups included classical plays. *Volpone*, Jonson's famous satire on commercial greed was put on by Manchester's Theatre of Action, where Joan Littlewood and Ewan McColl were beginning to build a permanent company, the germ of their later Theatre Workshop. Merseyside Left Theatre staged Auden and Isherwood's highly experimental *Dog Beneath the Skin*, usually considered too obscure for working-class audiences. Once again it was a varied scene; certainly not the return to 'legitimate conventional middle-class theatre' some historians have called it.

The greatest successes were, however, directly propagandist. The backbone of Unity's repertory was Clifford Odets' *Waiting for Lefty*, a play about a New York taxi strike (with anti-fascist and anti-war overtones), which turned the theatre into a strike meeting and was acted hundreds of times all over the country. Another trade union play was *Busmen*, a 'living newspaper' about the London bus strike of 1937, using real-life charcters and speeches; this was created by a group of actors, journalists and working busmen directed by John Allen, with music by Alan Bush and verse by Montagu Slater. In 1938, just after Munich, came the 'pantomime with political point', *Babes in the Wood*, which used one of the most popular of English theatrical forms to satirise the Chamberlain government and its ruling-class backers. It ran for six months with massive block bookings from the labour movement – the AEU, for example, took the whole theatre for six nights. This was indeed an anti-Tory and anti-fascist cultural triumph in a very local tradition.

The work was done on a shoestring by amateur actors and

without government subsidies. But from 1937 some help from the Left Book Club enabled Unity Theatre Guild to act as a technical, advisory, play-finding and script publishing centre for some 250 amateur groups all over the country and to run summer schools and training sessions for them. The amateur movement, however, was not the whole story. In 1934 a group of professional theatre people, led by van Gyseghem and including Barbara Niven and Miles Malleson, formed Left Theatre, consisting of professional actors who gave their services to perform plays of social or political value and take them out to working-class areas. Some of the group were Communists, others pacifists, others Labour. This company performed Montagu Slater's *Stay Down Miner*, based on his reportage of the Welsh miners' 1935 stay-down strikes against company unionism. And the little Group Theatre, put on plays such as Auden and Isherwood's *The Ascent of F6* – described by the *Daily Worker* as a brilliant attempt to debunk half-legends of heroism in the service of imperialism.

Film

Films were by far the most important medium influencing people's minds, but tightly controlled and censored not only by the state but by the industry's own board of censors. No anti-Nazi films could be made, and even a project to film *Love on the Dole* was banned as too controversial. The fight centred first on the right to show substandard 16mm films (especially the new Soviet sound films which were banned by the commercial cinemas) in ordinary halls to working-class audiences, without government or local authority interference. For example, the Royal Arsenal Co-operative Society alone gave 100 showings of Eisenstein's *General Line* in 12 months.

Though there was already an active group of left-wing film technicians, they lacked the capital to make full-length films, but were able to produce a few political shorts – a series for the Co-operative movement, newsreels of Hunger Marches and demonstrations by the Workers' Film and Photo League (founded 1935), Ivor Montagu's *Peace and Plenty* for the Communist Party (1939), and most important, several films by Montagu and a group of technicians on the Spanish Civil War. Meanwhile the Association of Ciné Technicians, formed in 1933 with Communists taking an active role, led the fight for government measures to save the very existence of a British film industry, in danger of being completely swamped by Hollywood.

And young left-wing directors joined in the new documentary film movement around John Grierson, in which the living conditions, skills and dignity of working people were for the first time allowed to speak for themselves on the British screen.[17]

Science, Planning and the People's Front

The work of scientists played a crucial part in the transformation of ideas.[18] Traditionally they had been rather cautious and conformist, standing somewhat apart from other intellectuals (partly because they were dependent on the approval of industry or the universities for financing their research). Many, however, had been deeply shaken by Hitler's coming to power in what was considered the scientifically most advanced country, and by the perversion and misuse of science which followed. Some had contacts with Germany and with victimised Jewish scientists, which brought home to them that the future of science was in danger. This didn't always lead to politicisation but many became involved in campaigns to help refugees (who were mostly prevented from working at their professions in England), or to refuse academic contacts with the universities that had persecuted their colleagues. This laid the basis for a serious left-wing movement with ideological effects far beyond the scientific community.

The organising initiative came from the young Marxist and near-Marxist scientists, some of whom as early as 1931 had been deeply influenced by the visit of a Soviet science-history delegation (led by Bukharin) and its famous publication *Science at the Crossroads*. J.D. Bernal, Hyman Levy, P.M.S. Blackett and Joseph Needham had been directly inspired by this vision of how science had developed as part of social production and what it could achieve in a planned socialist economy, in contrast to its frustration under capitalism. But as they admitted, their impact on the thinking of scientists at that time was negligible. Now a much wider prospect opened up.

Communist scientists had long been organising protests about the militarisation of science, and helping to inform people through exhibitions and lectures of the horrors of modern scientific warfare. Now they helped to revive the Association of Scientific Workers, which in 1935 adopted a new constitution committing it both to defend its members' salaries and conditions and to campaign on wider issues of science policy and funding so as to encourage research and employment. The

Association more than doubled its membership over the next two years. Through its efforts the British Association, the semi-official parliament of the profession, was persuaded to start a section to discuss the social aspects and uses of science. A Parliamentary Scientific committee was formed to lobby MPs and pressurise the government, and the first official contacts on policy were made between scientists and the TUC.

Left-wing scientists joined with the 'forces outside science' campaigning for change. The Socialist Medical Association was formed and affiliated to the Labour Party. The war-blinded doctor, Frederick Le Gros Clark, on the Committee against Malnutrition, worked in close co-operation with the National Unemployed Workers' Movement; physicists at the Cavendish Laboratory invited railway trade unionists in to discuss their work; medical students dressed the feet of the hunger marchers and some later helped to form the first British medical units with the Spanish Republican forces; J.B.S. Haldane visited bombed Madrid to advise the Republican government on Air Raid Precautions.

Scientists were more conscious than most of the horrors a second world war would involve. 'The millions who suffered in the last war are aware that to a large extent their sufferings were directly due to scientific developments and that science, far from having brought benefits to mankind, is in fact its worst enemy,' wrote Bernal in 1939. Younger radical scientists increasingly regarded the application of science to war as the worst prostitution of their profession. Yet a complete boycott of war research, even if it could have been organised (which it couldn't) would merely have left democratic countries at a disadvantage compared with fascist ones. Scientists disagreed as to what they should do; but both pacifist and non-pacifist scientists could agree in warning of the nature of modern war and the need for more research and expenditure on protecting the civilian population. Hence the successful campaign of the Cambridge Scientists' Anti-War Group, exposing the inadequacy of official air raid precautions by carrying out independent scientific experiments, which helped to spread the idea that the defence of the people was too important to be left to the government and its selected 'experts'.

The sense of urgency and hope is reflected in the books and theoretical writings produced by radical scientists after 1935, reaching out to non-specialists and to thinking workers on a remarkably wide scale. The Left Book Club (LBC) and the left-Labour *Fact* booklets included many titles on popular science, both theoretical and applied – Haldane on Air Raid Precautions, Hyman Levy on Marxist philosophy, Drs McGonigle and Kirby on poverty and public health, A.J. Clark on the patent medicine racket, Bill Beck and Harry Collier on the foundations of chemistry and biology. The Left Book Club books were discussed at meetings of its local groups, often with the authors as speakers. Here and there special LBC science discussion groups were set up in working-class areas such as the East End of London. The most influential Marxist statement, summing up a great deal of collective thinking by Communist and non-Communist scientists, was J.D. Bernal's *Social Function of Science* (1939), which documented in detail for the whole movement exactly how science was being frustrated by capitalism and fascism, what it could do immediately to raise living standards given enough pressure, and how in a planned socialist economy it could provide the technological means to end poverty and misery forever. Taken as a whole, they brought both confidence and vision to the wider movement, and helped to combat the irrationalism and fear which played into the hands of the right.

There was much, certainly that the Communist scientists and intellectuals of the 1930s failed to understand or foresee. The capitalist economic system turned out to have far greater powers of recovery and adaptation than they expected, allowing a massive expansion of science and technology and even long spells of full employment. Their writings of the 1930s naturally emphasise the immediate issues that seemed most urgent then – inadequate expenditure on medical and biological science, for instance, rather than the problems of population, ecology and pollution arising from its rapid commercial application after the war. Nevertheless they are far less simplistic and 'techno-economist' than they've sometimes been made out by later disillusioned socialists of the 1980s, whose 'radical science' often slides into anti-scientific despair. It is consistent with their whole record that after the war Communist and radical scientists of the 1930s were among the foremost in campaigning against the use of nuclear weapons.

Scholars and Academics

By 1938 the left had enough support among academics to launch *The Modern Quarterly*, especially designed to appeal to them and to provide an outlet for research articles that could not be accommodated in any existing left-wing publication. Its statement of aims committed the journal to be anti-fascist, anti-obscurantist, aiming at social revaluation of the arts and sciences and to 'devote special attention to studies based on materialistic interpretation of the universe, and to mutual relations between intellectual activity and the social background'. The majority of editors were Marxists, though not all the contributors had to be. Benjamin Farringdon wrote on ancient medicine, Needham and Levy on the philosophy of science, G.D.H. Cole on British capitalism and war preparations, F.D. Klingender on Goya. And there were important articles on economics, vindicating Marx against the idealism of Keynes and his school (Erich Roll) and appreciating (for once!) Maurice Dobb's *Political Economy and Capitalism* as 'an epoch-making book establishing the competence of Marxian economics to deal with concrete problems'.

A glance at this journal refutes the suggestion that in order to win influence in 'high science' circles the intellectuals had to conceal or play down their Communist convictions. By this time there were a good many scholars of great reputation in science and arts with Communists or left Labour sympathies and a generally Marxist outlook, and others (not at all naïve) who were happy to work with them in some kind of people's front alignment.

Daily Worker and Culture
The *Daily Worker* after 1935 gained enormously, both because more professional artists, writers and scientists were now available to it and because the party and the paper had fewer reservations about how their skills might be used. Culture in the broadest sense – including amateur as well as professional sport, hiking and dance-music, as well as 'high culture' – had a regular share of its terribly limited space. Book reviews covered novels and even poetry as well as directly political books. A regular column 'The Past is Ours', popularised the work of writers like Dickens, Swift, Defoe and Blake. From 1938 a weekly science feature by J.B.S. Haldane, probably the best science journalism available anywhere, did a lot to build sales. On the reporting side the 'capitalist-trained' journalist Claud Cockburn, previously of *The Times*, combined the roles of diplomatic expert, war correspondent, scandalous gossip-columnist and funny man, alongside the excellent veteran and likewise capitalist-trained

Walter Holmes, and under editors who were working-class leaders appointed by the party's Political Bureau – William Rust, Idris Cox and J.R. Campbell.

Religion
The Seventh Congress also signalled a break with earlier attitudes to religion, looking to co-operation with those of varied faiths against fascism and war. By 1935 the approach to religious people in Britain had already come a long way from the stuff produced by near-party journals like *Storm*, for instance a poem 'Opium of the People' which began:

> Any honest prostitute is better than a priest.
> Any decent cannibal would shudder at his feast.

After 1933 the root-and-branch attack on Christianity as such was stopped. Worldly or hypocritical aspects of the churches were still pilloried and sober Marxist analysis of religious illusions went on, seriously and without rancour, but the aggressive tone had gone. Communists working in local peace councils often found that Quakers and church people were among the most active and influential in exposing war preparations and rearmament. Clerics helped to lead campaigns against poverty and fascism; for instance Father Groser, a well-known Anglo-Catholic priest, became president of the Stepney Tenants' Defence League (which had a Communsit secretary), and led a deputation to the Home Secretary to ban Mosley's march through the East End. In 1936 the successful agitation against British universities attending the 550th anniversary of the University of Heidelberg began with a letter to *The Times* by the then Bishop of Durham.

In its pamphlet on *War and Culture* (1936) the Party noted the growth of 'an almost contemptuous attitude towards the Church' on the part of the ruling class. Duff Cooper had angrily attacked 'ignorant clergymen' who 'presume to give His Majesty's government advice on foreign affairs', and the Director-General of the Territorial Army complained that 'the clergy, in some cases, do not give the support we have the right to expect'. The rulers, said the pamphlet, 'can no longer afford to pay even lip-service to the humane teachings of Christ'.

A conscious alliance was now being sought with religious people as such, which became clearer in the late 1930s.

Communists contributed to discussions on the relationship between Christianity and Marxism (for example in John MacMurray's *Christianity and Social Revolution*) and the socialist Dean of Canterbury, Dr Hewlett Johnson, became the best-known cleric on the left through his *Socialist Sixth of the World*. In 1938 J.R. Campbell wrote in the *Daily Worker* that there was no reason why a Christian could not join the Communist Party. The influence of anti-fascist and socialist clergy and preachers within the united front was considerable, especially in areas like South Wales were religion was still an important element in the life of working-class communities.

British Freedom and National Traditions
A sense of national tradition was particularly necessary for the left in Britain. The British labour movement had a very strong pacifist, anti-national strain. Rejecting the imperialist 'patriotism' that had been responsible for the First World War, its activists could sympathise overwhelmingly with Abyssinia or Republican Spain. But to make their case convincing to the majority they had to come to terms with the national hopes and fears of Lancashire cotton workers and North-East coast shipbuilders, who believed that their own economic security required Britain to be great. In the 1930s Gracie Fields and George Formby were often more successful in appealing to such feelings than Communists were. But the Seventh Congress helped the left to reclaim patriotism and British freedoms. Instead of denouncing freedom as a liberal-bourgeois illusion, the movement now organised to defend it. The right to demonstrate and hold meetings against fascism and war had to be secured, not only against the Nazis and Mosley's bully-boys but against the encroaching power of the state.

The National Council of Civil Liberties, set up in 1934 with strong support among liberal intellectuals, monitored police violence against Hunger Marchers and anti-Mosley demonstrators, exposed the Sedition Bill which would be used against peace campaigners, and fought the censorship of books and films. With its help attempts by government and local authorities to stop the showing of Soviet and left-wing films in ordinary meeting halls were legally defeated, and the right of trade unionists to distribute recruiting leaflets outside factories defended in the Courts. Chaired by E.M. Forster, whose own art was deeply rooted in liberal protest against imperialism and sexual oppression, the Council included a variety of Labour and Liberal MPs alongside lawyers, journalists and publicists, some of them actually anti-Communist but prepared to use their influence for this common cause. It was on the subject of 'Liberty in England' that Forster addressed the Paris Conference of Writers for the Defence of Culture in 1935, saying that while British freedom was admittedly limited ('to a starving man it is not worth a plate of fish and chips') and in the colonies almost non-existent, to him it was still very much worth fighting for.

At the same time left-wing artists and writers showed how the fight for freedom reached far back into British history, recalling 'famous forebears' – the leaders of the Peasants' Revolt, the Levellers, the Tolpuddle Martyrs, the left-wing Chartists – whom the usual history textbooks largely ignored.

Reclaiming the Past

The recovery of the best in past democratic traditions for the left was not altogether simple, since unlike the French Communists, who had set the example, the British had to go back to the seventeenth century for their democratic revolution. Whereas the flag of France, was originally a *revolutionary* flag and The 'Marseillaise' a revolutionary song, the Union Jack and 'God Save the King' were not the same thing at all. On the other hand, England had the oldest working-class movement and that was the centre of the tradition that the Communist Party historians, writers and artists helped to revive and popularise.

There was as yet no organised group of Marxist historians, but a new idea of the past and its meaning came through individual works like Hymie Fagan's *Nine Days that Shook England* (on the Peasants' Revolt of 1381), *The English Revolution 1640* by Christopher Hill, Edgell Rickword and Margaret James, *The Levellers* by Henry Holorenshaw (actually Joseph Needham) and Allen's Hutt's *Post War History of the British Working Class* and *This Final Crisis*. The outstanding achievement was A.L. Morton's *A People's History of England*, read by many thousands as a Left Book Club choice and still a classic. Taken together these showed English history as a complex process of struggle, often tragic, yet potentially hopeful. The epigraph on Morton's title-page summed it up, quoting the mediaeval revolutionary John Ball in William Morris's story: 'Ill would Change be at Whiles, were it not for the Change beyond the Change'. The view was not sentimental but dialectical: the 'change beyond the change' was up to the reader. The *inspiration* was condensed in a splendid collection of first-hand extracts from the Middle Ages to modern times, *A Handbook of Freedom*: (selected by Jack Lindsay and Edgell Rickword, 1939).

May Day marches and ralies now began to offer a colourful alternative to the conventional 'patriotic' history advertised by military tattoos on the newsreels. In 1936 the London district of the party staged a march with 85 painted banners depicting figures and events in English history from Magna Carta through to the present day. The crowd cheered the banners of the socialist pioneers, Robert Owen, William Morris and Keir Hardie alongside those of Marx and Engels and those revealing the contribution to the international struggle – the strike on the *Jolly George* during the Hands Off Russia campaign, Easter Week with James Connolly and Padraig Pearse, the Invergordon Mutiny, the 1919 police strike and finally the emblems of solidarity with Spain.

Historical pageants became an important side of the party's and labour movement's propaganda – impressive because they not only spoke to and stirred great audiences, but actively involved literally thousands of party and non-party people as amateur actors, costume-makers, crowds and singers. André van Gyseghem as pageant director, Montagu Slater and Randall Swingler as script and song writers, Alan Bush as composer and choirmaster were responsible for organising many of these – for the co-operative movement in Wembley Stadium as well as for the party in the largest halls in London, Manchester, Liverpool, Glasgow and other cities.

The most remarkable of all was the Pageant of South Wales, sponsored by the South Wales Miners' Federation (SWMF) to celebrate May Day 1939 – the centenary of the Chartist rising. It was staged in three football grounds in West, Central and East Wales, with a cast of over 6,000 and drawing in every trade union and cultural organisation in the valleys – including twenty-eight choirs and eight silver bands with their traditional hymns and national music. The first part dramatised the demonstration and unjust trial of the Chartist leaders at Newport, using much of the original documentary records. The second told the story of the miners and their union from that time, from child labour in the Industrial Revolution to the General Strike, the devastation of the coalfield by unemployment, and finally the entry of a contingent of the South Wales miners just returned from the International

Brigade. The uniting of union and chapel people, traditional choral and solo singing and reciting, around their own democratic history was an image of the united people's front in action. Significantly the initiative came from Arthur Horner, one of the most convinced supporters of the broad alliance policy, who had recently become President of the SWMF. It was he who suggested to Lewis Jones, unemployed miners' leader, that he might write the history of miners' struggles in his now famous novels *Cwmardy* and *We Live*. Horner's commitment had already been made clear in a special message to *Left Review* (October 1936):

> Art and Literature, these can be our allies in the great struggle to defeat reaction and secure freedom. The old tendency to regard the working class as sufficient in itself, being able to do everything with its own 'pure hands', must be thrown overboard.

Spain

From the autumn of 1936 Spain was at the centre of all cultural work and a test for all that had been achieved. It is impossible to detail all the ways in which intellectuals and cultural workers showed their solidarity, in fund-raising, lobbying and direct propaganda. The Artists' International Association organised exhibitions of works to be sold for relief funds and a cabaret devised by Auden and Benjamin Britten, among other events. Montagu with a group of anti-fascist professional technicians, and support from the Republican government, made films, including *Defence of Madrid* and *Behind the Spanish Lines*. Unity and other theatre groups all over the country put on hundreds of performances of Jack Lindsay's mass declamation 'On Guard for Spain' and Randall Swinger's 'Arms for Spain' at public meetings to support the International Brigade. Auden's poem 'Spain' was sold as a pamphlet on behalf of Spanish Medical Aid, and enough good poems were written for John Lehmann to bring out an impressive anthology *Poems for Spain* in 1939.

In 1937 an international group of authors called on English writers to declare themselves in a brief message for or against the Spanish Government, for or against Franco and Fascism. Of the 148 replies printed in *Authors Take Sides* only five were against the Republic, including Edmund Blunden and Evelyn Waugh. Sixteen claimed to be neutral. These included T.S. Eliot, who felt at least a few writers should stay uncommitted; Ezra Pound, who considered Spain 'an emotional luxury to ageing and sap-headed philanthropists'; Vera Brittain, pacifist though anti-fascist. The rest were for the Republic. Their testimony ranged from Samuel Beckett's 'Uptherepublic!' to Liam O'Flaherty's 'As an Irishman I realise that the toiling masses of Spain are waging the same struggle which we have waged for centuries', V.S. Pritchett's 'Heart and soul for the people of Spain in their brave and stoic resistance' and Rose Macaulay's terse 'Against Franco'. Taken together they made an impressive demonstration of where British intellectuals stood, which it has proved impossible for the most biased of later historians to argue away.[19]

As everyone knows, a number of Communist and anti-fascist intellectuals went to fight in the International Brigade or serve in the medical units, alongside the majority who were industrial workers. The British movement could be proud of its unwavering intellectuals. For these were not romantic adventurers who thought war was fun. How clearly the decision to go to Spain was linked in their minds with the whole line of struggle after 1935 is explicitly shown in John Cornford's poem 'Full Moon at Tierz', composed while on duty at the front, and verses of which are used as the epigraph at the beginning of this book.

Some General Comments
The party's line on culture was simply the general line of the Congress – to build working class unity and a broad alliance against fascism and war and their main supporters in Britain. To this end cultural work went on at many levels, practical and theoretical, popular and specialised in a variety of forms and styles according to the occasion, the comrades available and the people we were trying to reach. There was no uniform levelling up – or down – to some ideal, homogeneous audience.

Within the urgent political aims, there was a new degree of flexibility and pluralism. Different trends and views were quite openly acknowledged and discussed in broad organisations and journals, rather than hushed up as disgraceful. Communists argued strongly and publicly for their views, but attached importance to contacting intellectuals with *really* different political outlooks. This relative toleration did not, however, extend to those regarded as Trotskyists, and political critics of the Soviet Union tended automaticaly to be labelled as agents of enemy propaganda, with whom no unity or constructive dialogue was possible.

In practice, most Communists felt free to follow their own tastes and judgements in the arts. There was no 'line' on form or content and there was considerable variety of opinion about styles.

Most of the published work including theoretical writing, seems by present-day standards remarkably accessible, though not patronisingly so. One must remember that there was as yet little basis for seminars and debates between different schools of academic Marxists – indeed it was a fight to get a hearing for Marxist ideas in university courses at all. Books on philosophy, economics and history were commissioned (by Gollancz especially) for general readers without specialist training, and had to be as readable and clear as a complex subject allowed. And if anything this seemed to encourage new and lively Marxist theoretical work.

It is sometimes said that the Seventh Congress led to a middle-class political culture, where the intellectuals instructed and educated the proletariat in the conventional forms approved by the ruling class. In practice it was not like that at all. The leading role of the working class in the broad alliance was always clear, and it was the working-class leaders who insisted most strongly on the importance of cultural work. Communist intellectuals and professionals worked in their party branches and generally felt that they learned more from the Communist workers than they could teach. Moreover, they were largely concerned with bringing their professional organisations into various kinds of practical activity alongside the unions or the unemployed. The experience thus gained was crucial in the long run for their professional and creative work, though admittedly the immediate demands were sometimes too heavy to allow time for personal creative work at all.[20] It is significant that so much of the work was concerned with developing popular cultural forms – as in the *Left Songbook*, a compilation of international songs of the labour movement, or the collection and revival of urban folk song and work-songs pioneered by A.L. Lloyd. As Edgell Rickword put it, looking back:

> The real triumphs … were not individual achievements. The real triumph was the drawing into the cultural ambit of a significant number of men and women who were barricaded out from participation in what was regarded as a middle-class preserve.[21]

The Left Book Club, in particular, has come in for a good deal of stick from ultra-left historians as a middle-class set up. In fact it presented a great variety of cheap Marxist and left-wing books to quite new readers. The books were followed up with meetings, discussions and sometimes political action. The assumption that because the members bought and read books they must have all been middle class is merely silly: especially considering the long tradition of working-class education and self-education in which so many Communist and Labour Party members and leaders had been involved. People like T.A. Jackson and J.R. Campbell were outstanding examples among many.

Women were leaders in almost every field of left-wing cultural work. Among the most active artists were Pearl Binder, Betty Rea, Nan Youngman, Peggy Angus, Felicia Browne. *Left Review* writers included Amabel Williams-Ellis, Sylvia Townsend Warner, Christina Stead, Storm Jameson and Nancy Cunard. Women scientists were to the fore in the anti-war movement, Dorothy Hodgkin and Nora Wooster among them, while Reinet Fremlin became organising secretary of the revived Association of Scientific workers. These were certainly not just a few token women. Novels and stories of the time often focus on the special situation and problems of women. Sexual politics was already a reality, though it was not called that. However, although some of the best-known writers of the left were homosexual, no open reference to their sexuality could be made, and there was almost no pressure for a change in repressive laws and attitudes.

The Soviet Union was the great source of hope and inspiration for the cultural work of the time. The sucesses of economic and industrial construction, achieved against tremendous odds; the high value placed there on education, science and the arts in spite of the material difficulties; the example of rational planning which eliminated unemployment – all this was immensely impressive to intellectuals frustrated by economic depression and cultural stagnation at home. Soviet films and eye-witness reports[22] brought all this alive at a moment when optimism was desperately needed and support became still stronger when the Soviet Union was the only country to send arms to Republican Spain. The 'Socialist Realism versus Formalism' debate had less prominence in the British cultural movement than one might expect, in spite of the tremendous prestige of the Soviet example in general. Much of it indeed was never translated for instance the controversy between Brecht and Lukács, neither of whom was widely known in Britain. Even some leading party figures seem largely to have ignored it as not directly relevant to British conditions, and few imagined that these could ever become hanging matters. Arrests of Soviet writers and cultural workers, so far as they were known about at all, were attributed by Communists to political activities, not to artistic ones. However, there is no doubt that the show trials of 1936-38, involving well-known cultural spokesmen like Bukharin and Radek (as well as the less-publicised arrests of internationally-known figures such as Meyerhold, Koltsov, Babel and Pilnyak) caused grave disquiet on the left, and severely damaged the broad alliance and the socialist movement. after 1937, indeed, there were few if any attempts to call broad international conferences of cultural workers.

From the time of the Munich agreement, and above all the fall of the Spanish Republic in March 1939, defeatism and apathy were beginning to erode support among intellectuals and others for the broad alliance, well before the Nazi-Soviet pact and the outbreak of the Second World War.

After 1939

The idea of a broad alliance was not, as is often assumed, simply snuffed out by the outbreak of war. Some sectors of the united front indeed fell apart. There was dissension and conflict but many of the writers, artists, scientists and technicians still felt they had common issues to fight for, not least through their professional unions. Despite the call-up, their cultural work continued in various forms through the phoney war and after the fall of France[23], until the entry of the Soviet Union into the war restored something more like the political conditions in which their alliance with the working-class movement had been formed. At that point new kinds of mass work took off, with anti-nazi films, touring theatre and concerts, post-war plans for science and building, and the work of left-wing intellectuals in the Army Bureau of Current Affairs.[23] All this had an important influence on the political thinking of ordinary people, which certainly helped to turn the vote against Churchill and for Labour in 1945.

Thus the influence of the Seventh World Congress long outlasted the 1930s. What changed the situation was not so much 1939 as the beginning of the Cold War in the late 1940s. And even that did not erase, at least for Communists of the generation of the 1930s, the style of work which the Congress had marked out. We had learned to regard every democratic organisation and every decent human being as a potential ally against the main enemy, and this we were never to forget.

NOTES

1. G. Dimitrov, *Selected Articles and Speeches*, London 1951, p. 99.
2. Ibid.
3. Ibid., p. 100.
4. Ibid.
5. Ibid., p. 129.
6. *Inprecorr*, 2 December 1935. Serafima Gopner was an old Bolshevik who joined the Bolshevik Party in 1903; she was active in Russia and arrested more than once. After the Revolution she was a leader in Ukraine CP. A member of Executive Committee Communist International (candidate) 1928-43 she was a delegate to 15th, 16th and 22nd Congresses CPSU. For Pollitt see *Inprecorr*, 30 October 1935.
7. James Klugmann in J. Clark, M. Heinemann *et.al.* (eds), *Culture and Crisis in Britain in the Thirties*, London 1979, p. 32.
8. For further information on the Artists' International see the excellent study by Lynda Morris and Robert Radford, *The Story of the Artists' International*, Oxford 1983.
9. In particular the International Conference of Writers in Defence of Culture, held in Paris in July 1935; the recalled conference committee in London, 1936; and the next full conference of the organisation in Madrid, 1937, where many of the previous participants attended in uniform on leave from the Republican forces.
10. *Storm*, copies of which are now very rare, was printed on the party's Utopia Press with the co-operation of some of its writers, and ran for four issues in 1933. Its hallmark, apart from political narrowness and bludgeoning language, was bitter contempt for any suggestion that effective writing might be a skilled craft to be learned. 'You say this story has no crisis, no climax like proper stories should. Sorry, mate – I'm no fiction artist.' This made things easy for the writer but very hard going for the reader. It was, however, favourably reviewed in *International Literature* (Moscow), in which the super-sectarian RAPP group was still strong.
11. Edgell Rickword, 'Culture, Progress and the English Tradition in C. Day Lewis (ed.), *The Mind in Chains*, London 1937.
12. This view, expressed by a correspondent in Left Review in 1935, drew a furious reply from Lewis Grassic Gibbon, author of *A Scots Quair*.
13. Pat Dooley, in a highly approving review of Mirsky's *The Intellectuals of Great Britain, Communist Review*, April 1935. *Left Review* later that year countered this judgment by devoting six pages to reprinting anti-war poems by Sassoon and Wilfrid Owen, as well as including sharp criticism by Alick West of Mirsky's book for presenting nearly all intellectuals as reactionary or fascist.
14. Some of the best of these pieces are reprinted in Edgell Rickword, *Literature in Society, Essays and Opinions*, Alan Young (ed.), Manchester 1978.
15. Properties were rigorously limited to a cloth cap for the worker and a top hat for the boss. Indeed when a Yiddish-speaking group used a wig to indicate a judge it was threatened with expulsion, according to Philip Poole, secretary of WTM at the time. See his interview in *Red Letters*, No. 10, for information on the movement before 1935.

16. For additional information and analysis of theatre developments see the articles by A. Van Gyseghem and J. Clark in *Culture and Crisis in Britain in the Thirties*, op.cit.

17. For additional information on film see ibid., articles by R. Bond and B. Hogenkamp.

18. For information (usually accurate) on left-wing science in the 1930s see G. Werskey, *The Invisible College*, London 1978.

19. Among them were famous names like Ford Madox Ford, J.D. Beresford, A.E. Coppard, Havelock Ellis, David Garnett, Geoffrey Grigson, C.E.M. Joad, Aldous Huxley, Arthur Koestler, Louis Macneice, Llewellyn Powys, James Stephens, H.M. Tomlinson, Helen Waddell, Rebecca West and Antonia White.

20. Thus C. Day Lewis, who worked hard for a time in the Cheltenham branch, selling the paper and speaking at meetings, eventually left the party not because of any disagreement over policy but because he found it impossible to function as a writer, though he liked and admired the workers in the branch as well as the party leaders he had met. (See his autobiography *Buried Day*, London 1960).

21. Interview in *The Review*, No. 11-12.

22. Too numerous to mention. Among the best-known were *Soviet Communism: a New Civilisation?* by Sidney and Beatrice Webb (London 1935) and *Moscow in the Making* by Sir Ernest Simon (London 1937).

23. e.g. renewed campaigns to improve ARP; Unity travelling shows entertaining shelterers in London tube stations; the continuation of *New Writing* and the foundation of *Our Time*; anti-Nazi broadcasts by Forster, MacNeice and others.

The Communist Party of India: From Leftism to United Front

CONRAD WOOD

The Communist Party of India (CPI) was formed in 1920 under the guidance of the Communist International. Before the 1917 Russian revolutions Lenin had worked out his ideas for the role of a revolutionary working class party in countries which had not yet experienced a bourgeois revolution. In such countries it was necessary to co-operate with bourgeois parties to achieve and complete the bourgeois revolution. But it was also essential to form a revolutionary socialist party which would maintain its independent organisation. For, paradoxically, the bourgeoisie would be unable and unwilling to carry through its own democratic revolution since it feared the revolutionary initiative of the common people. On the morrow of the bourgeois revolution, it would be necessary to proceed as swiftly as possible to the proletarian revolution.[1]

These ideas were of great political importance for India. They implied co-operation between Communists and the Indian National Congress (INC) against two enemies; those forces representing autocratic, pre-capitalist society (princes and great landowners) – the 'democratic' aspect of the revolution; and British rule – the 'national' aspect of the revolution. But an independent Indian Communist Party was also necessary. This Leninist policy was confirmed by the Second Congress of the Comintern in 1920, which declared:

> The Communist International must enter into a temporary alliance with bourgeois democracy in colonial and backward countries, but must not merge with it, and should under all circumstances uphold independence of the proletarian movement even if it is in its most embryonic form.[2]

At the 1920 Congress this policy was opposed, from a leftist position, by the Indian neophyte Marxist M.N. Roy, who argued

187

that such support for bourgeois movements would not be in the interests of the colonial masses and therefore the development of the revolutionary movement. He was criticised by Lenin and the Congress resolution made it clear that Communists should co-operate with 'nationalist revolutionary movements', that is those which aimed to transfer power from the imperialist bourgeoisie to an indigenous class.

In India, therefore, the prospect of Communist support for Congress action against British imperialism and its allies seemed bright. In 1920 the INC was passing increasingly into the hands of those who were willing to take actions which directly threatened the duration of British rule. Indeed, in 1920 the INC adopted the Nagpur Constitution, changing its aim from self-government within the Empire to *swaraj* (self-rule), a change indicative of its rapid (though still incomplete) transformation into the type of organisation which could undertake actions which would objectively further revolution in the Marxist sense. In addition, some influential Congress leaders had noted the Communist attitude to imperialism and had come to believe that Communism did not amount to the threat to Indian nationalism that the British represented it to be, while others thought that it might be an asset in the struggle against imperialism. To what extent Indian Communism could capitalise on this favourable situation depended on the extent of leftism in the movement.

During much of the 1920s Roy was entrusted by the Comintern with the task of nurturing the Communist movement in India. Although he showed a lingering adherence to leftism, he did, generally, guide the movement along the Leninist lines of 1920, by pressing for the formation of an illegal Communist Party and for the establishment of a 'front' organisation to fight within Congress against compromising tendencies and to develop the revolutionary trends in that movement. This 'front' organisation eventually took the form of the Workers' and Peasants' parties (WPPs). In these Communists played the key role. They combined support for Congress, so long as it fought imperialism, with an alliance with the petty-bourgeois 'left' of Congress. A policy of direct action was adopted towards the compromising leadership of the INC.

In 1928 the chances of such a Communist/left-nationalist alliance, with the object of forcing revolutionary confrontation with the Raj, appeared good. Jawaharal Nehru, who 'fresh from his internationalist and Communist connections in Europe',[3] had persuaded the 1927 Madras Congress session to pass a number of extreme anti-imperialist resolutions, was merely the most notable of a new generation of prominent Congressmen who were to help push Congress towards a degree of militancy not seen since the non-co-operation movement organised by the INC in 1921-22. Even Congressmen not of the 'left' had indicated their perception of a common interest between the nationalist and Communist movements over the Public Safety (Removal from India) Bill, which was 'especially directed' against the British Communists Spratt and Bradley who had been sent to India to assist the movement there. They declared that the Bill was directed against Indians themselves and would be used to persecute nationalists.[4] By early 1929 the Raj was noting 'a tendency for the political and Communist revolutionaries to join hands'.[5] One especial British fear was that Communism would not be ignored by 'those Nationalists who for the attainment of their ends look to the sanction of force' because Communism had a direct appeal to the masses among whom (the Government of India believed) the extreme nationalists had achieved little success.[6]

The source of these testimonials to the potency of Communism as a force to mobilise the masses was its advance among the Bombay workers in 1927-29. Gaining moral support from the activities of the British Communist Ben Bradley, the Bombay Communists found it easy to win the leadership of the textile millhands away from the moderate union leaders who had achieved little. Nor were their efforts confined to the Bombay mills. According to British Intelligence '(by) the end of 1928 ... there was hardly a single public utility service or industry which had not been affected, in whole or in part, by the wave of Communism which swept the country during the year.'[7] In the course of a five-and-a-half-month textile strike against 'rationalisation' in Bombay in 1928, the famous Girni Kamgar Union (GKU) was formed with Communist leadership and in few months its registered membership climbed from 174 to 54,000.[8]

Thus, by December 1928, participation in the national movement, along with the initiative, supported by British Communists, of assuming a key position in the labour movement, had placed Indian Communism on the crest of a wave. Communists had even come to hold important positions in Congress, being elected to the All India Congress Committee and controlling the Bombay Provincial Congress Committee (PCC).[9]

Even so this success had been achieved almost solely through

Communist-dominated unions and the Workers and Peasants' Parties. 'United Front' tactics had tended to become a substitute for the task of organising a strong independent Communist Party, in line with the decisions of 1920. This neglect assumed significance in the turn towards leftism heralded by the Sixth Comintern Congress of 1928.

Like Roy's leftism of 1920, this new leftism originated in an over-estimation of the degree of development of the colonial proletariat. It argued that this had occurred at such a pace that the national bourgeoisie was abandoning the revolution altogether and becoming counter-revolutionary. The 'Draft Programme of the International' declared that the 'revolutionary tendency' in the colonies was being 'temporarily paralysed ... by the treachery of the national bourgeoisie', which had become 'scared of the revolutionary mass movement'.[10] Conditions were therefore favourable 'for establishing the hegemony of the colonial proletariat in the popular mass struggle for independence'. The fact that the INC had under left-wing influence, just adopted the aim of complete independence, was interpreted as 'a pseudo-revolutionary formula to be used as a "threat" against the British government to extract concessions'. Thus leftism led the Comintern to interpret a real advance of the INC towards revolutionary confrontation with the Raj as a grave menace to the future of the Indian revolution.

The main task of the Indian Communists was, therefore, held to be that of exposing to the masses the true nature of the INC and especially to expose the petty-bourgeois intellectuals who were the 'left-nationalists'. They must 'demarcate themselves in the most clear-cut fashion, both politically and organisationally, from all petty-bourgeois groups and parties'.[11] This meant dissolving the WPPs, the one organisation through which they had influenced Congress and also to create separate revolutionary trade unions under the guidance of the Red International of Labour Unions (RILU).[12]

The WPPs were not, in fact, dissolved, though they no longer acted as a section of Congress. This was partly because the most experienced Indian Communist leaders were wary of adopting untempered leftism and partly because the advice of the British party ran counter to the ECCI line. However, any possibility of the CPI avoiding leftism was effectively ended by the events of the next few months. On 20 March 1929 almost the whole leadership was arrested and charged with conspiracy in what was to become famous as the Meerut Conspiracy Case. One of the chief objects was to behead the movement by including all leaders 'of any account ... in the case'.[13] The CPI found the task of adequately replacing them one of great difficulty, no doubt largely because of the 'neglect of the Party during the palmy days of 1928'.[14] Even in Bombay, where, exceptionally, 'other leaders of much the same type'[15] replaced the arrested men, they were, not surprisingly, inexperienced and young and not likely to discern the dangers of the developing leftism which was pressed on the CPI with increasing vigour during 1929.

At the Tenth Plenum of the ECCI in July the leftism of the Sixth Congress was pushed to greater extremes. The general consensus was that the Indian bourgeoisie had finally become counter-revolutionary[16] and that the 'real national-liberation movement in India was represented not by the last bourgeois-national congress but by the proletarian mass demonstration *against* this national congress'.[17]

The line was now clear. the advance of the revolution and the CPI was to occur via assault against the bourgeoisie and the Congress. There was now no longer any question of working within that body to strengthen a revolutionary against a reformist tendency: Congress as an organisation was written off as counter-revolutionary. Not surprisingly, therefore, the Plenum complained about the continued existence of the WPPs.[18]

Moreover from mid-1929 there was no question of support for any possible deviation from the Comintern line from any source within the international movement. The British Communist position on India had changed, with the WPPs no longer seen as fulfilling 'the needs of the proletariat'.[19] Roy was now opposing the new leftism and the writing-off of Congress, but had been publicly denounced at the Plenum as a Menshevik and as no longer a 'comrade'.[20] Under these circumstances the CPI was led further towards leftism by the new leadership. The strong position that had been built up in the labour movement suffered first.

Believing that they stood at the head of 'the growing revolutionary movement',[21] as they had been told by Kuusinen, and that in the past they had 'lagged far behind the sentiments of the broad masses',[22] the Indian Communists sought to convert strikes into revolutionary confrontations with government regardless of the real state of readiness for struggle of the workers.

Such tactics virtually destroyed the CPI's great achievement of 1928, the powerful GKU. In April 1929 the new leadership launched the Bombay millhands into an 'anti-victimisation' struggle which Kuusinen described as a 'political strike' which was 'the revolutionary answer' of the millhands to imperialist machi-nation.[23] In their revolutionary fervour the inexperienced Com-munist leadership of the GKU had chosen an unfavourable time for the millhands who were exhausted by the 1928 struggle.[24] In September the strike was called off with no success for the workers. The result was a slump of the GKU to a few hundred members[25] and the workers 'left in a mood of distrust of any leaders'.[26]

The precipitous decline of CPI strength in the trade unions was accelerated by their growing isolation within the movement. This in turn was the outcome of their sectarianism which promoted splits in the movement. At the December 1929 Nagpur session of the All-India Trades Union Congress (AITUC) the 'moderate' leaders split away to form their own federation leaving the Com-munists and nationalists to share control of the weakened parent body. Communist tactics of fighting at all costs to wrest control of the unions from the hands of the 'agents of the bourgeoisie', whether 'moderate' or nationalist, led, after Nagpur, to a protrac-ted battle culminating in a further split in the AITUC at the Calcutta session of July 1931.

The CPI by its leftist opposition to Congress provided its nationalist opponents in the struggle for the unions with allies, the Royists. After his expulsion from the Comintern Roy was deter-mined to combat its leftism by trying 'to capture the Indian Communist movement' which he hoped would 'enable him to make his own terms' with the Comintern.[27]

A key target was the Communist-led unions, and by early 1931 the Royists were in control of the GKU.[28] CPI union leaders were often left isolated in what were virtually 'paper' organisations existing parallel to unions led by the nationalist-Royist alliance. As the Meerut prisoners were to admit in a mid-1932 memorandum, nearly all the Communist-led unions passed into the hands of the Royists and their allies.[29] When the 1931 AITUC session was held in July, impending defeat for the Communists in the struggle for control of the organisation led to their seceding to form the 'red AITUC', which, according to their main nationalist opponent at this session, did not subsequently show 'much sign of activity except ocasionally in Bombay and in Calcutta'.[30]

But leftism adversely affected CPI fortunes in the political as well as the trade-union field. In the early 1930s Indian Communists had looked forward to a repetition of the type of situation that had arisen during the non-co-operation movement, a situation they believed would be ripe for a national rising against imperialism given the one great desideratum of 1920-22, the existence of a revolutionary party like the CPI.[31]

On the eve of the civil disobedience movement of 1930 the prospects for a spectacular advance of both the national revolution and the CPI appeared bright. The foundations of the Raj were such that Under Secretary of State Hirtzel even spoke of 'British rule' having lost 'a sufficient amount of political support to enable the King's government to be carried on'.[32]

As far as Congress was concerned CPI participation in the impending movement would certainly have been welcomed. Nationalist sympathy for the Meerut prisoners was manifest,[33] and Gandhi invited Indian Communists to co-operate with him in his plans for 1930.[34] In the event, because of its leftism, the CPI was unable to grasp its opportunity, for it saw Congress as Counter-revolutionary,[35] with left nationalists like Nehru and Bose the 'most dangerous obstacle to the Indian revolution', whose reactionary nature had to be exposed.[36]

With such a perspective the CPI's political practice during the crucial months of civil disobedience conformed to the estimate that 'the *real struggle*' was '*not between the Congress and British imperialism but between the Congress and the Indian revolutionary movement*'.[37] The CPI therefore not only tended 'to regard the whole anti-imperialist movement of 1930-31 as a purely Congress movement and to remain aloof from it',[38] but actually clashed with Congress at times during 1930. The most famous incident occurred at the Bombay Independence Day celebration which were terminated by a CPI-led invasion of the Congress platform resulting in a scuffle and the forcible hoisting of the red flag alongside the Congress flag.[39] The initial failure of the key Bombay working class significantly to participate in the civil disobedience movement,[40] no doubt partly due to CPI policy, resulted in great Congress efforts to win them,[41] with the organisation in August of a 'Congress Labour Week'.[42] This campaign helped convince the CPI that the 'real battle' was between the party and Congress, so that 'a vigorous struggle' for the support of the unemployed 'between the Congress and the Communists' resulted.[43]

However in its competition with Congress it was the CPI that was worsted. In August the non-CPI section of the GKU leadership joined Congress[44] and from this time millhands increasingly backed the Congress campaign.[45] Things were now looking black for the CPI. Its base among the millhands was badly eroded and its tactics were alienating the nationalist left with which such fruitful co-operation had been developing in 1928.[46] By February 1931 *Inprecorr* was speaking of the 'revolutionary masses' being 'welded together under counter-revolutionary leadership' and the consequent 'despair' of some Indian Communists.[47]

CPI fortunes reached their nadir in 1932. In May *Inprecorr* spoke of CPI 'passivity' and 'despondency',[48] and in July of 'hardly any resistance' to the machinations of the 'national-reformists' in the Calcutta trade unions.[49] By its sectarian tactics the CPI had destroyed the progress made in the labour and political movements up to 1928. The object of strengthening the party had not been achieved; indeed, the CPI was reduced to a few small groups riven with dissent.[50]

The first step away from leftism and towards recovery came in summer 1932 with advice from abroad after a request from Meerut prisoners concerned at the party's decline.[51] The advice correctly identified the immediate cause of CPI misfortune as isolation from the masses led by organisations, such as Congress and trade union bodies, which the CPI had labelled as irremediably inimical to the interests of the revolution. However no critique of the theoretical mistakes regarding the roles of the national bourgeoisie and 'left' nationalists, which had led to this isolation, was undertaken. Consequently the advice was only a very partial, inconsistent rectification of the leftist line. Advice on the need to renew contact with the masses by participating 'in all *mass* demonstrations organised by the Congress'[52] and by organising 'Communist fractions' in the 'mass organisations' of ' "left" national reformism'[53] was thus accompanied by support for extreme leftist formulations which had helped isolate the CPI from the masses in the first place. For example, left nationalists were identified as the 'especial' target for an '*uncompromising* struggle' whilst 'the worst enemies' of the Indian revolution were held to be not the imperialists but the Royists.[54]

Even so the CPI's acceptance of the revised line came only in 1933 when the release of most of the experienced leaders after Meerut[55] coincided with renewed international exhortation on the lines of those of 1932.[56]

In November 1933 a Calcutta meeting of the main cadres, convened by Adhikari, set about a CPI reorganisation involving the formation of a central organising 'nucleus', the barring of two of the main 1929-33 leaders from elective posts and the reunification of the key Bombay party.[57] A new political thesis which resulted from this meeting conformed to the revised line of the 1932 Open Letter but added its own original touch by making the first CPI advocacy of what later became known as 'collective affiliation'. Thus the Communists were 'to use the Congress platform', not as the CPI, but 'through some of the mass organisations of the toilers'.[58] This meant CPI-led 'mass organisations' actually joining Congress.[59]

This period also saw the first practical steps by Indian Communists to reunify the trade union movement. A late 1933 appeal had called for the uniting of CPI-led unions with 'parallel' unions,[60] but some unity in action was achieved in March 1934 when a Joint Strike Committee of Communists and Royists was formed to conduct a strike against wage cutting and rationalisation in the Bombay mills.[61]

In fact, after initial spectacular success, the strike collapsed amidst recrimination between the factions comprising the Joint Committee.[62] That the failure was partly due to CPI sectarianism was suggested by an *Inprecorr* analysis which spoke of some of the strike leaders called for 'purely Communist trade unions' during the second part of the strike after many of the experienced leaders like Adhikari had been arrested.[63] Even so, the first tentative CPI moves away from leftism had brought their reward. In the autumn the CPI was speaking of its 'rehabilitation' with the millhands[64] and the Bombay Governor of Communist domination of the city's unions.[65]

In 1934 the CPI also benefited from its abandoning of the policy of holding aloof from Congress. Thus Adhikari began to establish contacts with left-wing Congressmen[66] and the Bombay Congress session was the occasion for the distribution of CPI literature which influenced those who were to become Kerala CP leaders.[67] By January 1935 extending CPI contacts with the recently formed Congress Socialist Party (CSP) had resulted in an agreement for united action.[68] In April a further such agreement was reached between the CSP and the two trade-union centres, the AITUC and the Red TUC, which in the same month merged at Calcutta.[69]

Thus by early 1935 the CPI was participating in joint Bombay PCC-AITUC meetings festooning the platforms with banners praising Russia and the Comintern.[70] For the Raj the spectre of

Communist-nationalist collusion was reappearing,[71] alongside clear evidence of the CPI's advance.[72]

Nevertheless, as long as the CPI adhered to the general line of 1932 its advance was limited. Whilst Communists continued to brand the CSP as a 'manoeuvre' of the bourgeoisie to divert the revolutionary energies of the masses,[73] that party was likely to react, as it did in 1934, by banning Communists from membership.[74] Whilst (perhaps the less sagacious) Communists continued to launch attacks on Congress meetings the aim of collective affiliation was unlikely to be achieved.[75] The obvious need was for a new theoretical understanding which would hasten the halting steps away from leftism which had begun in 1932.

The decisive step came at the Seventh Comintern Congress in August 1935.[76] Here it was argued that imperialism was currently waging an 'intensified offensive' against the colonial peoples with political consequences of great significance'.[77] The antagonism between colonial and imperialist bourgeoisies had accentuated and the national-revolutionary tendency, as represented with the formation of left wings within bourgeois national parties was increasingly challenging reformism in those parties. In view of these developments 'anti-imperialist united front tactics' had assumed 'primary importance' for colonial Communist parties. However CPI work was held up as a model of how not to conduct such tactics. By demanding that the INC accept a united front programme including a demand such as 'the establishment of an Indian Workers' and Peasants' Soviet Republic' the CPI (in December 1934) had made proletarian hegemony a precondition for co-operation with the bourgeois Congress. Such 'Left' sectarian errors' could only make a united front impossible.[78] The CPI was thus urged to 'put a decisive stop to sectarianism' and 'in no case disregard work within the National Congress and the national-revolutionary and national-reformist organisations affiliated with it'. The Comintern had returned to the pre-1928 line of organisational independence for Indian Communism alongside full participation in the national movement to promote its revolutionary tendency against reformism. Moreover, work within the CSP was now clearly being urged.

Even so, not until after it was subjected to further pressure via the CSP decision to reverse its ban on Communists becoming members[79] and through a new thesis from British Communists (both in January 1936) did the CPI finally accept the break with leftism.

The new thesis, produced by R.P. Dutt and Bradley took the idea of collective affiliation and turned it into a means by which, along with other changes such as the democratising of its organisation and the dropping of 'the dogma of "non-violence" ' from its creed, Congress itself might be transformed into the desired united front. Of course the Communists would still maintain organisational independence but, as individuals, they would play a key role in the task of making Congress uncompromisingly revolutionary. This work would be effected not only by, hopefully, the affiliation of Communist-led mass organisations to Congress, but also by the CSP which 'as the grouping of all the radical elements in the existing Congress' had 'an especially important part' to play. It was necessary for the CPI to make clear its political differences with the CSP and vice versa, but this should be achieved through 'comradely discussion' which should not be an obstacle to 'common working on all the issues on which agreement can be reached'.[80]

To achieve the desired changes in Congress, unity of all national-revolutionary forces was thus essential. But it was clear that equally necessary was the reunification of 'the most consistently revolutionary force', the proletariat, so that the Dutt-Bradley thesis on unity in the political sphere was accompanied by an appeal for 'a united trade-union movement' since, '[in] this manner the united working class' would 'be able to bring its full strength to bear' in the united front. The ending of the last remaining divisions in the Indian trade union movement was thereby urged on the CPI as a key task.[81]

At first there was considerable opposition within the CPI to the Dutt-Bradley formulations,[82] but by spring 1936 a new CPI leadership had accepted the need to implement the new line and had grasped the hand extended by the CSP in January, Communists now being permitted to join that party on an individual basis.[83]

Even though leftism was to persist in the party, the new formulations had now been accepted as the guidelines for the CPI policy. It now entered a period when with the application of the new line it was to see an unprecedented growth in strength and membership.

The favourable effects on Communist fortunes were not long in manifesting themselves. At the Lucknow session of the Indian National Congress in May 1936, the party was able to come to an agreement with the Congress Socialists for mutual co-operation.

Partly as a result of this compact, Communists rose, during the second half of 1936, to influential and even dominating positions in CSP units in various parts of India, especially in the South. This growth of Communist influence within the CSP was not the result of sheer unscrupulous jockeying for power and the poaching of another party's membership, as has sometimes been made out.[84] It was, basically, a reflection of the genuine growth in the influence of the CPI at this time. Thus in August 1936 a member of the Secretariat of the Government of Bengal had cause to communicate to the Government of India the intelligence that Communist meetings and demonstrations had 'for many months past been frequent' and were 'increasing in frequency' in Calcutta and its suburbs.[85]

Within Congress itself a number of leading Communists now began to climb to important and influential positions. At the end of 1936, S.A. Dange, a Meerut prisoner who had been released from gaol in about the middle of the year, was elected both to the Faizpur Congress session and to the All-India Congress Committee itself.[86] Later, in 1938, Communists figured prominently among those elected to the Bombay Provincial Congress Committee, G.Adhikari receiving the highest number of votes given to any of the candidates in Bombay city.[87] Indeed, influence within the Indian National Congress was of great significance to the CPI in the revival of its fortunes in the years immediately after the Seventh Comintern Congress. In 1937 Congress ministries were formed for the first time in a number of Indian provinces, including the vital Presidencies of Bombay and Madras. Though these provincial governments had but limited powers, they were able to provide a more favourable, semi-legal environment in which the CPI could carry on its work. These developments were watched closely by the Governor of Bombay, Lord Brabourne, who reported in August 1937 that the provincial Congress government had given orders to cancel the ban on local Communist organisations and to relax the restrictions previously imposed by the British on all individual Communists.[88]

Not surprisingly, by 1938 this increased latitude meant that CPI activity began to be reflected in a further growth of mass influence. In the Bombay municipal elections of that year, the four Communist candidates who stood managed to beat the entire opposition.[89] CPI organisation and influence had developed to such a level at this time that the party was able to launch its first all-India weekly journal, appropriately called the *National Front*.[90]

Increasing strength was also demonstrated in the trade union sphere. By 1937 the biggest union in the Bombay cotton textile industry was the resurrected Girni Kamgar Union which, however, had only 5,500 members. It benefited from the relatively tolerant policy pursued towards it by the provincial Congress Ministry of 1937-39 as compared with the previous repression by the British. By June 1940 the GKU had 32,000 members, whereas the combined membership of all the rival trade unions totalled less than 7,000.[91]

The Second Comintern Congress had established that colonial Communist parties were faced with two basic tasks: firstly, to work in national liberation movements against imperialism and 'feudalism', and secondly, to organise Communist movements to conduct the anti-bourgeois struggle. Though the national movements by nature were bourgeois, no contradiction between the two tasks was admitted. In fact the two were seen as complementary since the completion of the national democratic revolution would ensure the conditions necessary for achieving socialism, whilst the building of Communist parties would mean strengthening the political expression of the class most consistently interested in the bourgeois revolution: the proletariat. Doubts about this thesis by those Communists who feared that the first task would necessarily hamper the second constituted the origin of leftism which, when it guided CPI work in the earlier 1930s, proved a severe handicap for Indian Communism. The lesson of these years was that *neglect* of the first task inevitably made success in the second impossible. Work within the national movement was necessary, if not sufficient, for success in building the CPI. The change of line which resulted from the Seventh World Congress led to co-operation between Communists and nationalists which transformed the fortunes of the CPI. It also had very important consequences for the Indian National Congress itself and so for the future of India, but these belong to the wider history of Indian nationalism.

NOTES

Abbreviations:
IOR = India Office Records;
PJ = Public and Judicial Department Papers
E = Economic and Overseas Departmental Papers

1. Lenin, 'Two Tactics of Social Democracy', *Collected Works*, Vol. 9, pp. 28-9, 49-50, 85-86.
2. Lenin, 'Preliminary Draft Theses on the National and Colonial Question', Collected Works. Vol. 31, p. 150.
3. Haig, Secretary to the Government of India, Home Dept., to Hirtzel, Under-Secretary of State, 19 January 1928. IOR L/PJ/6/1955, 365/28.
4. The Bill was introduced 'to provide for the removal from British India in certain cases of persons not being Indian British subjects or subjects of the States of India'. L/PJ/6/1967, 3788/28. Also Irwin to Hailey (Governor of United Provinces) 28 September 1928, IOR Hailey Collection, Vol. 13 c, p. 494. Also IOR Official Report of Legislative Debates, 12 September 1928, 638 and 15 September 1928, 825 in L/PJ/6/1967, 4259 and 4260/28.
5. Haig to all local governments (secret letter No. D342) 21 February 1929. L/PJ/6/1976, 792/29.
6. Ibid.
7. Government of India, Intelligence Bureau, *India and Communism*, Simla 1935, p. 127.
8. Union membership records in IOR, L/E/7/1347, 1827/30 and 1693/30. Though actual figures are not reliable the order of membership rise is correct.
9. *India and Communism*, p. 127, and M. Ahmed, *Communist Party of India: years of formation*, Calcutta 1959, p. 41. Also Report of the Commissioner of Police, Bombay, No. 1633/h/3717, 25 March 1931, L/PJ/7/78, 1847/31.
10. *Inprecorr*, 6 June 1928.
11. Theses on the Revolutionary Movement in the Colonies and Semi-colonies. Sixth Comintern Congress. *Inprecorr*, 12 December 1928.
12. Ibid.
13. IOR, Viceroy to Secretary of State (tel No. 257-S), *Halifax Collection*, (C 152) Vol. 15, p. 23.
14. *India and Communism*, p. 180.
15. Haig, secret letter No. D-342/29 of 24 June 1929.
16. See 'Theses on the International Situation and the Immediate Tasks of the Communist International', *Inprecorr*, 4 September 1929 and discussion contribution of Lot-In, *Inprecorr*, 9 July 1929.
17. 'Report of Kuusinen', *Inprecorr*, 20 August 1929.
18. See Lozovsky, *Inprecorr*, 11 September 1929 and Shubin, *Inprecorr*, 17 September 1929.
19. C. Dutt, 'The Class Struggle in India', *Labour Monthly*, July 1929.
20. By Lozovsky, loc.cit., and interjections by delegates during Kuusinen's speech, *Inprecorr*, 20 August 1929. According to a statement in *Inprecorr*, 13 December 1929, the Plenum had resolved to expel Roy from the Comintern although this was not publicly known in July 1929.
21. In his Tenth Plenum report, loc.cit.

22. P. Sch. (*sic*, P. Schubin or Shubin), 'The Conference of the Workers' and Peasants' Party of India', *Inprecorr*, 29 March 1929.

23. In his Tenth Plenum report, loc.cit.

24. According to a pro-Communist journalist of this period, M.G. Desai, one of the Communists arrested in March 1929 (Dange) had advised the millhands against a protest strike because of the weakened state the 1928 strike had left them in. 'Some Anecdotes of the Meerut Conspiracy Case', *New Age*, 5 October 1969.

25. M.D. Morris, *The Emergence of an Industrial Labour Force in India*, Berkeley 1965, pp. 184-5.

26. Note by B.N. Mitra, 16 April 1930; Viceroy to Secretary of State 23 April 1930, IOR, *Halifax Collection*, Vol. 6 p. 85.

27. *India and Communism*, p. 162.

28. Ibid., p. 164.

29. Ibid., p. 182.

30. S.C. Bose, *The Indian Struggle 1920-42*, New York 1964 p. 233.

31. This was Roy's belief expressed in his journal *Vanguard*; see Government of India, Intelligence Bureau, *Communism in India, 1924-27*, Calcutta 1927, p. 72.

32. Minute on letter D-o No. 315-P.A., H.W. Emerson (giving views of Punjab Government on political situation) to Haig, 3 January 1930, L/PJ/6/1995, 373/30.

33. Motilal Nehru had taken the offensive against the Government on this issue from the start (Viceroy to Secretary of State, [tel. No. 1161-S 1162-S], 21 March 1929, *Halifax Collection*, Vol. 15, p. 60) whilst both he and Jawaharlal helped organise a Meerut Prisoners' Defence Committee (see B.R. Nanda, *The Nehrus: Motilal and Jawaharlal*, London 1962, p. 311).

34. This was, apparently, the testimony of Meerut prisoner Ghate, see Communist Party of India, *S.V. Ghate, Our First General Secretary*, New Delhi 1971, p. 108.

35. 'Resolution of the All-India Anti-Imperialist League on the General Political Situation and the Tasks of the League' adopted at the All-India Anti-Imperialist League Conference convened in Bombay 24 October 1930 to establish the League. The formation of this body had been urged by the International Secretariat of the League Against Imperialism in an 'Open Letter to the Lahore Session of Congress', since, it said, 'the Congress cannot be regarded as an instrument for prosecuting an uncompromising struggle against imperialism', *Inprecorr*, 27 December 1929.

36. 'Draft Platform of Action' of the CPI, G. Adhikari (ed.), *Indian Communist Party Documents*, Vol. 1, 1917-22, New Delhi 1971, pp 3-12. This document appeared first in December 1930 and received 'wide circulation throughout India', *India and Communism*, p. 170.

37. V. Chattopadhyaya, 'The Indian National Congress against Revolutionary Development', *Inprecorr*, 6 November 1930.

38. 'Abridged Draft of Political Theses of the Central Committee of the CPI' *Inprecorr*, 20 July 1934. The correctness of this later self-criticism by the CPI seems confirmed by contemporary evidence; see for example the Governor of Bombay's comment with regard to the civil disobedience movement in May 1930 that the 'Communist and Workers' and Peasants' Organisations are watching and waiting' (Sykes to Irwin, 21 May 1930, *Halifax Collection*,

Vol. 24, p. 370), also a Bombay CPI document (quoted in the three Parties' Open Letter of 19 May 1932, see below, n. 48) of June 1930.

39. 'Bombay Special' to Home Department, New Delhi, (Tel. P No. SD148), 30 January 1930, L/PJ/6/1996, 770/30. Men who worked in Congress between the wars were often later to recollect this incident, e.g. M.R. Masani, 'the Indian Communists insulted on the sands of Chowpathy in Bombay the national flag of the independent India yet to be born', M.R. Masani, *The Communist Party of India, A Short History*, Bombay 1967, p. 29.

40. See Viceroy's telegrams to Secretary of State during May 1930, L/PJ/6/2009 for example No. 1451-S, 11 May 1930 (2357/30) and No. S688 25 May 1930 (2817/30).

41. Sykes to Benn (tel.), 20 July 1930, L/PJ/6/1998, 4116/30.

42. Government of Bombay to Secretary of State (tel. SD 523), 17 August 1930, L/PI/6/1998, 4653/30, L/PJ/6/1998, 4653/31.

43. Sykes to Irwin, 25 August 1930, *Halifax Collection*, Vol. 25, p. 740.

44. Sykes to Irwin, (tel.), 13 August 1930, *Halifax Collection*, Vol. 25, p. 688d.

45. Report of G.S. Wilson, Commissioner of Police, Bombay, 23 October 1930, L/PJ/6/1998, 6745/30.

46. Later Jaiprakash Narayan was to claim that though he had been converted to Soviet Communism in the USA in the 1920s, when he returned to India in 1929 and 'did not find the Indian Communists anywhere on the battle lines' he 'kept away from the CPI' and joined Congress. *Socialism, Sarvodaya and Democracy*, Bombay 1964, pp. 141-3.

47. 'The Next Tasks of the Indian Revolutionary Movement', by 'G.S.' *Inprecorr*, 26 February, 1931.

48. 'Open Letter to the Indian Communists from the Central Committees of the CPs of Germany, Great Britain and China', *Inprecorr*, 19 May 1932. (Referred to hereafter as 'Open Letter').

49. Rathan Singh (an exiled Indian revolutionary), 'The Struggle for the Indian Masses under Conditions of Colonial Terror', *Inprecorr*, 7 July 1932.

50. *Indian Communism*, p. 162 and 'Open Letter'.

51. *India and Communism*, p. 183 and Ahmad, *The CPI: Years of Formation*, p. 38.

52. 'Open Letter'.

53. Rathan Singh, loc.cit. The reference to 'mass organisations' clearly refers primarily to the trade unions.

54. 'Open Letter'.

55. The first releases, including Adhikari and P.C. Joshi, came in August, *India and Communism*, pp. 140 and 187.

56. 'The Indian Labour Movement', (unsigned), *Inprecorr*, 19 May 1933; V. Basak, 'The Present Situation in India, *Inprecorr*, 8 September 1933; 'Open Letter to the Indian Communists from the Central Committee of the Communist Party of China', *Inprecorr*, 24 November 1933.

57. See *India and Communism*, pp. 187-91 and Ghate's testimony in Communist Party of India, op.cit., p. 112. The two debarred men were Ranadive and Deshpande.

58. 'Abridged Draft of Political Theses of the Central Committee of the CPI', *Inprecorr*, 20 July 1934. According to the Intelligence Bureau, *India and Communism*, pp. 187-91, these were prepared by Adhikari on instructions from the November 1933 meeting and appeared in pamphlet form in February 1934.

59. Orgwald, 'A Conversation with Indian Comrades', *Inprecorr*, 29 March 1934.

60. 'For Trade-Union Unity in India', said to be an 'appeal worked out at the end of 1933 by a group of participants in the Indian trade-union movement', *Inprecorr*, 25 May 1934.

61. Government of Bombay to Government of India (letter No. SD-1602), 18 May 1934, P/83, File No. 7/5 – Political of 1934, Serial No. 341. Bombay Government to Secretary of State, (tel. No. 37), 29 April 1934, ibid. Serial No. 12; Maxwell, Home Department (Special) Bombay to Hallet, Secretary to Government of India. Home Department, Report for second half of January 1934, 1-6 February 1934, *Brabourne Collection*, Vol. 14.

62. Brabourne to Viceroy, 5 May 1934, *Brabourne Collection*, Vol. 14; Bombay Government to Hoare, 6 June 1934, P/83, Serial No./ 38; Maxwell to Hallett, report for second half of June, 1-7 July 1934, *Brabourne Collection*, Vol. 14.

63. 'Problems of the Anti-Imperialist Struggle in India', *Inprecorr*, 9 March 1935.

64. *India and Communism*, p. 200.

65. Brabourne to Hoare, 26 November 1934, *Brabourne Collection*, Vol. 14. That Brabourne was not referring solely to Royist control seems certain since earlier (Brabourne to Hoare, draft tel. No. 28, 10 April 1934, *Brabourne Collection*, Vol. 4), he had claimed that 'Practically all Textile and other Unions are in the hands of communist leaders, largely Meerut prisoners'. CPI influence in the Bombay unions almost certainly increased between April and November.

66. Biographical sketch of Adhikari, in Rao and Sen, *Our Doc*, New Delhi 1968, p. 7.

67. T.V. Krishnan, *Kerala's First Communist*, New Delhi 1971, P. 67.

68. Maxwell to Hallett, report for first half of January, 1-6 February 1935, *Brabourne Collection*, Vol. 14.

69. Weekly Report No. 15, Director, Intelligence Bureau, 20 April 1935, L/PJ/7/893, 2734/35, and S.D. Punekar, *Trade Unionism in India*, Bombay 1948, p. 334.

70. Maxwell to Hallett, report for first half of February, 16-21 February 1935, *Brabourne Collection*, Vol. 14; Knight, Secretary to Bombay Home Department (Special) to Hallett, report for second half of May, 1-6 June 1935, *Brabourne Collection*, Vol. 14.

71. Apprehension about the effects on Congress of any Communist support for CSP work in that body had been expressed by Government to India to Hoare on 16 October 1934 (tel. 38-C) L/PJ/7/484, 3736/34.

72. Viceroy to Hoare (tel. R. No. 1578), 28 June 1935, *Brabourne Collection* Vol. 17; Governor of Bengal to Hoare, 1 June 1935, *Templewood Collection*, Vol. 9, p. 224.

73. See, for example, R.P. Dutt, 'Congress Socialism', *Indian Forum*, October 1934.

74. M.R. Masani to R.A. Butler, 24 July 1935, L/PJ/7/893, 2810/35.

75. See for example details of the breaking up of the Independence Day celebration in Calcutta on 26 January 1935 by 'young communists', Government of India to Hoare, (tel. No. 396) 13 February 1935,

L/PJ/7/484, 488/35..

76. It is possible that the change in the line on India at this Congress came about partly because Spratt, who after his release from jail in September 1934 had toured India, sent the Comintern a report on the situation there, according to *India and Communism*, p. 205.

77. By Wang Ming in his report 'The Revolutionary Movement in the Colonial Countries', 7 August 1935. This was published in *Inprecorr*, 11 November 1935, but a revised and augmented version was published separately.

78. Of course 'proletarian hegemony' in the anti-imperialist movement was quite as much an aim of the Communists as, they assumed, 'bourgeois hegemony' was the aim of the Congress leadership. The point was that such hegemony could not be made a *condition* for the formation of the front.

79. Jaiprakash Narayan, 'Problems of Socialist Unity in India', a 1941 article in *Towards Struggle*, No. 170. No doubt this decision was influenced by the change in Comintern line of August 1935.

80. Dutt and Bradley, 'The Anti-Imperialist People's Front', *Indian Politics*, London 1936, pp. 2-13.

81. Ibid., pp. 14-24.

82. See the testimony of Communist C.V. Rao in Overstreet and Windmiller, *Communism in India*, Berkeley 1959, p. 162.

83. Ibid., and Ghate, quoted in Communist Party of India, op.cit., pp. 114-6. Ghate and P.C. Joshi were leading members of the new CPI Central Committee.

84. Overstreet and Windmiller, op.cit., p. 163.

85. E.N. Blandy, Bengal Secretariat to H.G. Hallett, Secretary to Government of India, Home Dept., 21 August 1936, Confidential DO No./ 2901-PS, 3786/36, L/PJ/7/451.

86. G. Adhikari, 'Shripad Amrit Dange: Five Decades of Toil', *New Age*, 5 October 1969.

87. R.P. Dutt, *India Today*, London, 1940, p. 472.

88. Report No. 13, Brabourne to Lord Linlithgow, Viceroy of India, 20 August 1937, IOR *Brabourne Collection*, Vol. 4.

89. Dutt, op.cit., p. 472.

90. Sankar Ghose, *Socialism and Communism in India*, Bombay 1971, p. 313.

91. Morris, op.cit., p. 192.

The Mole in the Crown – Memories of the Indian Underground, 1935-38

MICHAEL CARRITT

This account is based on my personal experience of discussions with some of the leading activists of the Communist Party of India (CPI) about the significance for India of the Seventh World Congress of the Comintern in 1935.[1] In these I participated to a limited extent, trying (hopefully but doubtfully) to explore the difficulties involved in applying the united front policy to the special problems of the movement in the Indian subcontinent.

All accounts based mainly on personal memories are bound to be subjective and mine makes no claim to be history supported by research into documents and other evidence from that period. The CPI was, throughout this period, a proscribed organisation and all the activists who had to cover their vast subcontinent were fugitives, on the run, living from hand to mouth on the generosity and hospitality of employed sympathisers who risked their own freedom by giving shelter. In such circumstances as little as possible is committed to writing – no minutes or decisions are recorded. And I suspect that few documents exist. In fifty years the voracious Indian ants will have done their job and anything left, so to speak, on the side of their plate will have mouldered away in the humidity of fifty monsoons. My own documents brought back from India were in a supposedly ant-proof trunk, but the trunk did not prove completely secure.

This trunk, with its contents, was borrowed from my house in my absence by the English police in (I think) 1941. They eventually returned the trunk empty, and I sometimes wonder whether they are still beavering away trying to decipher the Tamil, Urdu or Bengali script in the hope of breaking some sophisticated code!

They will find little. For the meetings I had with my Indian friends, few and far between, were not seated comfortably round a table with decisions recorded, but out in the open spaces of the Calcutta 'maidan' (a sort of Hyde Park) where two or three of us would meet at night, able to detect the watching eye or the listening ear and, if need be discreetly part company; or down in the marshy area of Ballyganj infested with malarial mosquitoes and secret lovers who had no bed to share; or, best of all, a 'chance' meeting on a bench by the side of the River Hooghly where we were interrupted only by the rude and noisy hooting of ocean-going ships being piloted up-stream to the docks. Of all the various party members I met in these secret rendezvous, I knew for certain only the names of three or four. The rest I knew by pseudonyms which had the disconcerting habit of changing from time to time.

I must explain briefly how I found myself in this association with fugitive inhabitants of the political underground. In 1929 I was selected for the Indian Civil Service (ICS). In the province of Bengal I had a year's training under an experienced District Officer (DO) who was assassinated by terrorists in my presence half-way through the year; his successor met the same fate a couple of months later. Despite these 'upsets' I managed to learn a great deal about the work of a DO, his overall responsibility for law and order in his district and a host of other administrative chores. I was soon appointed a magistrate with first class powers to sentence offenders for up to two years or commit them to Sessions Court. This was despite my inability to speak or understand the language and my having had no legal training. More important, in the long run, was my training in what was called 'Land Settlement' from which I learned the intricacies of the land tenure system in Bengal and the iniquity of the rack-renting landlord system legalised by the British-inspired Permanent Settlement Act of 1873.

After the year's training I held independent charge as DO in two sub-divisions – first in the scorched and dry western edge of West Bengal and later in the watery deltaic areas of East Bengal (now Bangladesh). Up to this point I was entirely non-political – a naïve and conventional product of the public school system – but during this period of some three years a succession of experiences began to disturb my pigmy liberal conscience and engendered a state of disillusion and anger in me *vis-à-vis* the claims of the British Raj to be benevolently leading the Indians toward equal partnership in the Commonwealth. At the end of 1934, taking the long home-leave due to me, I decided to seek the counsel and advice of English friends whom I knew to be sympathetic to the cause of Indian independence. I met G.D.H. Cole (not much help) and Leonard Barnes amongst the academics; I was lectured by Krishna Menon, later to be Foreign Secretary of independent India. I got much moral support from two MPs, Reginald Sorenson and Fenner Brockway, and I finished up sitting at a large table at No. 16 King Street facing Harry Pollitt, General Secretary of the Communist Party in Britain. I fancy that, in his friendly way, he was rather suspicious of me. However, I was then passed on to Ben Bradley, organiser of the League Against Imperialism.

To cut the story short I was asked to act as a courier and, on my return to India, to carry with me a large bundle of printed material, pamphlets and articles in *Inprecorr* covering the proceedings and resolutions of the Seventh World Congress of the Comintern – in particular the published speeches of Dimitrov, 'Ercoli' and Kuusinen on the united front against fascism. I also carried letters of introduction to P.C. Joshi, General Secretary of the CPI and was given two plans for contacting the movement in Bombay; these were to be memorised and destroyed.

I had in the meantime – in the late summer of 1935 – received a summons to return as soon as possible to Bengal to take up new duties as Under Secretary to the Government in the Chief Secretary's department, which was more or less analogous to the Home Office in Britain, responsible for police, law and order and political strategy in relation to the nationalist agitators.

This appointment ensured my presence in the metropolis of Calcutta instead of isolation in some distant out-station. It also dispelled any qualms I might have had about bringing in my baggage such a bulky parcel of proscribed literature since I enjoyed what amounted to diplomatic immunity from the curiosity of the Customs.

So, in the early autumn I arrived back in India. Plan No. 1 for making contact was a flop. Plan No. 2, which I had been told to use only as a last resort, was a spectacular success. It led me, sweating profusely up Malabar Hill, Bombay's select and healthy residential area with a view out to sea, and then along a broad tree-lined avenue to the luxurious residence of the Bishop of Bombay. Here I asked a suspicious and surly Indian butler if I could see the personal chaplain of the Bishop – and I was led into a small untidy room, almost like a monk's cell, where I met face to face the Revd Michael Scott.

Thus began our four years of collaboration, giving what aid and advice we could to the hard-pressed and over-stretched activists of the CPI. I spent the next day with him on the desolate Juhu beach and, having been put in the picture was given a contact address in Calcutta. I delivered to Michael Scott the large parcel of official reports of the Seventh World Congress which I had brought with me. Up to that time our friends had only read about the strategy of the United Front in the national press and the occasional cutting from *Inprecorr* that had filtered through the postal censorship. This bundle was literally torn from my hands and distributed amongst the leading activists, most of whom were then working underground in the Bombay area. There followed months of hectic summarising and translating into the four or five main vernaculars of the subcontinent for wider distribution. And, of course, all the time there was non-stop discussion of the new strategy and the issues raised by its application to the special circumstances of India – an undeveloped colonial country with virtually no political organisations such as are known in the West and with totally different problems in its separate provinces.

Meanwhile my private postal pipeline, which was virtually free from the risks of censorship, was flowing freely with proscribed literature from the West and correspondence from our friends in England. I must confess that whilst the general international news was useful and much appreciated, the advice and help tendered in the correspondence relating to India was not often very relevant since it failed to distinguish the problems of the industrial workers in the West from those of the peasantry and unskilled workers in backward economies.

This irrelevancy was fuelled by a smouldering resentment in the CPI that, when postal and personal contact with the Comintern had finally ceased to function because of government vigilance they (the CPI) had been placed in the 'care and protection' of the British CP. And the British CP was itself fully occupied with its own united front problems with a Labour Party which was notoriously unconcerned with the problem of imperialism; as Lenin had said, the reformism of the British labour movement was indirectly due to the comparative benefits they enjoyed from the surplus wealth flowing into the country from the exploitation of India and the colonies.

Anyhow, be that as it may, the two comrades selected by the British CP to 'oversee' the Indian situation were peculiarly vacuous in their advice on our on-the-spot problems. And, as often happens, the messenger (in this case myself) delivering unwelcome news is apt to have to shoulder the blame!

Neither did Michael Scott or I at any time have direct access to the inner councils and discussions of the Indian leadership. Our white skins combined with the illegality and anonymity of the membership would have aroused enough curiosity, if not actual suspicion, to confuse the situation. Apart from which we had no status in their party – nor indeed did we enjoy any official status in the British CP. We came out there as couriers, we established an effective postal link and only by degrees and without any deliberate aim we acquired the 'guru' position of unofficial advisers.

For all that, however, we were only respected observers on the side lines, watching the game, encouraging the players, from time to time giving them advice; even on some occasions we were asked to adjudicate in a dispute between players. But we were, first and last only onlookers – and proud of the privilege of our ringside seats. Neither of us was well read in socialist literature (I less than Michael), neither of us had participated in the political movement at home, and neither of us (he less than I) had moved amongst the workers and peasants of India

*   *   *

To what conclusions all these discussions led can best be summarised by recalling a meeting with P.C. Joshi some eighteen months later. I was attending a 'durbar' (Governor's public levee) when a message came from Michael Scott to say that Joshi urgently wished to meet us in the bazaar.

He stood waiting for us at the corner of a street as arranged, accompanied by an unnamed companion, an older man with peculiarly deep-set eyes. He, the companion, spoke little and that in a halting and idiosyncratic English that I found difficult to understand.

P.C.J. was a slightly built figure, looking with his large spectacles more like a student than a revolutionary, much less the leader of the Communist Party of all India, small as it was. He was, in fact, not such a youngster as he looked and had been one of the accused in the Meerut Conspiracy case. For an Indian he was of pale complexion, coming from an upper class family in the North – the same district, I believe, as the home of Jawarharlal Nehru.

Unlike his usual cheerful self he now seemed in poor form. The reason for this was soon apparent: he had eaten nothing for twenty-four hours; he was penniless and without any place to lodge since his undercover arrangements in Calcutta had, for some reason, broken down. This kind of crisis was by no means unusual in the life of an underground political fugitive. His family, like most in India with sons or daughters in the political struggle, were willing enough to support him modestly, but neither from his point of view nor theirs was it easy or wise for him to go anywhere near his own village and walk into a police trap.

The immediate food and money problem was easily solved by Michael and myself; we rather shamefacedly turned out our pockets and found enough loose change to keep him going for more than a week. The lodging problem was a bit more tricky. P.C.J. was naturally anxious not to compromise any of the local people and our contacts were few and unsuitable. Eventually I took him under my own roof in the flat in Galstaun Mansions where he slept on a sort of back verandah and was to masquerade (if any questions were asked) as my private bodyguard – the sort of cover that nobody, except the Intelligence Branch themselves, would dream of questioning.

That done – and it was now getting very late – our essential business for discussion came up; namely, P.C.J.'s report on the tactical implications of the Seventh World Congress policy for a united front of *all* Indian nationalists against British rule.

The anonymous Indian comrade then led us through some narrow passage ways to a derelict site of rubble long-since overgrown with tufts of coarse grass. Here he pointed to a chunk of fallen masonry and said 'comrades now sit'. And with these words he departed silently.

When we were seated P.C.J. began to speak, and I shall try to summarise his description to us of the long talks that had taken place within the Communist leadership since my delivery of the Seventh World Congress reports and relevant documents.

'We accept', he said, 'the general policy of the united front against the common enemy as outlined in the report of Wang Ming to the Congress; that means that we accept too the criticism of our sectarianism in relation to other sections of the national movement in the past.

'Inevitably there have been amongst us some reservations when it comes to the practical application of that general slogan in all the complexity of the Indian situation, varying from province to province. But these reservations are not serious. In the last eighteen months we have talked enough and the time has come for us to put into practice our decisions.

'The common enemy against whom all true Indian nationalists must unite is imperialism, not fascism which does not exist here nor does the situation here lend itself to the development of an indigenous fascist movement in the foreseeable future. For one reason the foreign financial and commercial interests are so strongly based and making such profits that they do not need to call up the bully boys to terrorise the politically unsophisticated masses.

'The framework and organisation (however sketchy) of that movement against foreign rule already exists in the form of the Indian National Congress (INC).

'The INC is *not* a political party in the general meaning of that phrase but rather a broad movement. It has one single unifying purpose – to achieve liberation from foreign rule – Indian independence. It has consequently, no detailed programme or manifesto of political demands whether fiscal, economic, social or whatever else. No attempt is made to present a picture agreeable to all concerned of what this India of tomorrow will be like; liberation must come first and its future society will be shaped by Indians elected by Indians under an Indian constitution.

'As a consequence of this consensus on the movement's objectives there arise no questions of negotiation between disparate groups or special interests sitting down together to bargain over their interests in order to achieve a coalition of unity for independence.

'It is, in fact, a united front itself embracing all who desire independence and with whose central aim the CPI is entirely united and agreed. Because, however, it is a non-party-political united front it includes all sorts of groups and classes with whom the CPI has little common ground other than the struggle for independence.

'One important factor which facilitates the unity of the Indian national liberation movement is the absence of that acrimonious schism in the Western working class movements between a reformist, social-democratic or 'moderate' wing and a revolutionary wing. This schism has plagued the countries of the West and largely helped fascism to power. But in India there is virtually no reformist labour party or organisation. The CPI, though small in the number of its activists and having to work underground spread over a vast subcontinent, holds decisive influence in the All-India TUC and the All-India Kisan Sabha (peasant congress), although it must be admitted that the latter enjoys only a very rudimentary organisation and leadership; and it is anarchic, spontaneous and sporadic in its activities.

'There are, it is true, several self-styled spokesmen for the labouring masses in factories and railways, good men with the most worthy intentions, such as N.M. Joshi, who belong to no party (except for vague allegiance to the National Congress); nor have they any group of followers, much less a party, but who have acquired membership of the phoney Legislative Assembly by election or nomination and, who, with the approval and patronage of the British Raj, air the workers' grievances and represent them, whilst discreetly functioning as a safety valve.

'One other small group is the Congress Socialist Party (CSP) – not a party at all but a few intellectuals within the INC who have their journal, do propaganda for a future socialist India and whose status and loyalties are those of ordinary Congressmen. They have no other party organisation, no mass following nor direct influence with workers and peasants. We have spent a lot of time arguing with them – with Asoke Mehta, Masani, Kripalani and the maverick J.P. Narayan – about unity on the left. But whilst they would benefit by sharing our influence in factory and field we feel it is necessary to preserve our special contribution to the united national movement, that is as the organised party whose role is to raise the political level of the working people and to draw them into the anti-imperialist front; and that can only be done by our attending to and promoting the economic and social grievances of these people at ground level; and that, in turn, is something which the heterogeneous INC cannot do and of which many of its well-to-do supporters are afraid.

'On the other hand this group of radicals exert an influence within the INC out of all proportion to their numbers as well as having access to Nehru himself. So we must maintain a good relationship with them even if it consumes much valuable time in these 'unity' talks.

'So much for what may be termed the 'positive' aspect of the INC as the framework of the movement for national liberation – and our proposed role within it. But there is a reverse side to the coin,' and here P.C.J. paused for a minute to recover his breath.

Then he continued. 'The INC in its origins was essentially bourgeois, expressing the aspirations of the Indian upper classes to share in the exploitation of the vast potential wealth and resources of that country, to muscle in on the preserves of the British and no longer to be confined to drawing rents from the land. Gandhi, when he left South Africa where he had led the Indian community, was approached and offered financial sponsorship by the bourgeoisie to lead the movement on their behalf in India.

'Amongst these industrialists who financed the national movement in its early days were the textile mill owners in Bombay and Ahmedabad, notably the Birla family which still continues furtively to finance the INC because they resent the British government's fiscal policy which favours the import of cheap Lancashire cotton goods at the expense of Indian industrialists.

'It includes also a lot of small-scale Indian entrepreneurs in the commercial world who want to break through the monopoly enjoyed by the British 'Managing Agents' who control a variety of enterprises (coal mines, tea plantations, jute mills) and organise the exports and their sale on European markets.

'In spite, however, of these bourgeois aspirations behind the INC origins (and their continuing pressures) the movement during the last two or three decades has changed substantially and broadened its appeal to more and more sectors of the middle class – all those who find their aspirations and expectations frustrated by the power of British domination of the economy. Not least in this respect are the educated professional classes and their children whose qualifications lead them to no career in the professions.

'So inclusive has the INC become that as far as the bourgoisie and middle class are concerned only the toadies remain consistently loyal, that is the big landowners whose interests are closely and constitutionally tied to the existing system, the locally recruited government services in all branches of the administration, and those contractors who are satisfied with the crumbs that fall from the table of British exploitation of Indian resources.

'Nevertheless, in spite of these rapid developments in our country, the nationalist movement still remains today essentially bourgeois in its composition, its outlook and its methods of struggle against imperialism. It has no detailed policy for meeting the immediate problems of the exploited industrial worker and still less to satisfy the demands of those millions of rack-rented small peasantry or landless labourers.

'So the bare-footed peasant in his loin-cloth feels some embarrassment in marching and shouting slogans alongside the sons and daughters of the small-time landlords who squeeze him for rent whilst being themselves squeezed by the big landowners above.

'Nor is it easy to explain to the illiterate and politically unsophisticated industrial or rural workers that the British Raj is the main and common enemy of all. To them the Raj is an abstraction, something not seen or recognisable and, therefore, not open to attack.

'As one village elder, more articulate than most, said to me,' P.C.J. continued, ' "We know our own devils, we know the money-lender devil, the landowner devils and the small sub-landlord devils underneath them; we know the overseer devils who drive women coolies, with babies on their backs, to work in the tea gardens or down the mines; we know the big devils who own the textile mills in Bombay and Ahmedabad – and lots of other devils who bleed us white. And we know, too, the corrupt police who protect and encourage all the lesser devils to torment us. But who is this Super-Super-Devil, called Imperialism? We do not know his face; he is not seen here. We know all these local devils and we know the paths by which they go at night so that we can attack them with sticks; we know the barns where they store their rice so that we can set fire to them; we know how to break down their fences by night so that the cattle can trample their paddy crops. But who is this super-devil, the British Raj? We do not know his face nor where his barn is, we do not know how to hurt him."

'Thus you can see that the movement amongst the peasantry is, in fact, essentially spontaneous, sporadic and anarchic; it has neither the leadership nor the understanding at this stage to join with any degree of enthusiasm a united front with the *bhadra-log* (gentry) against an abstraction like the British Raj. They are prepared in anger to use criminal violence to express their grievance by physical action of revenge, but their political organisation, the Kisan Sabha movement, exists more in theory than any reality.

'It is, therefore, not opposition or antagonism that the INC faces from the industrial and rural poor so much as apathy and their failure to understand either the abstractions or the methods of the non-violent middle class ideology of that broad movement.

One might say that just those aspects of the INC which give it strength as a broad movement leave the unsophisticated masses in a state of comparative apathy or indulging in their own sudden outbursts of spontaneous anger against the known devils.

'And it is precisely amongst these unsophisticated masses that the CPI with its very limited resources in effective man-power and having to work underground, exercises its main influence.'

*   *   *

Such in summary and as far as memory goes back to that evening 48 years ago, was the picture drawn for us by P.C. Joshi and his analysis of the political situation eighteen months after the Seventh World Congress.

Day really was now beginning to break and P.C.J. was clearly exhausted but Michael Scott with his relentless tenacity still wanted more. 'So what now?' he asked. 'Where do we go from here in order to make that specific and recognised Communist contribution to the national movement which no one else can make?'

P.C.J. pulled himself together and agreed that that was the urgent issue upon which there were still divergent views within the leadership. The arguments in favour of the first option were – since the main power base of the CPI to date was in the textile mills of Bombay and Ahmedabad and, consequently in the AITUC operating from Bombay, it was there that we could exploit our prestige when secretly co-operating with the INC. It was there that our friends, the radical CSP wing of the movement were most active; in short Bombay was our main stronghold, provided the best cover for a proscribed party membership and the best contact with the INC. One additional and incidental argument in favour of the concentration of our limited forces in our main centre was that since the new united front policy was likely to throw up urgent day-to-day problems it was essential to have a majority of leading comrades on the spot instead of being dispersed over the whole of India, their wherabouts often unknown and the postal service being taboo. In those circumstances it would be virtually impossible to maintain a genuine political consensus at the centre of the leadership.

In favour of the other option it was argued that our special role within the national movement, and one which no other group could perform, was with new emergent and potentially revolutionary forces in the subcontinent – the small and scattered industries, coal mines and tea plantations but above all with angry rural masses whose apathy towards the INC has been already mentioned. After all they made up the majority of the population, and only we were able to give some leadership and political consciousness to their largely anarchic revolt against landlords and authority.

In taking this second option the CPI would of course, have deployed its meagre resources over a very wide area and thus weakened a leadership that was already threatened by internal rivalries and the legacy of past dissensions. In the end this dispute was resolved in some sort of compromise – to try and achieve both objectives as far as possible; for politics, as we are told, is the art of the possible.

But the sun was now up and we were running unnecessary risks by any further trespass upon the day ahead. So wearily we went our separate ways after instructing P.C.J. how to find my flat for his temporary shelter.

*   *   *

At the end of 1937 or early in 1938, when I was already thinking of resignation from my position in India, partly because I felt I could no longer give much political help and partly because the danger of detection, even by the bumbling Intelligence Branch, was increasing, I arranged through Michael Scott for a meeting with one or other of the leading comrades in Bombay. He managed this very quickly but was unable to accompany me across India to Bombay.

My tryst was to be on the familiar Johu beach where I had first made contact with the CPI in 1935. So, on a sultry afternoon I found myself once more waiting in the blown spray and the sound of the breakers for an unnamed, unknown conspirator. Nothing was changed from my previous visit – the same silent fishermen in the middle distance, feebly casting their hopeless nets into the hopeless sea; the same wet sand on one side and the scruffy and hostile sand-dunes on the other.

Eventually two figures emerged from the dunes on to the sand of the beach at a point about half-a-mile north of where I was sitting. They stood looking first to the right and then to the left like pedestrians about to cross a motorway that had no traffic; then slowly they walked towards me engaged in animated discussion and gesticulation.

One of the two I recognised at once – not because I had seen him before but from his description given to me. His name was A.K. Ghosh, later to become the CPI's General Secretary. He was a peculiar looking individual; for a Bengali he was very tall and his height was accentuated by a bony and very thin body, an elongated neck and a *huge* wobbly Adam's Apple. He was indeed a striking figure in his ugly and ungainly way. But he grinned with charm at our meeting.

To my surprise he was accompanied by this other who was introduced to me simply as 'our friend here' – the kind of introduction that is adequate and wise in such circumstances. The 'friend' was short, plump and jolly; he talked fluently in good English and with considerable confidence. I believe he was an ex-terrorist who had abandoned the revolver for Marxism; the fore-runner of others to follow.

We settled down into the soft sand, partly shaded from the midday sun by a tuft of tall, coarse grass, and we talked. There was no agenda for our discussion nor any organised procedure such as obtains in the labour movement in the sophisticated West.

Soon, and inevitably, we came on to discuss 'the tactics of the united front against fascism' in its Indian context. I prepared to extract myself in reverie or a quiet doze in the afternoon sun; we had chewed that theoretical rag (and its application in a variety of hypothetical situations) often enough and to such little purpose.

But within a few minutes I realized that this was something new. 'Our Friend', as I must continue to call him, was speaking, fast and fluently, and with a note of feeling and detailed knowledge in his voice that seemed to indicate a history of personal experience of the fascist or Nazi régimes.

The time had come, he was saying, to cease the back-and-forward discussion of these theoretical and hypo-thetical issues with all the opportunities that they provided for factionalism within our movement. The next immediate and practical danger for us came, he argued, from Subhas Bose who had recently held office as President of the Indian National Congress. The danger was crucial for the national liberation movement in general and the left in particular; Bose, a man of great ability (who years before had spurned an offered appointment to the ICS), and influence within the Congress, had recently made surreptitious contact with both Mussolini and Hitler to discuss the possible role of the Indian nationalist struggle in the event of war in Europe – the opening of the backdoor of imperialism and the tying up of troops in the Far East.

In fact, neither dictator took Bose very seriously but later, with the opening of the Far East theatre of war after Pearl Harbour the Japanese were to adopt Bose and his army (INLA). The numbers in that army were not inconsiderable – some 20,000 it is said, although it was not of very high military quality and despised by the Japanese, who used it as a kind of 'labour' battalion in Burma and allowed it to die in the jungle.

That is all later history, but our friend on Juhu beach saw more clearly than the rest of us the threat presented by Bose and the urgency of it. Liberation with fascist aid would be no liberation for India, least of all for the workers and peasants. And whilst it was certainly true that Bose's influence with the working class was minimal, his appeal to the elements in the Indian Army, in the lower levels of the administration and amongst militants in the student movement, was increasing – and to some extent at our expense.

We had got to present, and fight for, the principle, he concluded, that collaboration with fascism is no road to national liberation, much less a socialist society; there could be no deal with Hitler and Mussolini even against the British Raj. This was not a question of abstract theoretical discussion; it was a simple issue of survival as a movement for there were plenty of people in the country who could and would opt for collaboration.

There was silence; a long thoughtful silence. I don't know what A.K.G. was thinking; one must assume that already he had milled over these arguments with 'our friend' and accepted him as spokesman for this occasion.

It was dusk. 'Well,' said A.K.G., 'we had better be going unless you want to spent the night losing your way in pitch darkness through these lousy dunes. You go first, Bashir [my party name] and we'll follow in twenty minutes.' That was the last I saw of them.

*   *   *

I conclude with the same apologia as that with which I started. This is not a piece of serious historical research into the 1935 turning point in the history of our movement. It is, on the contrary, the story of an old *pallachari*[2] concerning long-ago events and arguments, strung together on the slender and fragile thread of his memory's eye. The only and modest claim made is that the stories of an old *pallachari* are marginally of supplemental value in a human way to the meticulous records of the critical historian.

NOTES

1. The full story of how I came to find myself involved with the CPI is told in my booklet, now being published, *A Mole in the Crown*.
2. I am indebted to my friend Godfrey Heaven for introducing me to this modern Greek word which is used by the villagers with tolerant affection to refer to the old men sitting in the sun drinking their glass of wine (on the house?) and entertaining visitors with their oft-repeated stories of the brave days of the Resistance – and their heroic role therein; and here the speaker smilingly taps his forehead and adds ... 'dear old boys, they are a bit soft now'.

Class and Nation in Ireland

C. DESMOND GREAVES

A three hundred page book, emerging like a butterfly from the chrysalis of a college thesis, has recently presented the Trotskyist interpretation of the history of the Communist movement in Ireland. Its author is Mr Mike Milotte.[1]

Eight times in all, feints and flourishes apart, he tilts at the windmill of what he calls the Comintern's 'stages strategy' which he claims 'artificially separated the national struggle from the struggle for socialism' and was derived from the needs of Soviet foreign policy. He presents the matter in the form of a question:

> Was it the case that the struggle for socialism could not commence in earnest until the country had been united and its independence secured? ... Or was it the case that national unity and independence could only be secured through the triumph of the working class and socialism, and the spreading of the revolution to Britain, Europe and beyond?

He thinks the Irish Communist movement answers the first question in the affirmative most of the time (an oversimplification as we shall see) and calls this support for the 'stages strategy'. At the same time he puts his finger on an issue that has exercised the Irish labour movement over several generations. If national independence cannot be achieved until after capitalists have been overthrown, leaving aside all socialist foreign missions, then they cannot logically be enlisted in the national struggle. The slogan is, so to speak, class against class. On the other hand if national independence takes precedence they can be logically so enlisted. The slogan is people's front.

The issue arose in the debates of the First International. Some of the English had objected to Irish sections on English soil. In May 1872 Engels, who had sympathised with the Fenians, stated what has usually been recognised as the classical position of Marxism:

In a case like that of the Irish, true internationalism must necessarily be based on a distinct national organisation, and they were under the necessity to state in the preamble to their rules that their first and most pressing duty as Irishmen was to establish their own national independence.[2]

This view was not universal among Irish socialists. According to Jim Connell, who wrote the words of the socialist anthem the 'Red Flag', there was a strong Bakuninist tendency in Dublin in the stormy 1870s. Socialism was not on the agenda in Ireland and the small groups who held meetings and study circles flirted with various international fashions, from 'progressism' to the British ILP. Classical Marxism re-appeared briefly during the industrial upheavals of 1889-90, when former Land Leaguers like Pete Curran, joined with Engels's correspondent J.A. Poole and others to hold the first May Day meeting in Phoenix Park, and tried to join in one grand alliance the emergent labour movement, Fenianism and the now dethroned Parnell. But the economic prosperity that had prompted the wages movement collapsed quickly and the movement fell apart. The socialists were sects again.

That Connolly, when he returned to Dublin in 1896, brought back the classical principle is clear. He wrote of the party he founded that its members were:

a few workingmen whom the writer had succeeded in interesting in his proposition that the two currents of revolutionary thoughts in Ireland, the socialist and the national, were not antagonistic but complementary, and the Irish socialist was in reality the best patriot, but in order to convince the Irish people of that fact he must learn to look inward upon Ireland for his justification and rest his arguments on the facts of Irish history, and be a champion against the subjection of Ireland and all it implies.

In 1902, however, the Irish Socialist Republican Party (ISRP) became heavily influenced by the teachings of Daniel De Leon, in reaction against English and French opportunism. Connolly fought the 1903 municipal elections on a platform of pure socialism. He did not raise the demand of national independence. He did not even propose a programme of reforms. His vote slumped. There were disputes in his party, and he left for America, there to unlearn quite rapidly the De Leonism he had temporarily embraced.

He remained in the USA seven years. Largely as a result of Larkin's industrial activities, the socialist sects that survived Connolly's departure were brought together again in September 1909, and Connolly was induced to return as organiser of the Socialist Party of Ireland (SPI). A year later he became Belfast organiser of the Irish Transport and General Workers' Union, and in 1914 its acting General Secretary. He was no longer able to devote much attention to the SPI.

But his demand for a national orientation in the Irish labour movement emerged clearly in his famous polemic with William Walker. At the 1911 Galway meeting of the Irish TUC the proposal to establish an Irish Labour Party fell victim to Walker's amendment that the ITUC affiliate to the British Labour Party. This clearly implied acceptance of the principle that the Irish workers would have socialism (if this is what the British Labour Party stood for) when the British wanted it. In the discussion that followed Connolly wrote:

> The Socialist Party of Ireland considers itself the only international party in Ireland, since its conception of internationalism is that of a free federation of free peoples, whereas that of the Belfast branches of the ILP seems scarcely distinguishable from imperialism, the merging of subject peoples in the political system of their conquerors.

Walker was of course accommodating himself to the prejudices of Belfast Orangeism. Ulster Protestantism was being groomed for an ugly counter-revolutionary role.

In passing it may be worth remarking that it has become fashionable among young academics to blame Marx for not recognising the principle of Ulster exceptionalism. The answer is of course that in Marx's last years the Land League had united practically the entire adult tenantry of Ireland, and those who care to look up old newspapers will find many reports of anti-landlord demonstrations by Ulster Protestant farmers in what is now the six county area. The alliance of Catholics and Dissenters, so important in the 1790s, was not so quickly broken up as has been claimed, and when Marx died there were few Orange halls not in need of a lick of paint. The great investment in Orangeism followed Randolph Churchill's decision to play it as a card against Gladstone's Home Rule. One recalls Thyssen's investment in Nazism. And indeed every twelfth of July, Belfast had a Nuremberg rally.

A distinct Irish Labour Party was established at the 1912 Clonmel meeting of the ITUC on Connolly's motion. By then Home Rule was expected. Connolly's *Reconquest of Ireland* was written with a view to stating a labour platform in the coming federal parliament. At the same time he had little confidence in the bourgeois leaders of the Irish parliamentary party if their class interests were threatened. He had already shown in *Labour in Irish History* how frequently the bourgeoisie had raised the banner of Irish independence only to betray it. When betrayal came again in the form of acceptance of the principle of partition he made his prophecy:

> Such a scheme as that agreed to by Devlin and Redmond, the betrayal of the national democracy of industrial Ulster, would mean a carnival of reaction both North and South, would set back the wheels of progress, would destroy the oncoming unity of the Irish labour movement, and paralyse all advanced movements while it endured.

Connolly did not therefore reject all consensus between the workers and the national bourgeoisie. But he recognised that their class interests made them dubious partners. On the other hand petty bourgeois groups, language, sports and cultural organisations supported the workers in the long hard-fought lock-out of 1913-14. But he made no test even of this. When at the outbreak of the First World War the bourgeoisie went over shamelessly and almost unanimously to the side of British imperialism, Connolly co-operated in the Irish Neutrality League with Arthur Griffith, one of the most resolute critics of Larkin and the ITGWU.

Indeed he did not exclude the possibility that sections of the bourgeosie might in certain circumstances adopt a position of support for a native government in which the working class enjoyed a high degree of hegemony. In an important article published in the *Workers' Republic* of 15 January 1916 – several days before he sealed the final alliance with the republicans – he wrote of a 'first stage of freedom' in which 'all factories and workshops owned by people who do not yield allegiance to the Irish government immediately on its proclamation should at once be confiscated.' Whether this was practical politics or not is not the point. Connolly clearly implied the possibility of bourgeois compliance. As for the duration of the 'first stage of freedom' obviously this would depend on the relation of class forces.

The insurrection of workers and petit-bourgeois in 1916 was defeated and Connolly was executed. Classical Marxism went into abeyance for five years. When the Irish TUC met at Sligo in August 1916, there was no protest at Connolly's execution, no demand for the release of prisoners, or even for compensation for workers whose homes had been wrecked by the military. Opposition to the war was replaced with neutrality. This neutrality reappeared in 1918 when Labour offered no candidates rather than decide whether to participate in or abstain from the Westminster Parliament. The result was that Labour had no representation in the revolutionary assembly (Dáil Eireann) that was set up in January 1919.

The origin of this neutrality was the desire to preserve unity with the North. Connolly had asked 'why sacrifice all Ireland for a part of Belfast?' His successors did not heed him. From the time the counter-revolutionary base was established in North-East Ulster, the Protestant working class had been made accomplices in the oppression of the Catholics. They thereby forfeited all capacity for independent political action. But what about the unity of all Irish workers on a class basis? The Northerners would sacrifice it instantly for the sake of their tacit accord with the Unionists. If they wanted unity the Southerners must sacrifice their position in the national movement. And this they did.

It is my opinion that Connolly would not have accepted this. The alternative was to take part in the national revolution as principals, and work from that position to the reunification of the working class. As things were, Dáil Eireann showed not the slightest interest in the Belfast engineers' strike of January 1919, and the Northern unions rejected the offer of financial support from the ITUC. As the national movement advanced its influence was increasingly felt in the North. In the local elections of 1920, the Belfast Unionists held 37 seats, Labour won thirteen and the combined Nationalists ten. In the famous speech at Finaghy field in which Carson heralded the savage pogroms of July 1920 that initiated the counter-revolutionary offensive, he pointed to the danger of 'the combination of the republican question with the Labour question', and acted to prevent it. Labour, not represented in the Dáil, took no part in the Anglo-Irish negotiations of 1921. It took no stand on the resulting settlement, and when the entire national movement split down the middle and the stage was set for dis- astrous civil war, it professed neutrality, thus in effect siding with the stronger party, the Provisional Government established by Britain.

The fortunes of labour were directed by able, honest and dedicated men. But they *reacted* to the national movement rather than attempting to lead it. There was much revolutionary talk but little revolutionary strategy. They had no conception of striving for working class hegemony within a movement united against imperialism and thereby nurturing the forces that would ultimately make for socialism. They anticipated that some time the national struggle would be over and then they could throw themselves into what they considered the normal class struggle. Mr Milotte's distinction between a supposed stages strategy and a pure class approach is thus not valid. They are the two sides of one coin.

The Socialist Party of Ireland was reconstituted in 1917, but could make little progress in the disturbed state of the country. During the Anglo-Irish negotiations a left-wing led by Roderick, son of James Connolly, secured control, changed the name to Communist Party of Ireland and applied for affiliation to the Comintern, which was accepted. The party recognised the primacy of the national question, denounced the treaty settlement, and took part in the civil war in the Dublin area on the side of the Republicans against the Provisional Government. It faded out in the era of bitterness and disillusionment that is so graphically depicted in O'Casey's three Dublin plays.

For a time the Comintern recognised Larkin's Irish Worker League, though it never prospered. When Seamus McGowan, Sean Nolan and others attempted to establish a second Communist Party the Comintern instructed them to dissolve the organisation. Larkin could win a Dáil election on his personal charisma, but he was incapable of building an organisation. He could not delegate. The modern period opened on 2 March 1930, when there was held in Dublin a conference of delegates from Revolutionary Workers' Groups (RWG). It was agreed to prepare for the re-establishment of a Communist Party of Ireland. While the conference was sitting a congress of small farmers was in session at Galway. Fraternal messages were interchanged. On 5 April the weekly *Workers' Voice* began publication.

By 1930 the shape of modern Ireland was discernible. The revolutionary era was now a memory. The partition régime, though detested, had stabilised. The treaty had been followed by a savage onslaught on working class conditions. Trade union membership had fallen away. The strongest union, the ITGWU which had 100,000 members in 1922, had only 15,000 in 1929.

The jails were crammed with Republican prisoners, though this in itself was a sign that the IRA, though defeated in the civil war, was still a power in the land. Sinn Fein persisted with its policy of abstention from parliament. But in 1927 De Valera took Fianna Fáil, a breakaway from Sinn Fein, into Leinster House, and for the first time the successors to the Provisional Government had reason to fear for their majority. By 1930 there was an increasing realisation that the new Ireland had come to stay. The fight for freedom must be continued under new conditions. At the same time the working class, on the defensive for seven years, despite rapidly mounting unemployment, began to think of advance.

That readjustment was so slow is easily understood. The generation active in 1930 had lived through what Frank Gallagher called the 'four glorious years'. They remembered the mass demonstrations carrying red flags and singing the 'Red Flag', control of the people while British soldiers looked on helpless, the peoples' courts that handled cases while the crown courts stood empty, the guerrilla activities of the active service units, the land seizures and the so-called Soviets. With such intense national experience just behind them the Irish people must necessarily take years to adjust to politics that were so radically transformed and begin to react once more to international influences. It would be fair to say therefore that the development of Comintern strategy had less relevance to Ireland than to most countries. The Irish situation was largely clarified by the end of 1934, and the Seventh World Congress of the Comintern set a welcome seal on a position for the most part already arrived at.

In 1928 the Comintern abandoned its earlier tactic of seeking a united front with the Labour and Socialist International. The new slogan was class against class which was vague enough to guarantee misunderstanding and demand constant exegesis. The issue was sharpened at the Tenth Plenum of Executive Committee held in July 1929. It was then stated that 'The ECCI imposes on all sections ... the obligation to intensify the fight against Social Democracy which is the chief support of capitalism'. This was of course not class against class in the common or ordinary meaning of the words, but Communists against the alleged main prop of capitalism. Degras cites a *Pravda* article of the period which wrote that social democracy was 'already a component part of the fascist system'.[3] It is hard at this distance in time to resurrect the expectations and preoccupations that gave currency to this opinion. On the whole the leaders of international communism at this time were young. Perhaps they had not yet noted how seldom does any intention take shape as it was conceived.

Parallel with the denunciation of social democrats for holding back the workers from revolution, there was condemnation of the 'national-reformist' bourgeoisie for preventing the victory of national liberation in the colonial world. The remedy was to develop the 'united front from below' – to seek unity with members while attacking their leaders.[4]

The first editorial of the *Workers' Voice* bore the headline, 'Our policy: class against class'. The object was:

> the establishment of an Irish Workers' Republic, through which all power will be in the hands of the working class, and which will socialise all means of wealth production for the benefit of the producers, and guarantee to working farmers the use of such land as they can work without the exploitation of others.

It might be objected that even allowing the sharing of power with sections of the farmers, as the interchange of greetings implied, there was work for a generation here. The answer is of course that these were not experienced draughtsmen and none of their early statements should be subjected to legalistic scrutiny.

The *Workers' Voice* also declared for 'complete independence from British and any other imperialist robber state, and the unity of Ireland under workers' rule'. There was to be an election for the new Dublin City Council, and the *Workers' Voice* declared, 'We are against all of them, Cumann na nGaedheal, Fianna Fáil and the Labour Party.'

The *Workers' Voice* of 19 July 1930 wrote:

> The Irish bourgeoisie are no longer 'oppressed' by British imperialiam, but are ruling Ireland, North and South, in alliance with British capitalism. They have abandoned the struggle for a Republic ... Not a single move can now be made for independence without a struggle to overthrow the Irish capitalist class ... This means that the old slogans of 'Ireland against England', 'Independence', 'Republic' must now be replaced by the slogan of class against class.

The Labour Party was characterised on 6 September:

> The role of the Irish Labour Party conforms to the same role as the British Labour Party and social democracy throughout Europe, as

being one of active agents of capitalism in carrying out the policy of capitalism under a cloud of democratic phrases, and, at the same time, using all the oppressive machinery of the state to break the resistance of the workers against the capitalist offensive.

Two points should be noted. No distinction is made between the two forms of British influence. In the six counties it consisted of overall state control. In the twenty-six there was an independent state available for a government that wished to use it. Second, the British and Irish Labour parties are placed on a par, though one was in government and the other was not. But as Marx observed of the workers who supported the Gotha programme, which declared all their opponents 'one reactionary mass', they acted not on what the programme meant, but on what they thought it meant. Statements of the 1930s cannot be judged by the standards of the present day.

What would be described today as a crude and sectish approach was not without appeal to workers impatient of the long retreat before reaction. The RWG were involved in important industrial actions. Most spectacular of all was the Belfast unemployed struggle of October 1932 in which for the first time since 1907, there was fraternisation between Catholic and Protestant workers and a joint struggle for an increase in outdoor relief rates.

The world economic crisis had ended emigration. In 1932 there was a net reflux into Ireland for the first time in living memory. There was no export of discontent. Terrified of a repetition of the revolutionary upsurge of 1918-21, the Cosgrave government redoubled its repression. The jails, full enough already, had more crammed into them. Organisations were banned wholesale, including the RWG. But in the election of January 1932, Fianna Fáil won a majority and formed a government with Labour support on a programme of empty the jails, abolish the oath of allegiance to the king of England, and withhold the land annuities (repayments of land purchase mortgages advanced by British governments to Irish farmers).

When De Valera enacted this last measure and placed tariffs on British imports while subsidising Irish exports, the British response was to clap a 20 per cent tariff on Irish goods imported into Britain. The 'economic war' began. It was the fraternal work of J.H. Thomas.[5] It injured most the big agricultural interests behind Cumann na nGaedheal. Within months these were trumpeting the virtues of remaining in the British Empire. When Hitler came to power in February 1933, they learnt to strut around in blue shirts and give the Nazi salute.[6] They evoked so strong an antagonism, and so effective an opposition among the rank and file of the IRA, that De Valera brought back the coercive legislation of his predecessors to curb them, and at the same time put a rein on the left.

But where did these events leave the strategy of class against class? The Irish bourgeoisie had been revealed not as one class but as two. One section was embroiled with British imperialism. The other was stabbing it in the back. Clearly the previous analyses had been too simple. This was represented to the Comintern by Sean Murray.[7]

De Valera went to the country again in January 1933. He wanted endorsement for his policies, and to free himself of dependence on the Labour Party. The RWG issued a statement on the election that owed precious little to the politics of class against class. The issues before the Irish people were:

> Irish independence versus the British Empire.
> For or against the British Government's coercion of the Irish people.
> For or against the payment of £5,000,000 in annual tribute to Britain.
> For or against the Cosgrave agents of British imperialism in Ireland.

This was in effect advice to vote Fianna Fáil. And there can be no doubt whatsoever that it was absolutely correct. Classical Marxism had triumphed over the doctrinaire. The Revolutionary Workers' Groups were amalgamated into the Communist Party of Ireland in June 1933. Already, under the influence of the Nazi victory in Germany, there were those in the Comintern who were seeking policies to meet the new danger. The Comintern was consulted over the manifesto of the new party, and advised an uncompromising national stand.[8] The manifesto was entitled *Ireland's Path to Freedom*. Introducing it, Sean Murray, who became General Secretary, spoke of 'breaking the imperialist rule and uniting the revolutionary forces as a first step on the road to social emancipation', and emphasised:

> The national struggle is the prime question with which we are faced in Ireland. It is necessary, therefore, that we understand the stage we have reached in the struggle. If the Irish capitalists had done what they should the national question would be solved.

The gravemen of his argument was that now that it was clear that the bourgeoisie had betrayed the nation, it was necessary to persuade the working class to save it. But he recognised the need for allies. The big farmers had come out openly on the side of the imperialists, but no movement for national or social liberation could be successful if it did not take account of the reserves of the revolution in the countryside. He expressed confidence that unlike Sinn Fein and other groups with sectarian anti-working class attitudes, the Communists could bring together workers from Waterford and Shankill who could meet on no other basis.

The changes resulting from the ousting of the comprador bourgeoisie by the industrialising, affected the republican movement. The leadership was divided, but the majority were prepared to give Fianna Fáil a chance. That De Valera was prepared to tolerate harassment of the Communists which placed them in a position not far removed from semi-legality, the worst persecutors being the adherents of the blueshirts he claimed to be fighting, did not alarm them. There were many Communists in the IRA and these were faced with a choice of which organisation to adhere to. On the other hand there was a minority that wished to undertake a public agitation distinctly more radical than that of De Valera. A number of these launched a republican political organization called Saor Eire which included workers and small farmers. It failed, the CPI believed, because of the dead hand of the urban middle class.

Following a split in the Army Council that led to their resignation, Peader O'Donnell, Frank Ryan and George Gilmore called a preliminary conference at Athlone, with the object of launching a political republican movement. O'Donnell was close to Sean Murray and there is no reason to doubt that he was consulted at an early stage. The Athlone manifesto called for the building of a mass movement for the purpose of making 'the Republic a main issue dominating the whole political field' and indicated its expected component parts:

1. Industrial workers who are being dragged into degrading working conditions to found a factory system at a time when the experiences of Europe and America are there to warn us of the horrors ahead.
2. In the Gaeltacht areas which must be in close support of the Irish working class … The Gaeltacht youth must get help to tumble its walls and get free access to the broad ranches.[9]
3. Small farmers and petty traders are strongly represented in Republican organisations and here is urgent work, for this section of the nation can only free itself as the ally of the working class.

This manifesto was a plea for the restoration of the grand alliance of 1919, which had been allowed to drift into capitalist control thanks to the unwillingness of the Labour leaders to identify themselves with the Republic.

There were theoretical unclarities. Occasionally the cart was put before the horse:

> We believe that a Republic of a united Ireland will never be achieved except through a struggle which uproots capitalism on its way.

This was presumably not intended to imply that it was possible to introduce socialism in a country still under foreign domination. It probably meant that the struggle for national independence should be waged without undue concern for capitalist interests. Arthur Griffith had made a fetish of these and had thereby handed over the greater part of the republican movement to the bourgeoisie at a time when they had no organised party of their own. Fifty years is a short time and the experience of the 'four glorious years' would be present to the minds of all but the youngest.

The CPI, while commenting on certain confusions in the manifesto's presentation, gave full support and plunged into the campaign that followed. Groups were established all over Ireland. The demands of the wage-earners were joined to those of the land-hungry small farmers and rural labourers. A network of tenant leagues demanded improved housing in Dublin, Cork and Waterford. The growing wages movement was supported. In Belfast a movement of the unemployed was set in train and attracted a number of Protestants. Two 'James Connolly Workers' Republican Clubs' were established in traditionally Unionist areas. Between April and September 1934 it seemed there was a 'little 1919'.

But there were differences. State power was in the hands of a native government which claimed to be republican, and not as in 1919 in the hands of palpable aliens whom it was patriotic to defy. And the majority of the IRA leaders, to their own consciences upright patriotic men, were in the grip of an ideology. They despised and feared politics. Fianna Fáil appeared to be saying the right things, if what they said mattered at all. They were not even prepared to offer an independent challenge to the pro-British blueshirts, even though the government was fighting them through legislation identical to that which had imprisoned themselves. There was a fear that 'politics' (which means the politics of the left) would endanger the integrity of the military movement.

Their right-wing stance was shown in June 1934, at the annual commemoration of Wolfe Tone at Bodenstown. A number of Protestant Republican Congress supporters carried a banner inscribed 'Shankill Road Belfast Branch. Break the connection with Capitalism'. This was an outrageously leftist slogan for the time. But had the IRA leaders had some tiny place in their hearts for all Irish people, they would have rejoiced at the fact that Belfast Protestants were rejoining the nation, and allowed them to say what they liked as long as they were doing it. What happened was that the IRA attacked the Belfast contingent, and then went home to deplore partition. As an illustration of the danger of incorrect theoretical formulations, it may be remarked that the Shankill slogan corresponded exactly to the Athlone proposal to 'uproot capitalism on the way'. The Belfast contingent wanted a united republic and thought this was the way to get it.

These contretemps notwithstanding, the Republican Congress which met in Rathmines, Dublin, on 28 and 29 September was well attended. There were 186 delegates from workers' organisations and Congress branches. Fourteen trade unions and trades councils were represented, along with delegates from the Labour Defence League, Labour against Fascism, the Unemployed Workers' Movement, Tenant Leagues, Communist Party, Northern Ireland Socialist Party and Republican Socialist Party. Delegates came from Dublin, Belfast, Cork, Waterford, Galway and Kilkenny.

But there were differences over tactics which were national enough in the circumstances. A programme like that of the Republican Congress required governmental implementation. If you thought bourgeois nationalism an extinct volcano, then you must form a new party and try to replace Fianna Fáil. If you felt there might still be a few rumbles in the old crater, you might think a sufficiently vigorous agitation might suffice to start a fresh eruption. Roddy Connolly, Michael Price and others wanted the new party. Sean Murray, Peadar O'Donnell and their supporters favoured the agitation. On balance they would seem to have been right.

A more serious difference arose on the question of strategy. Roddy Connolly defined the Congress objective as a 'Workers' Republic'. This was taken to mean socialism as the next step.

Peadar O'Donnell thought such a strategy would limit the appeal and exclude important allied strata. He wanted 'the Republic', the road of 1919 traversed again without the accompanying errors. This was to attempt to recreate the exuberant optimism of the 'four glorious years'. Sean Murray wanted neither to return to the past nor forge too rapidly into the future. He asked simply for 'an Irish republic', which would seem to have been the wisest thing. Murray and O'Donnell won the day by a small majority but the leftists refused to co-operate and the Republican Congress never accomplished either purpose.

It was a year after these events in Ireland that the Seventh World Congress of the Comintern was held in Moscow and the class against class slogan was discarded. The aim became the broad united front against fascism and war. There was thus retrospective endorsement of the people's front that had been attempted in Ireland. In his speech to Congress, Sean Murray admitted an earlier lack of clarity in handling the national question. In the beginning the Irish Communists had thought De Valera part of the camp of imperialism. Now they saw the national bourgeoisie as vacillators, and their own task as preventing the vacillation.[10] This analysis had clear implications for the two trends at Rathmines. If it had been available would it have made any difference? It might, but it is one of the tribulations of small nations not to have much say in the timing of world events. The Moscow Congress nevertheless endorsed the position taken up by James Connolly and reaffirmed classical Marxism in Ireland.

The Seventh World Congress coincided with anti-Catholic pogroms that were the worst Belfast had seen since 1922. The Unionists were determined to break decisively the fragile unity that had been achieved as a result of the unemployed struggles of 1932. The atmosphere was not conducive to the building of broad unity, though unquestionably the effort was made to hold together the tacit alliance of advanced trade unionists and nationalists. In the South reactionary forces attacked democracy under the cloak of religion, especially after the fascist conquest of Spain in the guise of a civil war.

The position of the CPI was extremely difficult. A special tribute should be paid to the heroic work of Sean Murray, whose vision was largely responsible for the formation of the James Connolly Battalion of the International Brigade which acquitted itself so nobly on the battle field. It included Belfast Protestants as well as Southern Catholics, and members of both communities lost their lives. Some of the most prominent of the younger leaders never came back, and one can still mourn the loss of men like William MacGregor and Charles Donnelly. The Connolly Battalion is perhaps the best reply to those who are anxious to belittle the work of the CPI during the 1930s.

NOTES

1. Mike Milotte, *Communisn in Modern Ireland*, Dublin 1984. As a corrective see Sean Nolan (ed.), *The Communist Party of Ireland, Outline History*, Dublin n.d.
2. K. Marx and F. Engels, *Ireland and the Irish Question*, London 1978.
3. Degras, *The Communist International*, 1919-43. London 1971, Vol. 3, p. 36.
4. To modern readers there seems an air of unreality about many of the debates in the Comintern. When some time in the late 1960s I reminded R.P. Dutt of the decolonisation debate at the Sixth World Congress of 1928, he started to laugh.
5. J.H. Thomas was the railwaymen's leader who called off sympathetic action by his members in support of the locked-out Dublin workers in 1913, making their defeat inevitable. He subsequently participated in the Tory-dominated 'National Government' of 1931 and was later disgraced for leaking budget secrets.
6. The 'Blueshirts' were traditional reactionary 'strong arm' brigades consisting of the sons of the more prosperous farmers, and these played a considerable part in the crushing of the resistance of the agricultural labourers following the establishment of the Free State in 1922.
7. It must have been in the late 1930s while I was staying at the home of Sean Murray in Belfast that he described a meeting of the Anglo-American committee of the Comintern at which the Chairman, Harry Pollitt, reminded him of Comintern policy when he proposed a softer policy towards Fianna Fáil.
8. Sean Murray told me that at one point he suggested making reference to high-spots of 'loyalist' tradition in order to reach out towards the Orangemen. One of the Soviet members replied, 'No nation can tolerate a Vendée.' (Vendée was the centre of revolt against revolutionary governments in France 1793-1800.)
9. Gaeltacht areas; areas where Irish is the predominant language.
10. I remember asking Sean Murray in July 1939 to state succinctly CPI policy towards the De Valera government. He replied, 'We support it.'

Fifty Years of People's Fronts

ERIC HOBSBAWM

Fifty years ago, in 1936, the first Popular Front governments were formed in France and Spain; that is to say, coalitions of Communists with social democrats and certain middle-class parties which were not seen as the immediate preliminary to revolution and working-class power. Such governments had always before then been condemned by the revolutionary left. They were regarded as typically social-democratic, likely to be dominated, directly or indirectly, by the bourgeoisie, and therefore likely to divert the movement from its real task, which was to make revolution. The only major exception to this might occur in colonial and semi-colonial countries, where – according to the Programme of the Communist International (1928) – the dictatorship of the proletariat was not the immediate aim of the Communists, but a more or less rapid transition from a bourgeois-democratic to a socialist revolution would have to take place.

Without going into the complex history of earlier Communist discussions, let me simply say that people's front or coalition governments of the kind I have sketched were quite new and shocking in the 1930s, and raised serious debates within the revolutionary movement which have not ceased to this day. Before the war two Popular Front governments failed. The French never overcame its internal contradictions and the half-heartedness of the Socialists who led it, and faded away in 1938. The Spanish was faced with Franco's rising, and went down in defeat in 1939. But people's front governments, in the form of governments of anti-fascist unity in the war against Hitler were formed during and after the war, if anything on an even broader basis than had been envisaged in the 1930s. In 1946 there were few countries which did not have them. They were the rule in the People's Democracies (which were so-called precisely because

235

they were not then supposed to be exclusively Communist governments), and in the West there were Communist ministers in Austria, Belgium, Denmark, France, Italy and Norway until they were expelled or resigned with the coming of the Cold War. In the colonial and semi-colonial countries governments of a broad anti-imperialist front were, of course, also common and less controversial.

For several years after 1947 people's front governments – outside the areas of colonial liberation – were neither practicable nor encouraged, but since the 1960s there has been a return to this type of perspective, notably in Italy, France and Spain. Since the mid-1970s the major issue in Italian politics has been the entry of the Communist Party into government, either as part of a majority of the united parties of the left or as part of a grand coalition, a sort of national government excluding the neo-fascists and the extreme right. So the issues raised by such governments are not merely historical but belong to practical politics.

Revolutionary Perspectives after World War I

The international Communist movement was founded on the assumption that a world revolution, or at least a revolution in important regions of the world, was both practicable and imminent. That revolution would not necessarily take the Russian form, but nevertheless the October Revolution was in a profound sense the model both of what ought to and would happen, and of the strategy, tactics and organisation for making it happen. This is why the new Communist International insisted on the most rigid and exclusive conditions for joining it. It wanted an effective world party of revolutionaries. It obviously wanted to exclude from this movement and its national sections the right-wing social democrats who had betrayed proletarian internationalism in 1914, and revealed themselves as deeply committed to capitalist society or even – as in Germany – as its main saviours. However, it also wanted to exclude anyone even partly committed to the non-Bolshevik way, anyone unwilling to break with social-democratic tradition and organisation in the most total and public manner.

In the excitement of the moment there were, after 1918, plenty of people and parties willing to declare themselves Communists or even, carried away by the mood of global revolution or the radicalisation of the masses, to affiliate with the Communist International. What the International wanted, however, was not an influx of the miscellaneous left, but an international Bolshevik party. If thus deliberately rejected most of those wanting to join it, leaving the quite important group of left-wing socialist parties – or at least those unwilling to make the total break – to float vaguely in the space between social democracy and the Comintern. Several of them tried briefly to organise themselves into the so-called 'Two-and-a-Half International' or Vienna Union before drifting back to social democracy after 1922, for want of anywhere else to go.

This approach made sense only on the assumption that the Russian revolution would soon be followed by other revolutions, or that an international revolutionary crisis offering similar perspectives would very soon recur. In 1918-20 this seemed a perfectly realistic assessment. It is quite unhistorical to blame Lenin, in the light of hindsight, for setting-up an International on the basis of splitting the old international movement – or what remained of it – on the narrowest and most exclusive basis. The situation looked, and was, revolutionary. In such a situation the masses would follow the most consistent revolutionaries. The vital thing was to see that these were consistently and effectively revolutionary, rather than to convert a larger percentage of the old non-Bolshevik socialist parties into Communist ones at the cost of compromise.

Exploring Alternative Strategies

Hardly had the Comintern established itself effectively when it became clear that its original hopes would not be realised. From the early 1920s it had to operate in a non-revolutionary situation, at least in most of Europe, though in much of the colonial, semi-colonial and dependent world a revolutionary situation could be said to exist, or to be probable, or even imminent. However, at this stage the great majority of Marxists did not regard the colonial revolutions as the immediate forerunners of the 'dictatorship of the proletariat' and socialist construction. As the programme of the Communist International put it in 1928:

> as a rule, transition to the dictatorship of the proletariat in these countries will be possible only through a series of preparatory stages, as the outcome of a whole period of transformation of bourgeois-democratic revolution into socialist revolution.

We need not here discuss the debates, mainly centred on the Chinese revolution, which were eventually to lead to a different view of the political prospects of colonial liberation.

From 1921 the Comintern thus found itself in the difficult situation of having to work out a strategy on the assumption that further October Revolutions were not in fact likely to take place. This was awkward. As Karl Radek put it at its Fourth Congress (1922): 'It is particularly difficult in a period when there are no popular revolts to pursue a Communist political policy.' It was doubly awkward, since the very principles on which the International had been constructed now made it more difficult to mobilise, and co-operate with, those large sectors of the movement which it had been designed to exclude. The Comintern found itself in a position rather like an army equipped for offensive, breakthrough and pursuit, which suddenly and unexpectedly finds itself obliged to settle down to a lengthy siege.

To do it credit – and the Communist International receives little enough credit nowadays – it set about seriously rethinking its European strategy almost immediately, with the launching of the United Front policy in 1921. However, the discussions about the new strategy and the new perspectives were confused by four important factors. *First* and foremost, the hope of a European – or at least a German – October were not abandoned but only postponed; at first briefly, but after the failure of insurrection in Germany in 1923, for a longer period – perhaps until the next capitalist crisis. Alternative strategies were therefore still largely seen as something designed to fill in time until a new revolutionary crisis made a new and better-prepared October possible.

Second, opinion within the new Communist parties was divided and, on the whole, unenthusiastic. Those who had joined them had done so precisely because they wanted revolution and a total break with the old social-democratic tradition. They were ready to follow the line, but left to themselves, most of them sympathised with what was increasingly clearly a sectarian position. This was very marked in the German Communist Party.

Third, the divisions and arguments within Communist parties were unfortunately but necessarily entangled with the internal struggles and debates within the Soviet party in the 1920s. This was particularly evident in the period 1928-34, when a policy of almost suicidal sectarianism was imposed on the parties from Moscow. That such a policy had some support within the parties is undoubted; but I don't think it would have established itself in the British Communist Party, for example, without Moscow.

Fourth, and more defensibly, the task of turning the new Communist parties, so largely composed of former social democrats, syndicalists or small left-wing sects, into proper Leninist parties, remained. After all, the case for Lenin's type of party (with or without its Stalinist developments or deformations) was not simply that such a party was required to make insurrection. It was required for any form of effective struggle for, and construction of, socialism.

Popular Front Strategy

So, though alternative strategies were explored within the Comintern in the 1920s, and occasionally surfaced, it was not until the 1930s that they were systematically developed. The movement had, vaguely, looked forward to the coming world crisis of capitalism as something which would somehow automatically produce a revolutionary situation. Instead it produced the most staggering and undeniable débâcle, assisted, without any doubt, by the ultra-sectarianism of the Comintern line after 1928.

In early 1933 the entire European perspective of the International lay in ruins. Hitler was in power in the country to which Lenin had once hoped soon to transfer the headquarters of international socialism, and the German CP was in exile, in concentration camps, or a hunted, illegal rump of cadres. Italian fascism felt strong enough actually to let some Communists out of jail in an amnesty in 1932. The only other CP in Western Europe with major support, the French, had been reduced to 28,000 members and 12 seats in Parliament. It was no longer possible to deny that the failure of the world revolution to occur in 1917-20 had been more than a temporary setback. The defeat of 1928-33 was clearly of more lasting significance, even though for another year or more officially the Comintern maintained that all was well, though with an increasingly strained air. What was more to the point, the movement was not only beaten but pursued. Fascism was advancing on all fronts. Something had to be done, if only to mobilise an effective defence.

It is not necessary to repeat the way in which the International came to adopt the Popular Front strategy, or the elements in earlier discussions within the Communist movement which anticipated it and from which it was developed. We know that it was pioneered in France in 1934, and officially adopted by the International at its Seventh Congress – the first for seven years –

in 1935, which totally reversed the former policy of seeing social democracy as the main enemy. The new line was put forward in two powerful and visibly heartfelt reports by the new General Secretary of the International, George Dimitrov, and his assistant – also new as a spokesman for the International – Palmiro Togliatti, or, as he was then known, 'Ercoli'.

The point I wish to make here is that the Popular Front strategy then adopted was more than a temporary defensive tactic, or even a strategy for eventually turning retreat into offensive. It was also a carefully considered strategy of advancing to socialism. It was, in my view, the first, and so far still the only, such strategy evolved for countries in which the classical insurrectionary situations of the type of the October Revolution or of other types were not to be expected, though not necessarily impossible. This does not mean that it was bound to succeed. No strategy is *bound* to succeed, though some are bound to fail. The search for the magic pill, certified by white-coated or red-flagged scientists, and absolutely guaranteed to cure cancer, cholera, rheumatism and the common cold or their political equivalents, belongs to the field of self-delusion and advertisement rather than to the field of politics.

Unity the Core

Just to remind ourselves: the core of the popular front strategy was unity. It was a set of concentric circles of unity: at its centre the united front of the working-class movement, which in turn formed the basis of an even broader anti-fascist people's front, which in turn provided in the relevant countries the base for a national front of all those determined to resist fascism in the form of the danger from Hitler, Mussolini and the Japanese, and finally – even more loosely – an international front of governments and peoples – including the USSR – against fascism and war. Each of these circles had, as it were, a different degree of unity.

The object of the united front was the reunification of labour movements split mainly between social democrats and Communists. This was quite clear in the trade union field, where the merger of separate socialist and Communist (or other) unions into a single comprehensive trade union federations was envisaged – and sometimes as in France, achieved. Mergers of socialist and Communist parties into a single working-class party were not seriously envisaged in practice, since the conditions for such unity laid down by Dimitrov amounted to asking social-democratic parties to become Communist ones by committing themselves to 'the dictatorship of the proletariat in the form of Soviets' and 'democratic centralism' of the Bolshevik type. Nevertheless the question of the political reunification of the labour movement, 'of a single political mass party of the working class' was formally declared to be urgent, and in the form of a merger of existing parties rather than of attracting the masses away from social democracy to the Communists.

The people's fronts and the broader national fronts were to have a rather looser unity – they were in fact alliances – though, in the course of the anti-fascist struggle a more permanent unity came to be envisaged, in the form of People's Democracies or the Western governments based on the unity of all anti-fascist resistance forces. The international unity was more *ad hoc* still; though once again, at the peak of the wartime alliance – but this was after the abolition of the Comintern – the Russians envisaged something like its permanent or semi-permanent prolongation into peacetime.

Strategically, the basic principle of the new policy was to:

> find a *common language* with the broadest masses for the purposes of struggling against the class enemy, to find ways of finally overcoming *the isolation of the revolutionary vanguard* from the masses of the proletariat and all other toilers, as well as overcoming the fatal *isolation of the working class itself* from its natural allies in the struggle against the bourgeoisie, against fascism. (Dimitrov.)

In short, the working class had been defeated because it had allowed itself to be isolated; it would win by isolating its main enemies.

Defensive and Offensive

The novelty of this strategy was to use the same weapons for defensive and offensive purposes. For the people's front was, from the start, envisaged not simply as a necessary short-term alliance of desperation against an enemy who threatened forces which had nothing in common except the fear of this threat. This might be so, as it were, on the extreme outskirts of anti-fascist unity. Thus the British Communist Party shocked its allies in 1938 by proposing to extend its support to Churchill, just as Churchill in 1941 shocked his supporters by unhesitatingly extending it to Stalin – both on the same grounds, namely that even the Devil was a good enough ally against Hitler, if he was prepared to fight him. However, governments of the anti-fascist people's front, based on working-class unity, which were the logical outcome of the policy, were from the outset also envisaged as possible elements in the transition from capitalism to socialism. The Comintern was extremely cautious and qualified in its formulations of this question, but clear enough to state that: 'It may be that in a number of countries the *united front government* will prove to be one of the most important transitioinal forms.' More generally, it was clearly stated that the fight against fascism was the main way forward in the struggle for socialism. To defeat it would also be to strike a major blow at capitalism.

The arguments for this, though not often stated with great clarity in public, were as follows. Fascism was the logical expression of monopoly-capitalism, which had reduced the effective control of the economy to a handful of ultra-powerful corporations or groups – the 'two hundred families', as the French put it. These crucial groups of concentrated capitalist power, in a period of revolution and intensifying class struggle, saw their main salvation in fascism at home and abroad. As the French reactionaries put it frankly, when faced with a Popular Front government in their own country: 'Better Hitler than Léon Blum.' In fact, the bulk of French big business took the logical step of collaborating with the Germans, and much of private industry after the war was expropriated, not on the grounds that it was private, but on the grounds that it had so collaborated, e.g. the Renault works. Under these circumstances the call for anti-fascist struggle was in effect also the call for struggle against the most powerful, dangerous and decisive sectors of monopoly capital. It was not a struggle against the bourgeoisie as such, but, as Manuilsky argued in his survey of the Congress (*Inprecorr*, 17 December 1935):

> Whilst we are undermining the power of these elements, we are at the same time undermining the power of the bourgeoisie as a whole, because ... [it] is indissolubly connected with the most reactionary, most chauvinist and most imperialist elements of finance capital.

This was excessively optimistic, for two reasons. First, because not *all* bourgeoisies, and not even all groups of monopoly capitalists, joined the fascists and thus made themselves vulnerable to attack on this ground. The Americans and the British eventually fought fascism. Second, and more seriously, because it assumed that fascism was a lasting phase of capitalist development, that bourgeois democracy was permanently abandoned as no longer compatible with capitalism, so that the defence of liberal democracy became objectively anti-capitalist. In the 1930s this was not implausible. Most of us believed it. But, as it turned out, fascism was a temporary and regional phase of world capitalism, which after 1945 returned to a modified and bureaucratised version of liberal democracy.

Period of Anti-Fascist Unity

However, in the 1930s and 40s the front line between fascism and anti-fascism was indeed that of the class struggle, and the popular front strategy enabled the left to fight it with the maximum number of allies, all the more so as it was evidently defending itself, its allies, and its nations, against fascist attack. What is more, in so far as this defence was necessarily armed – as in Spain and later in the Second World War – it turned into a revolutionary struggle in which the Communists were able to increase their influence, sometimes decisively, by virtue of their obvious effectiveness and leadership. Let us not forget that the period of the strategy of anti-fascist unity eventually led not only to something that had been hardly conceivable in Western Europe, namely armed guerrilla warfare – on a much larger scale than anything in, say, Latin America since the war – but also, and more important, to the extension of socialist power to large parts of Eastern Europe. Much of this was due to the Red Army, but by no means all. Yugoslavia, Albania, probably in a large degree Bulgaria and – until suppressed by British intervention – Greece, all had genuinely home-grown liberation movements.

Moreover, from the narrower point of view of the success of Communist parties, the period of anti-fascist unity was as brilliantly successful as the 1920s had been disappointing. There was no Communist party, however insignificant, which did not gain relatively enormous ground. I have mentioned the disastrous situation of these parties in 1933. Twelve years later, at the end of the war, the European parties were at their all-time peak, except for the German one which (in West Germany) never recovered from Hitler, and the Spanish which shared the defeat of the Republic by Franco.

In France and Italy the party was, or was on the way to becoming, the majority party of the working class for the first time. Even in countries where it had never established any support comparable to that of the socialists, its vote rose dramatically: 13 per cent in Belgium (or more than double its best previous performance), 12.5 per cent in Denmark (or more than five times its previous best), 23.5 per cent in Finland (or almost double its previous best), 10 per cent in Holland (or about three times its previous best), 12 per cent in Norway (or double its previous best), 10 per cent in Sweden (or almost double). Even in Britain, you may recall, the two Communist MPs elected in 1945 mark the high point of the party's modest electoral achievement.

In one sense the period of anti-fascist unity was therefore an undoubted success. It reversed the global trend towards fascism, defeated fascism, and furthermore got the Communist parties out of their sectarian isolation. If the French and Italian Communist parties replaced the socialist party as the major party of the working class in their countries, it was due to the experiences of the anti-fascist period. On the other hand the possible contribution of people's front governments to a transition to socialism is much more debatable.

Debate in the International Movement

There was indeed a deep, if not always acknowledged, division on this question within the Communist movement. The USSR was primarily interested in its own security – mainly against German aggression – and in diplomatic alliances to safeguard it. I think it is safe to say that it was seriously interested in people's fronts chiefly from this point of view, and not from the immediate point of view of making revolutions or the prospects of transition to socialism in other countries. Since the defeat and destruction of the USSR would have been a fatal setback to the movement everywhere, Communist parties were also prepared to subordinate everything to the defence of the USSR, though this did not prevent them having plans for advancing to socialism in their own countries.

But what plans? There was a left-wing view which still believed that a return to the classical revolutionary perspective was essential. If a broad front was necessary at all – and within the Comintern Bela Kun, Lozovsky and some others were far from convinced – it should simply, as it were, get the golf-ball of revolution out of the bunker into which it had got itself by 1933, after which the game would go on as before. The peoples' front slogan led to an enormous revitalisation and strengthening of the left, both in France and Spain. The victory of Popular Front governments produced a spontaneous radicalisation in the masses in both countries, which – some people argue – ought to have been used to make a bid for power in France, and which actually produced a social revolution in Spain, when Franco made his insurrection. I do not want to discuss the criticisms of Communist policy which have been made about these episodes, beyond saying that I do not believe there was a revolutionary situation in France in 1936, and that in Spain the need to defeat Franco inevitably dominated the policy of the Popular Front government.

Policy of the Long Haul

But within the Comintern there was another perspective, though it was only hinted at, because those who had previously put forward such views had been damned or expelled as right-wing deviationists, for example Georg Lukács, who between 1928 and 1956, was forced out of politics and into literary criticism for this reason. Antonio Gramsci (whose friend Togliatti was now one of the chief spokesmen of the International) had elaborated a policy based on the assumption that the lost opportunity of 1917-20 would not recur, and that Communist parties must envisage not a short front offensive but a lengthy war of position – a policy of the long haul. In effect, they must win the leadership of a broad alliance of social forces, and *maintain* this leadership during a prolonged period of transition, in which the actual transfer of power was only one episode.

In the West Communists were not confronted with a state which had only to collapse for the working class to seize power. The state was only the first line of the bourgeoisie's defence. Behind it there was a whole system of bunkers and fortresses – the institutions of civil society which established the legitimacy of bourgeois rule. Again, unlike the East – I quote Karl Radek (1922):

> in the West the working masses are not so amorphous ... They are members of parties and they stick to their parties. In the East, in Russia, it was easier to bring them into the fold of communism after the outbreak of the revolutionary storm. In your countries it is much more difficult.

Or, as Dimitrov put it in 1935:

> It is a common mistake of a leftist character to imagine that, as soon as a political (or revolutionary) crisis arises, it is enough for the

Communist leaders to throw out the slogan of revolutionary insurrection, and the masses will follow.

The struggle for hegemony over a long period implied two things: that even in the West the slogan of an immediate transition to the 'dictatorship of the proletariat' was correct only in exceptional circumstances, and *second*, that it was wrong for the Communists to refuse to take any interest in government until after they had made their own revolution. On the contrary, the more they did so, the more they left hegemony in the hands of the bourgeoisie, and condemned themselves to subalternity.

Now in so far as the Popular Front governments were seen as possible régimes of transition to socialism, they therefore implied that the dictatorship of the proletariat was not the immediate programme of the Communists, and that there would be an intermediate phase between the rule of the bourgeoisie and socialism. (I am not here discussing the meaning of the term 'dictatorship of the proletariat', which has now such associations that many Western Communist parties are abandoning it.) But as I have tried to show above, there was a major weakness in this analysis. It made sense on the assumption that capitalism was fatally weakened by the defeat of fascism. As we have seen, this was not so. After the war it still made sense – though a bit less – on the assumption that capitalism would not recover. But as we know, it did. It made sense on the assumption that the Popular Front government was decisively tilted to the left, so that it could not drift back into being a bourgeois coalition with a socialist or Communist appendix. But, outside Eastern Europe after the war, this was not so. On the contrary, the governments of anti-fascist unity in Western Europe could get rid of their communists whenever they wished, and in any case kept them in subordinate positions, where they took the blame for unpopular government policies, for example as ministers of labour.

It is true that in Eastern Europe after the war – 1945-47 – there were genuine alliance governments, and not merely Communist régimes in fancy dress, although the left wing in the Communist movement – led at the time by the Yugoslavs – regarded this as undesirable. Thus Dimitrov in 1946 said: 'Our immediate task is not the realisation of socialism, but the consolidation of the democratic and parliamentary system.' 'People's Democracy' then was not yet a synonym for the dictatorship of the Communist party, nor was a single way of development –

patterned on the USSR – imposed on the East European states. But with the coming of the Cold War this ended, and little was left of the perspective of a gradual transition to socialism in accordance with conditions in each country, except the name 'People's Democracy' which was now meaningless.

Situation in which People's Fronts Arise

The criticism of people's fronts and broad alliances by the Western ultra-left envisages similar development. Such governments are rejected unless they are the immediate precursors of socialist power, i.e. unless they stop being people's fronts and turn themselves into 'dictatorships of the proletariat'. Here the present ultra-left echoes, among others, the opinions of Leon Trotsky, who dismissed the Comintern's policies in the wildest and most sectarian manner, though he had earlier made some very sound criticisms of the Comintern's disastrous sectarianism before 1934. He actually seems to have believed that people's fronts 'doom the working class to impotence *and clear the road for fascism*' (my emphasis – E.J.H.). Trotsky and other ultra-radicals at the time rejected the very idea of the broad anti-fascist alliance, and when it became clear that it stimulated a striking revival and growth of the movement, rejected it for not immediately proceeding to make a classical revolution. In the 1970s ultra-leftist attitudes towards Chile have been along the same lines.

This was and is to misunderstand the situation in which people's fronts arise. Broad alliances of groups and parties, including people's fronts, are necessary only when the working-class party is not strong enough to win on its own: it rarely is. But when such alliances or fronts are necessary, they therefore consist of a variety of groups and organisations with very different opinions, some of them not even socialist. They are united only against a common enemy, or for a common programme which represents only the first step for some participants, whereas for others it marks the furthest point to which they are at the moment prepared to go. This follows from the fact that they are neither socially nor politically homogeneous. In short, if they are to be more than brief political interludes, the socialists within such alliances *must* convince and carry along their allies, or at least neutralise them. If they fail to do so, they simply revert to being a relatively impotent minority group. Indeed, they might even be worse off, if their policy had antagonised formerly allied, neutral or indifferent strata, allowing these to be mobilised by the class enemy.

Some Criticisms

The Italian Communist leader Berlinguer quite rightly pointed out that this is so in countries such as his, whether there are people's fronts or not. Even if the Italian CP were to get 51 per cent of the votes – or even a lot more – and establish a pure Communist government, it would still have to carry most of the other 49 per cent with it. The Italian analysis of the tragic Chilean experience is that Allende failed not simply because his Popular Unity was unable technically to defeat the military, but because it alienated large sectors of the population which it ought to have carried with it, or at least not allowed or stimulated to become bitterly antagonistic. It thus isolated itself at the very moment of danger, and provided the military plotters with both an excuse for their coup and at least a temporary mass base of social support for it. In short, socialists must not allow themselves to forget strategy and politics – isolating the adversary, winning friends and influencing people – by falling into the trap of arithmetic – whether in the social-democratic manner by counting votes or the ultra-radical manner by counting guns; which is not to say that either can be neglected.

Furthermore, the problem of winning political support does not disappear even when the revolutionaries are actually in effective possession of power. Portugal is a sad example of a country in which they lost a historic opportunity, partly by relying too exclusively on the backing of a military state power whose revolutionary maturity and homogeneity they overestimated, partly by the old leftist error of supposing that even in a revolutionary situation *all* the masses will automaticaly rally to the revolutionary slogans. They neglected the real distribution of political forces in their country – the fact that the workers and landless peasants were only a minority, the Church's influence, and the ease with which the small and middle peasants of the North could be mobilised by anti-Communist slogans.

This is not to say that Popular Front governments ought not to be criticised. They may not try to advance towards socialism at all, and therefore be no more than ordinary temporary coalitions. I think the French Popular Front of 1936 is open to this criticism. They may rely too much on being, as it were, carried in the right direction by inevitable historical forces. As suggested above, this was the weakness of the argument that the defeat of fascism must entail the decline of capitalism, or that capitalism after the war would not be able to recover its initiative and dynamism. This meant that Communists who entered such governments did not do enough to change the political structures of their countries. For instance, it may be argued that the Italian Communist Party in 1945, when it had the weight of anti-fascist insurrection behind it, neglected to destroy the structure of the old fascist bureaucracy and the political power of the Church, relying too much on a new and admittedly very progressive Constitution which they helped to draft. Again, people's fronts may be criticised for failing to appreciate the very serious problems of transforming heterogeneous and mutually suspicious coalitions or electoral alliances into effective reforming governments. This criticism can certainly be made of the Chilean Popular Unity. They may finally sometimes be criticised for not sufficiently appreciating the basic fact that government in itself is not power; that reforming governments which go too far for the ruling class may be overthrown by it, or its allies, or its foreign supporters.

The Strategy which Reaction Fears

Still, when all these criticisms have been made, the people's fronts remain to this day the socialist strategy which most frightens the enemy. They are not scared of barricades going up in Milan or Paris. On the other hand, they have always regarded unity as the main danger. Why did the Americans spend so much energy and money in the 1950s splitting the national and international trade union movements and any progressive or socialist party (such as the Italian) willing to co-operate with Communists? Why did ideologists invent the myth that nobody could ever co-operate with Communists without being swallowed by them – unless to discourage such co-operation? (In fact, such alliances have, as often as not, benefited the non-Communists, who got rid of the Communists when they had served their purpose. Communists have never regarded this as a reason for condemning all alliances on principle.) Why that other myth according to which no people has ever freely voted a red government into office?

Why did the US government from time to time in the 1970s, through its ambassadors, warn European socialist parties against having anything to do with Communists? Why did they – and do they – repeat daily that the entry of communists into any government, whether Italian or Nicaraguan, is intolerable? Why did the Italian reaction, as we now know, conspire secretly to make coups against governments willing to include the Communist Party, and cheer – perhaps even assist – the ultra-left assassination of the Christian-Democratic statesman most favourable to this policy? Because they are afraid of the strategy of the broad alliance. They would much prefer the revolutionaries to isolate themselves, the more sectarian in spirit, the better, They know that in most countries where socialism has come, it has been brought about by broad fronts led by Communists – whether in the form of people's fronts or not – rather than through the isolated action of revolutionary Marxists. No war of liberation could have been won on any other terms.

It is sometimes a good thing to remind ourselves of what the enemy fears most. Today, in spite of two generations of criticism from the left, what he fears most – especially in the developed countries of Europe – is still the sort of strategy first systematically adopted by the international Communist movement in the 1930s.

Notes on Contributors

Tony Atienza is a retired history master and comprehensive school head teacher. He lectures in local history and family history and is currently cataloguing the archives of the International Brigade Association.

Noreen Branson has worked for the Labour Research Department for many years. She is author of the recent *History of the Communist Party of Great Britain 1927-1941*; her previous works include *Poplarism, 1919-25, Britain in the 1920s* and (with Margot Heinemann) *Britain in the 1930s*.

Sue Bruley wrote her thesis on Communism and feminism between wars. She teaches history and politics and is a feminist and a member of the Labour Party.

Michael Carritt served in the Indian Civil Service from 1929 to 1938, as District Officer and Magistrate and afterwards as Under Secretary in the Political Department. Disillusioned with British rule he discussed the decisions of the Seventh World Congress with underground trade union and peasant leaders.

Jim Fyrth has worked in adult education since 1947, much of the time with shop stewards and other trade unionists: his books on trade union and industrial subjects include *The Foundry Workers* (with Henry Collins), *Science, History and Technology* (with Maurice Goldsmith) and *Political Action* (with Ann Taylor).

Desmond Greaves is General Secretary of the Connolly Association and edits its monthly, the *Irish Democrat*. His works include *The Life and Times of James Connolly* and the history of the Irish Transport and General Workers' Union.

Margot Heinemann joined the Communist Party in 1934 and was for some years on its London District Committee. She was a research worker at the Labour Research Department and subsequently Lecturer in English at Goldsmiths College, London and at New Hall, Cambridge. Books include *Britain's Coal, Wages Front, Britain in the 1930s* (with Noreen Branson) and *Culture and Crisis in Britain in the 1930s* (edited with Jon Clark *et al.*)

Eric Hobsbawm is Professor Emeritus in Economic and Social History, Birkbeck College, University of London. His many books include *Labouring Men, The Age of Revolution, The Age of Capital, Primitive Rebels, Bandits* and *Industry and Empire*.

Monty Johnstone is a member of the Executive Committee of the Communist Party and former editor of *Challenge*. He writes and lectures on Marxist political theory and international working-class history.

Martin Myant is Lecturer in Economics at Paisley College of Technology and editor of *Scottish Marxist*, journal of the Scottish Committee of the CPGB. He is author of *Socialism and Democracy in Czechoslovakia, 1945-48* and *Poland: a Crisis for Socialism*.

Geoff Roberts works in NALGO's Education Department. He was organiser of the 1978 Communist University of London and was Communist candidate in East Lewisham in the 1983 general election. He has recently completed a study of the Nazi-Soviet Pact.

Conrad Wood lived in India for six months in 1974-75, collecting material for a doctoral thesis on Indian history. He has contributed articles on Indian politics to several journals and newspapers including the *Journal of Indian History* and *Modern Asian Studies*.

Index